English
Poetry
1900–1950

An Assessment

I am not speaking of those hundreds of persons who follow blindly a tradition which has no longer any meaning, and produce the thousands of books of verse which plague the world; nor am I speaking of pot-wallopers ... I am speaking of the genuine poet.

F. S. Flint

English Poetry

1900-1950

An Assessment

C H Sisson

Methuen
London and New York

First published in 1971 by Rupert Hart-Davis Ltd
Reissued 1981 by Carcanet New Press Ltd
330 Corn Exchange Buildings, Manchester M4 3BG

First published as a University Paperback in 1981 by
Methuen & Co. Ltd
11 New Fetter Lane, London EC4P 4EE
Published in the USA by
Methuen & Co.
in association with Methuen, Inc.
733 Third Avenue, New York, NY 10017

Printed in Great Britain by Billings, Guildford

British Library Cataloguing in Publication Data
Sisson, C. H.
    English poetry 1900-1950.—(University paperbacks; 752)
    1. English poetry — 20th century — History
    and criticism
    I. Title
    821'.91209   PR601

ISBN 0-416-32100-3

Acknowledgements

For permission to reprint copyright material, acknowledgement is gratefully made to the following: To the Hamlyn Publishing Group for quotations from *Collected Poems of Richard Aldington*. To Faber & Faber Ltd for quotations from *Poems, The Orators, Look Stranger*, and *Collected Shorter Poems*, by W. H. Auden; and from *Collected Poems 1930–1955* by George Barker. To Sidgwick & Jackson Ltd for quotations from *Weeping-Cross and Other Rimes* by A. H. Bullen. To Faber & Faber Ltd for a quotation from *Talking Bronco* by Roy Campbell. To the Literary Trustees of Walter de la Mare and the Society of Authors as their literary representatives for quotations from *Complete Poems of Walter de la Mare*. To Faber & Faber Ltd for quotations from *The Complete Poems and Plays of T. S. Eliot*. To William Empson and Chatto & Windus Ltd for quotations from *Collected Poems of William Empson*. To Robert Graves for quotations from *Poems 1914–1926*. To the Trustees of the Hardy Estate, and Macmillan, London and Basingstoke for quotations from *Collected Poems of Thomas Hardy*. To the Society of Authors acting as the literary representative of the Estate of A. E. Housman, and Jonathan Cape Ltd, for quotations from *Collected Poems* by A. E. Housman. To the Executors of the James Joyce Estate, Jonathan Cape Ltd, and the Society of Authors acting as the literary representative of James Joyce, for a quotation from *Chamber Music*, and to the Society of Authors acting as the literary representative of James Joyce, for quotations from *Pomes Penyeach*, by James Joyce. To Mrs Patrick Kavanagh for *Lines to Yeats* (first published in *The Holy Door*), and to MacGibbon & Kee Ltd for quotations from *Collected Poems of Patrick Kavanagh*. To Mrs George Bambridge and Macmillan, London and Basingstoke, for quotations of Rudyard Kipling. To Mrs Anne Wyndham Lewis for *Grignolles*, and for quotations from *One Way Song*, by Wyndham Lewis. To

Christopher Murray Grieve for quotations of Hugh MacDiarmid. To Harold Owen, and Chatto & Windus Ltd for quotations from *The Poems of Wilfred Owen*. To Faber & Faber Ltd for quotations from *Poems* by Clere Parsons; quotations from *Cantos*, *Collected Shorter Poems*, and *A Lume Spento*, by Ezra Pound; and quotations from *Annals of Innocence and Experience*, and *Poems 1914–1934*, by Herbert Read. To Edgell Rickword for quotations from *Collected Poems of Edgell Rickword*. To the Estate of Isaac Rosenberg, and Chatto & Windus Ltd for quotations from *The Collected Works of Isaac Rosenberg*. To Faber & Faber Ltd for quotations from *Collected Poems of Stephen Spender*. To Mrs M. Thomas and Faber & Faber Ltd for quotations from *Collected Poems of Edward Thomas*. To M. B. Yeats and Macmillan, London and Basingstoke, for quotations from *Collected Poems of W. B. Yeats*, *A Full Moon in March*, and *Last Poems and Plays*.

Contents

Introductory Note   11

Chapter *1*   Preliminaries : A. H. Bullen.
The nineties : Lionel Johnson ;
Ernest Dowson ; John Davidson   13

Chapter *2*   Thomas Hardy ; Rudyard Kipling ;
A. E. Housman   25

Chapter *3*   The influence of prose on verse :
Ford Madox Ford ; Walter de la
Mare   44

Chapter *4*   Imagism : F. S. Flint ; Richard
Aldington ; T. E. Hulme ; the verse
of James Joyce   54

Chapter *5*   Edward Thomas ; Wilfred Owen ;
Isaac Rosenberg ; Harold Monro   71

Chapter *6*   Ezra Pound   96

Chapter *7*   T. S. Eliot   125

Chapter *8*   W. B. Yeats   155

Chapter 9   Herbert Read; Robert Graves;
Edgell Rickword; the influence of
the prose of James Joyce and D. H.
Lawrence   180

Chapter 10   The thirties : W. H. Auden ; Stephen
Spender; Clere Parsons; William
Empson   202

Chapter 11   Wyndham Lewis ; Roy Campbell ;
Hugh MacDiarmid   222

Chapter 12   The forties : George Barker ; Dylan
Thomas ; Patrick Kavanagh ; David
Gascoyne   242

Chapter 13   Conclusion   260

Introductory Note

The object of this book is to show where the best English verse of the first half of the century is to be found, to indicate what its qualities are and—since these things are not separable—what sort of men wrote it. Many names which were once well known, and some which still are so, do not appear in the book. It is not a history of reputations. A number of men who have written one or two good poems apiece are left out to make the outline of the history clearer. There is no lack of anthologies where traces of these occasional producers can be found. The only Americans included are Pound and Eliot, the latter of whom settled here while the former operated powerfully on the London scene.

Even with these limitations, more than thirty poets find a place in the history. A moment's reflection on any other fifty years of English literature will suggest that the number is too large rather than too small. In the end only a few figures are left in any epoch. There is of course another view of literary history, according to which it is made up of movements swirling from decade to decade or even in quinquennia. There is a theory that it has to do with changes in the poetry trade. One recent editor says of the fifties: 'It was not until the Poetry Book Society was formed, and the P.E.N. sponsored an annual poetry anthology, and the Fantasy Press, Oxford, commenced its influential series of pamphlets devoted to the young that British poetry began to struggle back to health.'[1] Such social and political history is largely ignored in this book. Even serious 'movements' are valued only for the work they have left behind.

[1] Robin Skelton, introduction to *Poetry of the Forties*.

Chapter One

Preliminaries : A. H. Bullen

The nineties : Lionel Johnson ; Ernest Dowson ; John Davidson

I

The penumbra of the twentieth century stretches back into the nineteenth—as far as you like, in fact. People will get born at odd times; they will die inconsiderately; and they will do their best work when the humour takes them. One certain thing is that they will learn to speak, first of all, from those immediately about them and a bit older than themselves. If they belong to the class of persons we are here considering, those addicted to the writing of verse, they will at some time, and however much they deny their sources afterwards, be profoundly influenced by poets of the preceding generation—though again, to speak of generations in succession supposes a tidiness with which human life is not in fact arranged. Moreover, it is no use looking at dates of birth to see what poetry was accessible. There are the accidents of publication, such as that which led to the impact of Hopkins (1844–89) being delayed. Hopkins was published only in 1918, having, during his life-time, had advice on the proprieties of writing from Robert Bridges. Bridges was born in the same year as Hopkins and died in the year of the latter's second edition, having meanwhile been much reprinted himself and crowned with numerous laurels, now faded, including those of the Laureateship. There are other less prominent accidents of accessibility, in a world which does not guarantee the prominence or even the circulation of the best writing, and in which poets are born in circumstances that not only favour unequally their personal obscurity but determine how long it takes them to become acquainted with the best literature that is current in their day. There are the accidents and foibles which bring about unlikely influences or the influence of opposites, as that of James Thomson (1834–82), the author of *The City of Dreadful Night*, or John Davidson (1857–1909) on T. S. Eliot. If literature has a history, it is the history of obscure cross-currents and connections, and it is very rarely what contemporaries

imagine it to be. The contemporary obscurity of William Blake —
as of several other now favourite subjects of the Sunday supplement *literati* — is fabulous. Marvell was known as a political
satirist and pamphleteer and his *Miscellaneous Poems* were published in 1681, three years after his death. George Herbert sent
the manuscript of *The Temple* to Nicholas Farrer from his death-
bed, to be made public or burnt. The poems of Thomas Traherne
(1636–74) were first published in 1903.

None the less, when one looks back from a sufficient distance
one manages to discern a sort of loose common character which
can be attributed to the literature of a period. This is because
there is a general, completely inartificial conversation among
contemporaries of which what remains as the literature is, in
some sense, the finest expression. All the winds blow through
Shakespeare; they do not all blow through William Collins or
Landor. Yet Collins and Landor are fine poets, of a minor kind,
which means that they are major indeed compared with most
even of the creditable performers likely to be enjoying contemporary recognition at any one time. But major or minor — as well
indeed as versifiers of no account — have an inevitable relationship
to the talk of the period as well as a more specific relationship to
one another's techniques. It is easier to recognize the common
character of a period from a distance, but a history, whenever
written, must be some kind of a guess at it.

2

Among the minor writers at the turn of the century is one who is
remembered with respect as the editor and publisher of a number
of charming anthologies of sixteenth- and seventeenth-century
verse as well as of the works of Thomas Campion. This is A. H.
Bullen, who felt his way among neglected work with a fine tact
for the minor purities of language without which no major work
is done. It is impossible to estimate the contribution of such a man
to the perceptions of more productive writers. Bullen was patently
groping in the direction of the sort of refinement of language
which had to be achieved if the century was to find its voices. He
died in 1920, and it was not till his last three or four years, long
after his main work as editor and publisher was finished, that the
small volumes of his own verse appeared, in editions respectively
of twenty-five and thirty copies. It would be useless to pretend that
most of this verse does not have the antiquarian flavour which

might be expected from such a man — and that means something different from the common vulgarities of the manufacturer of sham antiques — but there are a few epigrammatic verses which are well worth notice for themselves. There is this:

> You've told how waking, in the middle night
> You turned your longing arms to left and right
> In love's embrace; alas! she was not there
> And you lay lonely in your dazed despair.[1]

And this from *Callimachus*:

> Their Crethis, with her prattle and her play,
> The girls of Samos often miss to-day:
> Their loved workmate, with flow of merry speech,
> Here sleeps the sleep that comes to all and each.

Those who think such a small achievement negligible have not reached the point from which the study of poetry starts. And it may astonish even a sympathetic reader, in our illiterate age, to know that behind this was a man for whom 'the writings of the Fathers...Origen, Clement of Alexandria, Irenaeus, Lactantius, Augustine, Tertullian, and Gregory, became at last almost as familiar friends as Lucretius, Propertius, Theocritus, Euripedes, Plato, Athenaeus, Aulus Gellius'[2] and others. Few ages have had more pedantry and less learning than our own.

> When in Elysium I shall seek out those
> Who've much delighted me in verse or prose,
> Kindly Crinagoras, I will never rest
> Until I find your shade among the Blest;
> And sure I am that you will not repel
> Me who have loved you long and loved you well.[3]

It is the very fall of the voice of this gentle scholar, who could not afford to visit Greece, this lover of hedgerows who was 'before all

---

[1] *The Middle Night.*
[2] From the introductory note to *Weeping-Cross and Other Rimes.*
[3] *To Crinagoras of Mitylene.*

else, a simple-minded man; simple in his habits, and contented with simple pleasures'.[1]

> Be wary; practise incredulity
> Which makes the soul subtle and sinewy.[2]

It could not be said that he did not speak out before he died, and that is all anybody can do. This last couplet, in particular, is loaded with the man who wrote it. Free from any suspicion of fashion, Bullen caught the indubitable rhythm of the twentieth century, a language free from pretension as from any effort to be 'poetical', words that follow speech so closely that the reader is hardly aware that he has not merely overheard the sentence. But any rubbish will not do; the lines have the weight of long experience and digested thought.

Bullen's achievement provides some sort of clue to the history of the verse of our period. In some sense, any poetical development presents itself as a purification of language. This is well understood in relation to the movement associated with the names of Waller, Denham and Dryden, who left a long posterity to prove their case and in the end turned the country into a stable which had to be cleaned by Collins, Blake and Wordsworth, for no style holds that long. It is less easy to see, in one's own time, that writers who are doing anything are cooperating in a similar common task. Yet that is so, though in our day there is less likelihood of success, indeed every unlikelihood of it, in the technologically-inflated world which seems to stretch before us. The language must be renewed. 'Make it new', as Ezra Pound ordered. Bullen performed only a tiny scraping operation preparatory to such a task. But that is worth something. Moreover, he found his way to re-establish a link between verse and the language that is spoken. And this, as much as anything, is what the history of 1900–1950 is about.

3

If we look at the nineties in this light of this hypothesis, we shall find confirmation in some of the things Yeats tells us about his associates in the Rhymers' Club. 'The nineties' is, of course, an

---

[1] Introductory note.

16   [2] *Epicharmus' Counsel.*

artificial conception, and the Rhymers' Club did not write poems —any more than the Athenaeum does; but Lionel Johnson, Ernest Dowson, John Davidson and Yeats himself were workmen of importance by any standards which would be reasonable in a history of fifty years, and their technical practice was important, in varying degrees, for the writers who followed them. The vague and notorious aura of the period matters less. That was, in a sense, little more than a side-effect of the disintegration of Victorian morality and, to an extent which cannot easily be judged, of the beginnings of an era to be dominated, to an unprecedented extent, by the vulgar press. The proportions of the scandal of Oscar Wilde, which after all was no more than a row between an overblown wit and a tiresome peer, were certainly due to the menace of that sinister power as, in a different style, was the Dreyfus affair in France. People were so taken aback at the novel fury and confusion engendered by the press in these two controversies that it must have seemed that the size of the questions was what journalists said it was. The fuss about Beardsley's drawings had much the same low origin, and we are not yet at the end of the period when money is to be made out of giving prominence to just a little more obscenity than people in general are accustomed to. It matters little that the moral indignation is now always on the side of the Wildes or the Beardsleys, or rather of those who, however devoid of wit as of draughtsmanship, are their sociological successors. There is, of course, a more serious element in the atmosphere of the nineties, which can only be appreciated by those who get near enough to their work. This is the subjectivism, or introversion, which may be regarded as deriving from Walter Pater. There is the obsession with 'exquisite moments', the attitude of 'the aesthetic critic' who 'regards all the objects with which he has to do, all works of art, and the fairer forms of nature and human life, as powers or forces producing pleasurable sensations, each of a more or less peculiar or unique kind'.[1] This had led by the nineties to such confusions as that involved in Lionel Johnson's remark—which for effect he attributed to Newman— that the profession of letters was a third order of the priesthood. The philosophy of 'exquisite moments' and the excitement they can bring is, of course, a refined version of the sensationalism of the press, but if this brooding on feelings is an effeminate thing as

[1] *The Renaissance.*

compared not only with the more integrated attitudes of earlier centuries but with the religious and social controversies of the earlier Victorians, it carried with it heightened attentiveness to words and rhythms which was a necessary preliminary to the further development of the language.

What Lionel Johnson had to say to Yeats, explicitly according to *The Trembling of the Veil*, implicitly if one merely compares the practice, at that time, of the two men, is that it was wrong to regard words made to be read as 'less natural' than words made to be spoken. The account Yeats gives of Johnson's reading of his poem *By the Statue of King Charles at Charing Cross* gives point to this. 'Meaning and cadence,' says Yeats, 'found the most precise elocution... It was as though I listened to a great speech.' What the Rhymers' Club wanted — and what perhaps frightened Francis Thompson away — was verse which 'could hold the attention of a fitting audience like a good play or good conversation'.

4

'A great speech' is not a piece of conversation. Nor is it necessarily great literature. Indeed, it is most unlikely to be the latter. Cicero and Burke have literary merits of a kind the twentieth century thinks little of, and no doubt we under-rate them, but there is no denying the dangers of eloquence. Yeats's impression of *By the Statue of King Charles* is exact. The verses are meant to be spoken, and one can well imagine the appropriateness of Lionel Johnson's 'musical monotone' as a vehicle for their delivery.

> Sombre and rich the skies;
> Great glooms, and starry plains.
> Gently the night wind sighs;
> Else a vast silence reigns.
>
> The splendid silence clings
> Around me: and around
> The saddest of all kings
> Crowned, and again discrowned.
>
> Comely and calm he rides
> Hard by his own Whitehall.

There is a deliberate pathos which is an oratorical trick, and the 'vast silence' and the 'splendid silence' are meant to be impressive and do impress. There are rhetorical questions:

> Which are more full of fate:
> The stars; or those sad eyes?
> Which are more still and great:
> Those brows; or the dark skies?

Only a great sobriety of tone prevents one from feeling that the effect is overdone. Occasionally it is overdone:

> Although his whole heart yearn
> In passionate tragedy

—which is very near a heavy-handed newspaper sensationalism. But the poem as a whole is certainly one of the triumphs of the decade, conveying something of the sombre atmosphere of Victorian London as well as of the pity of its nominal subject who is, as it were, magnified by a fog. The subject was of course, for Johnson, a profoundly sympathetic one, and he could not have written the poem if it had not been. The phantasmagoric quality is partly due to the difficulty of a public subject for so bookish a poet involved in a movement which insisted upon 'emotion which has no relation to any public interest'.

If the language of conversation had been what the Rhymers wanted, they might have found it in Christina Rossetti, but it is clear that the more artificial and limited rhythms of her brother Dante Gabriel were more in their minds. Better still — because it would have taken them out into a fresher atmosphere — they might have found it in Clough. But Clough, probably, could not be of service to them because what they were, properly, intent on was the exclusion of words which did not carry their full weight. Lionel Johnson's contribution remains a sort of purged rhetoric.

> Beyond the straits of Hercules,
> Behold! the strange Hesperian seas,
> A glittering waste at break of dawn:
> High on the westward plunging prow,
> What dreams are on thy spirit now,
> Sertorius of the milk-white fawn?[1]

[1] *Sertorius.*

Johnson was as it were aspiring to some sort of public statement, which was something to try for. He died in 1902, at the age of thirty-five, having been groomed for his role by Winchester and Oxford, and supported in it by a private income.

5

Yeats said that Ernest Dowson's verse was 'Song, though song for the speaking voice', and the description serves to distinguish Dowson's contribution from the 'great speech' of Lionel Johnson. Dowson is a profoundly sympathetic figure, to the extent that one is led to suspect the sympathy he evokes. It is partly that, as Arthur Symons said, 'he used the common-places of poetry frankly, making them his own by his belief in them' — but it is the second part of this characterization which is important. It is partly, it must be admitted, that he exhibited without effort the weaknesses of conduct — and of physique — appropriate to a poet in the tradition of Verlaine. This character was fixed on him by the introduction Symons wrote to the collected *Poems*, with its picture of him playing a quiet game of cards with the girl for whom he entertained a suitably hopeless passion, and then going elsewhere to pursue the roles of one who could not 'resist either the desire or the consequences of drink. Sober,' Symons goes on, 'he was the most gentle, in manner the most gentlemanly of men; unselfish to a fault, to the extent of weakness; a delightful companion, charm itself. Under the influence of drink, he became almost literally insane, certainly quite irresponsible. He fell into furious and unreasoning passions; a vocabulary unknown to him at other times sprang up like a whirlwind; he seemed always about to commit some act of absurd violence.' It is not, however, for his touch of alcoholism that Dowson is to be remembered. He was no less than Lionel Johnson given to the art of good writing — 'a rare thing in England', Pound said in 1914, and it is certainly not less so now. Dowson had too that sense of using the classics which is part of the continuity of our literature; 'the Horatian Cynara or Neobule', as Symons says, 'were still the natural symbol for him when he wished to be most personal.' Indeed, the assimilation of his personal feelings to the traditions of our language, or of European language, may have been surer than Johnson's. One can understand Pound, looking in 1914 for a hardening of the medium, finding more traces of what he wanted in Lionel Johnson, but the 'small slabs of ivory' Johnson seemed to have produced look softer now, for the most part, while the best of Dowson's verse — and it is very little — retains a life of its own because of its intimate rhythm. One has to swallow, in this, the facility of the feeling:

> A little while in the shine of the sun,
>   We were twined together, joined lips, forgot
> How the shadows fall when the day is done,
>   And when Love is not[1]

— but the verse is not negligible; it has a fall of its own. Throughout these verses this individual tone comes and goes; it flickers and is lost. In a short epigram, even, it is hardly maintained throughout:

> Because I am idolatrous and have besought,
> With grievous supplication and consuming prayer,
> The admirable image that my dreams have wrought
> Out of her swan's neck and her dark, abundant hair:
> The jealous gods, who brook no worship save their own,
> Turned my live idol marble and her heart to stone.[2]

It is, however, in the poem in which Eliot noticed 'a slight shift of rhythm', *Non sum qualis eram bonae sub regno Cynarae*, that Dowson left the surest traces of himself.

> Last night, ah, yesternight, betwixt her lips and mine
> There fell thy shadow, Cynara! thy breath was shed
> Upon my soul between the kisses and the wine;
> And I was desolate and sick of an old passion,
>   Yea, I was desolate and bowed my head:
> I have been faithful to thee, Cynara! in my fashion.

It is certainly unfashionable stuff — nonsense if you like, though not complete nonsense — but it contains a contribution to prosody. Not everyone who lives thirty-three years does anything so useful. Dowson was born in the same year as Johnson, in 1867, and died two years before him, in 1900.

[1] *April Love.*
[2] *Epigram.*

6

The third figure of the nineties who managed to produce work of some use to the poets who followed and not merely, like Arthur Symons or Oscar Wilde, verses with a certain period charm, was John Davidson. He was by ten years the senior of the other two but was born further from London and nearer to poverty, in Renfrewshire and as the son of a minister of the Evangelical Union. At thirty he was still schoolmastering in Greenock. He is one of those provincial voices which come to break on the smoothness of the capital with a usefully jarring note. He had the bumptiousness such a situation requires, reinforced by the characteristics of his province and of his father's religion. He had a prehensile and miscellaneous mind, with the common aspiration of bringing into his thought scraps of scientific information only half digested. All this made him a complement to the Oxford courtesies and scholarship of Dowson and Johnson, the gallicizing of Symons and the hierarchic aspirations of Yeats. If it was Swinburne who set him alight when he was twenty-one, it was Shaw who lent him money when he was fifty. The New Woman put in an appearance in a rather hideous poem published in 1894. Davidson was a man of new worlds and unlicked philosophies.

He liked to thump the table. He was a good Scots preacher, like his father, with a doctrine perhaps less out of line than he supposed with the extreme protestantism he inherited. 'This is a great part of my immorality,' he says in his long introduction to *The Theatrocrat*, 'that, instead of a myth, children should be told, as soon as they begin to express their wonder, that they consist of oxygen, hydrogen, nitrogen, carbon, calcium, kalium, natrium, sulphur, phosphorus, iron, magnesium, silicon; that the principal human elements are also the principal constituents of the whole Universe, and that all the elements are forms of one substance. They should also be shown experimentally the qualities and properties of these elements; and gradually, instead of catechisms and the grammars of dead languages, obtain a knowledge of the poetry of evolution: a poetry that does not require to be taught or learnt; that requires only to be told and shown to be known, welcomed, and remembered, because it is already subconscious in the Matter of which we consist.' Anyone contradict that? he seems to inquire hopefully. Then he goes on: 'Thus a child would know at once that there has been no philosophy, no religion, no literature hitherto; that there is nothing for him to learn; that everyone must make for himself his own philosophy, religion, literature.' It is rubbish, of course, and in a well-known tradition. The iconoclastic 'dare' needs to be supported by a certain egotism. Davidson certainly had that. There is also a genuine gritty substance under his big talk, and it is when this gets into the texture of his verse that he is at his best.

It is a question how often that happens. Much of the verse is loud-mouthed with the insistence of Davidson's personality rather than telling because of what it says. A test piece is *A Woman and her Son* from *New Ballads* (1897). There is little doubt that, at forty, Davidson is still arguing out the personal agony of his adolescence.

> 'You married then a crude evangelist,
> Whose soul was like a wafer that can take
> One single impress only.'
>   'Oh, my son!
> Your father!'
>   'He, my father! These are times
> When all must to the crucible — no thought,
> Practice, or use, or custom sacro-sanct
> But shall be violable now. And first
> If ever we evade the wonted round,
> The stagnant vortex of the eddying years,
> The child must take the father by the beard,
> And say, "What did you in begetting me?"'

There is nothing of importance in that for anyone except John Davidson. The lines have the stress of the consulting-room or they are melodrama. The poem carries this brawl on to

>   'Mother, rejoice;
> For I shall make you glad. There is no heaven,
> Your children are resolved to dust and dew:
> But, mother, I am God. I shall create
> The heaven of your desires'

—and so to a final comment which, if true enough, is not an insight which illumines the dreary scene, nor a piece of versification which can give pleasure, though there is craftsmanship in the last short line.

23

For both were bigots — fateful souls that plague
The gentle world.

There is a touch of illumination in *Thirty Bob a Week*, which is, justly, Davidson's most famous ballad, and a restraint which enables him to express his condition rather than to shout about it. There is the rhythm of speech and not of mere harangue.

It's a naked child against a hungry wolf;
    It's playing bowls upon a splitting wreck;
It's walking on a string across a gulf
    With mill-stones fore-and-aft about your neck;
But the thing is daily done by many and many a one;
    And we fall, face forward, fighting, on the deck.

And there are, in Davidson, the sudden vivid locations:

In the Isle of Dogs by Millwall Dock[1]

or

As I went down to Dymchurch Wall.[2]

He did not pass those places without leaving a ghost. He is a nagging, unfinished figure, whose technique was not equal to the new poetry he proclaimed. He walked into the sea off Penzance in 1909, an elderly and belated member of Yeats's tragic generation. Hugh MacDiarmid, then a boy of seventeen, 'felt as if the bottom had fallen out of his world'.

[1] *In the Isle of Dogs.*
24   [2] *In Romney Marsh.*

Chapter Two

Thomas Hardy; Rudyard Kipling; A. E. Housman

I

Among the poets writing in 1900 who have an undoubted importance in the new century, there was one who had his roots deep in an already remote epoch. Thomas Hardy was born at Lower Bockhampton, in the parish of Stinsford, Dorset, in 1840. The railway had not yet come to Dorchester. Hardy's father, a master mason from an old local family which included Nelson's Hardy among its connections, played the violin Sunday after Sunday in the gallery of the village church, where the version of the psalms by Tate and Brady was still in fashion. The ballads had not yet been forgotten in the countryside. Hardy was educated, first, at the village school, then in Dorchester, which is within walking distance. At twelve he started Latin with 'the old Eton grammar and readings of Eutropius and Caesar' and learned enough to return often to Horace, Virgil and a Latin Testament in later years. At sixteen he left school and became an articled pupil to an architect and church-restorer in Dorchester. He afterwards worked for a time in London, and his architecture served intermittently to support him until his novels brought him in enough to live on. In Dorchester as a boy he saw a man in the stocks and attended a public execution. There was hard and solid reality behind the bookish observations Lionel Johnson made, in *The Art of Thomas Hardy* (1894), about Hardy's kinship with the past. 'Certainly,' Johnson said, 'at Cerne Abbas or at Abbotsbury, the sight of those old granaries, where bundles of straw protrude through noble windows, calls up the same thoughts, with which the scholar looks upon Virgil's very plough, still furrowing the earth of Italy, as does Mr Hardy's picture of calves, sheltered under old arches, who cooled "their thirsty tongues by licking the quaint Norman carving, which glistened with moisture".' There is, however, no trace in Hardy of the townee attitude — now largely unfashionable in relation to this country, but flourishing as ever, in relation to foreign peasantries, with thousands of those who take their holidays ever further afield in order to find suitable objects — of simpering over picturesque poverty. Hardy was, moreover, at pains to destroy the sort of picture of the countryman which might present itself to a 'philanthropic lady', as his article on *The Dorsetshire Labourer*, published in *Longman's Magazine* in 1883, explicitly says. He had a great admiration for the trade unionist Joseph Arch (1826–1919), whom he had seen and listened to during the latter's early attempts to organize agricultural labourers in Dorset.

The fact that Hardy's memories went back to a time and place which retained many ways from a much older date is important, not for its antiquarian interest, but because it gives his view of humanity a certain depth in time. One of the most alarming prospects of the technological world — if prospect is the right word for something that is already upon us — is the achievement of a society in which change is simultaneous and world-wide, so that the lessons of earlier epochs are expunged before they are understood. But Hardy was not only a man of the past. He was a provincial. 'A certain provincialism of feeling,' he wrote, 'is invaluable. It is of the essence of individuality, and is largely made up of that crude enthusiasm without which no great thoughts are thought, no great deeds done.'[1] The combination of an imaginative reach into the past with a dogged insistence on his right to his own differences gave Hardy a strong protection against the easy flow of prejudice which is of all things the most inimical to poetry. Add to that a powerful eroticism, concealed under a quiet and somewhat secretive exterior, and one has the elements of his famous pessimism, which was a sort of unhoping spirit of independence. There is no doubt that he has put himself into Michael Henchard's will, in *The Mayor of Casterbridge*:

> That Elizabeth-Jane Farfrae be not told of my death, or made to grieve on account of me.
> & that I be not bury'd in consecrated ground.
> & that no sexton be asked to toll the bell.
> & that nobody is wished to see my dead body.
> & that no murmurs walk behind me at my funeral.
> & that no flours be planted on my grave.

[1] Quoted by Florence Emily Hardy in *The Early Life of Thomas Hardy*.

& that no man remember me.
To this I put my name.

It is true that, a few weeks before his death in 1928, Hardy said 'he had done all that he meant to do', but he added that he did not know whether it had been worth doing'.[1] He had a way of looking down on completed works, and finding that they were not good.

When John Lane produced his bibliography of Hardy in 1894 he revealed that much of the 'earliest work' — he had been 'told, on good authority, the entire work of two years — was in verse'. Of this work Lane believed that 'everything, with the exception of one poem, was destroyed'. The 'one piece of salvage' was said to be the ballad which was later called *The Bride-Night Fire*. Lionel Johnson's book was exclusively about Hardy's work as a novelist. There was at that time no other public manifestation of Hardy's art, except the poem published by Lane as an appendix to Johnson's book, and perhaps three other poems which had appeared in periodicals and were by then lost in obscurity. But when Hardy's first volume of verse, *Wessex Poems*, was published in 1898, he added a note to the effect that many of them 'were written long ago' and that 'in some few cases the verses were turned into prose and printed as such, it having been unanticipated at that time that they might see the light.' It is an astonishing bit of literary history, and the moral is that one should beware of contemporary reputations. It was towards poetry that Hardy had directed his first literary efforts. It is even alleged that he first desired to get into print as the author of a novel because 'he could not do so as a poet without paying for publication'. The *Wessex Poems*, his first volume of poems, appeared in 1898, but the second poem in it bears the date 1865. Hardy had been writing verse for thirty years while reputations were made and unmade around him. 1865 was the year of Kipling's birth and *Barrack-Room Ballads* was published in 1886. A number of early poems are scattered around in Hardy's later volumes, and were released to the world forty or more years after their composition. When we consider the casual style of Hardy's verse, which gives it so important and influential a place in the history of English poetry in the twentieth century, and the fact that that style was largely formed when the earliest poems were written, we have to concede

[1] Notes by F. E. H. in *The Later Years of Thomas Hardy*.

that this unobtrusive, if now prominent, figure was an innovator to an extent which the passage of time has done much to obscure.

For two reasons the peculiarities of Dorset life are less prominent in the poems than in the novels. In the first place, Hardy's poems — or a great many of them — are personal in the sense that they relate more or less immediately to his own life, which means that they reflect London and the miscellaneous chances of a wider world as well as the local scene. Secondly, in the shorter speech of poetry Hardy is naturally less concerned with accidental circumstances and more with the essentials of passions which are much the same in any time and place. But the local scene is not out of view for long in the pages of the *Collected Poems*, whether explicitly, as the stage for a dramatic episode such as *At Winyard's Gap*, or more unobtrusively as a hovering background. And Arthur, in *The Famous Tragedy of the Queen of Cornwall*, is the 'Over-king of Counties'. This attachment to a place is so far from being a freak of Hardy's art, or a piece of stage management, that it is in fact the mere consequence of his sober observation and the truth of what he has to relate. His imagination is really an imagination; it uses images to clothe his thought, and they are assembled from things actually seen and intimately known. It must be admitted that his forays into abstraction, the Spirits and Pities of the *Dynast* choruses, are less impressive than the fates embodied in a woman waiting for her lover or in the branches rustling on a Dorset hillside.

As for the subject-matter of Hardy's poetry, it cannot altogether escape the charge of a certain obsessional brooding on the more emotional moments in the relationships of men and women. The reader hardly needs the researches which attempt to track down the movements of a long dead girl in Puddletown to tell him that this poet found a certain sort of involvement almost irresistible, and returned again and again, in his study where he sat every morning, to some of the more poignant episodes. Indeed, passion remembered, the contrast, sometimes with rather obvious irony, between one year and another year long past, is a recurrent theme. The indulgence of memory became almost a vice. He lived with his memories between an erotic impulse and a shudder.

Do they know me, whose former mind
        Was like an open plain where no foot falls,

But now is a gallery portrait-lined,
    And scored with necrologic scrawls,
Where feeble voices rise, once full-defined,
    From underground in curious calls?[1]

This habit of mind is projected on the figures who people the
poems. An almost crude example — but not ineffective, and there
is often a certain melodrama about Hardy's effects — is *The Carrier*,
who always kept a place vacant for his long-dead wife who used
to ride with him. Hardy cannot miss a train and have to put up at a
casual inn at the junction without dreaming of past assignations:

    Thus onetime to me…
Dim wastes of dead years bar away
Then from now. But such happenings to-day
    Fall to lovers, may be!

    Years, years as shoaled seas,
Truly, stretch now between! Less and less
Shrink the visions then vast in me. — Yes,
    Then in me: Now in these.[2]

There is also in Hardy an observation of nature which is impelled
by a profound fellow-feeling, so that even the most insignificant
creatures arouse a curiosity not really different in kind from that
which he accords to men and women. He sees in his study one
August night

    A sleepy fly, that rubs its hands[3]

and he can sit indoors, listening to the wind, and say with precision
what is happening outside. It is a combination of his sense of the
confrontation of past and present with his profound sympathy with
the events of nature which give so powerful a completeness to such
a poem as *The Last Signal*.

    Looking hard and harder I knew what it meant —
    The sudden shine sent from the livid east scene;

[1] *In a Former Resort After Many Years.*
[2] *The Missed Train.*
[3] *An August Midnight.*

It meant the west mirrored by the coffin of my friend there,
    Turning to the road from his green,

    To take his last journey forth — he who in his prime
    Trudged so many a time from that gate athwart the land!
  Thus a farewell to me he signalled on his grave-way,
      As with a wave of his hand.

The friend was William Barnes.

No single poem, and no short selection, can give an adequate impression of the weight of Hardy's achievement as a poet. The sheer bulk of closely-felt impressions, covering sixty years or more of his writing life, is without parallel in our literature. He is no Wordsworth, hardening as the years go on, and the last poems are as lively as, and deeper than, the first. The whole *oeuvre* is united by temperament and by a style which did not harden simply because it was nothing more than the words and rhythms that it was natural for Hardy to use, in his persistent impulse to set down the truth as he saw it. At all times in Hardy's writings there are awkwardnesses of expression. He neither kept such things for defiant show nor seems to have wished to get rid of them. In the end they seem to be less awkwardnesses than aspects of his speaking mind, like a particular lurch or other movement which is habitual to some bodies. The rhythm of the verse, with its hesitations, sudden speeds, and pauses which are almost silences, is the very rhythm of thought. One understand why, in the last poem of his last volume, *He resolves to say no more.*

  O my soul, keep the rest unknown!
  It is too like a sound of moan
      When the charnel-eyed
      Pale Horse has nighed;
  Yea, none shall gather what I hide!

  Why load men's minds with more to bear
  That bear already ails to spare?
      From now alway
      Till my last day
  What I discern I will not say.

In 1903–8 *The Dynasts* was published. The theme had occupied Hardy for twenty or thirty years; in a sense he had grown up with it. For, his connections with Captain Hardy apart, memories of the

Napoleonic Wars and of the preparations to meet the invasion which did not come were still alive in the Dorset of his youth. George III's residence at Weymouth, and his ministers going to and from there, meant that Hardy had an intimate knowledge of at any rate one of the centres of consultation in these actions. It suited the retrospective cast of his mind to choose for his most ambitious work a theme which had so many physical associations for him. When he decided on a dramatic form — even though a form, as he says, for 'mental performance' only — he had in mind a peculiar good fortune of his youth, 'the old Christmas mummers' who had been an accepted and ordinary part of his early years. He remembered 'the curiously hypnotizing impressiveness' of their 'automatic style — that of persons who spoke by no will of their own' and conceived of a similar 'monotonic delivery of speeches, with dreamy conventional gestures'. It was something at once novel and ancient that he was proposing. The ironies and fates brood somewhat heavily over this large and shapeless drama, but, clumsy as the machinery is, it corresponds accurately enough to the tensions in Hardy's mind not to be more than superficially absurd. Accustomed to the scale of operation of prose fiction, Hardy ploughs on through scene after scene in which the blank verse is saved by its very flatness, for he is pretending to nothing that he does not mean to say. It is Hardy's lack of pretension — more in evidence in his verse than in his prose — which is his profoundest contribution to the literature of the twentieth century.

Hardy has this to say about the relationship of prose and verse (the source is a speech made to the Royal Society of Literature in 1912, when he was seventy-two):

For my own part I think — though all writers may not agree with me — that the shortest way to good prose is by the route of good verse. The apparent paradox — I cannot remember who first expressed it — that the best poetry is the best prose ceases on examination to be a paradox and becomes a truism. Anybody may test it for himself by taking any fine lines in verse and, casting off the fetters of metre and rhyme that seem to bind the poet, trying to express the same ideas more freely and accurately in prose. He will find that it cannot be done: the words of the verse — fettered as he thought them — are the only words that will convey the ideas that were intended to be conveyed.[1]

Another short critical masterpiece deserves to be remembered in

[1] 'A Plea for Pure English'.

this place. It is dated from Max Gate, Dorchester, in 1914, and addressed to the Editor of the *New York Times*:

In answer to your question of which is the best short poem I have read in the English language I can only say that I fail to see how there can be a 'best' poem, long or short; that is, one best in all circumstances. This attempt to appraise by comparison is, if you will allow me to say so, one of the literary vices of the time, only a little above the inquiry who is the biggest poet, novelist, or prizefighter, although not quite so low down as that deepest deep of literary valuation, 'who is the biggest seller'.[1]

2

If Hardy was a poet who took to prose until, so to speak, the world was ready to receive his verse, Kipling was a prose master who used verse when it suited him, without much changing his attitude towards words. He is a wholesome writer in the sense that there is remarkably little *literary* nonsense about him, not because he did not care about the refinements but because, on the contrary, he was a deliberate craftsman who was not content unless he had done a good job. Yet he was so far from writing merely to exhibit his craftsmanship that he seems always to be bursting with what he has to say.

Rudyard Kipling was born in India in 1865, eight years after the Mutiny and twenty years after Patrick Vans Agnew, a twenty-five-year-old civil servant murdered in the course of his duty, had died in Multan with the words: 'We are not the last of the English.' The period of reconstruction after the Mutiny determined the character of the imperial period. In a way these Victorian years were an exhibition of national self-confidence, but they began with something different. The proclamation of 1858 accepted the differences of caste and creed in India as something not to be meddled with by the British, who thus admitted that these foreign ways were too difficult for them and that it was better for them not to act according to their own lights. At the same time, Dalhousie's view that the native states were an anachronism was set aside out of gratitude to the princes who had saved our bacon in 1857–8. The British became spectators and manipulators of the wonders of India rather than radical managers and reformers. They presumed to a patriarchal care, on which great energy and seriousness were expended, without inquiring too closely what the children were up to. Although no doubt the

[1] 'Which is the Best Short Poem in English?'

resources of official information grew as the years went on, the English consciousness of India shrank, and a sort of earnest frivolity set in.

For a small English child in India there was another side to all this. He might be unnaturally important, as the son of a princely race, but he was left to talk to the servants and their connections and so to learn their language and, for a few years, to live below the surface of the Raj. For an inquisitive and imaginative child the experience was profound and determining. Kipling learned as much of this world as any child could and it remained there, in the back of his mind, when the foreground came to be filled with more common place Anglo-Saxon concerns. He was sent home at an early age, and the arrangements made for his up-bringing were such that he certainly suffered from lack of affection and might, even, be regarded as having been seriously deprived. He came out of this epoch with a sort of cocky victory, and at the age of seventeen went back to India to take up journalism, his short sight preventing his entry into the army, which might otherwise have been his career. The India he returned to was different from the one he had left, for his perspectives were different. He was now the young sahib with a profession, mixing at the club with 'none except picked men at their definite work', as he says in *Something of Myself*. The later years brought travels in various parts of the Empire, as well as in France, and in spite of years in Sussex he remained an imperial product, a sort of outsider, only half in sympathy with the native English. But he remained a 'picked man' at his 'definite work' of writing. Short stories, novels and verses were turned out as only a very highly qualified professional could make them. And Kipling, whether as entertainer or political spokesman or both, was addressing himself to a public he knew and which was there. *Plain Tales from the Hills* were aimed at a public as definite as that addressed by the men who wrote for the Elizabethan and Jacobean theatre — a public of sahibs and mem-sahibs, public-school boys and their ladies, and a wide peripheral group who looked with more or less approval and respect on doings of that class, and felt themselves sharing in a national and ultimately a defensive task. If the public was, for a poet, a less satisfactory one than Shakespeare's or Ben Jonson's, that was not Kipling's fault.

The reader cannot avoid questions about Kipling's personality. The tale of *Baa, Baa, Black Sheep* — in the volume of *Wee Willie*

Winkie — which reflects the years in England when he is supposed to have been abandoned to extraordinary tyranny at the hands of a bullying foster-mother, is certainly a Hell, and, some might say, so is the school of *Stalky & Co*. 'When young lips have drunk deep of the bitter waters of Hate, Suspicion, and Despair,' Kipling says, 'all the Love in the world will not wholly take away that knowledge.' That solemn sentence is to be recalled beside the sinister expression of the Black Sheep's aversion from his fellow-pupils: 'Some of them were unclean, some of them talked in dialect, many dropped their h's, and there were two Jews and a negro or someone quite as dark.' There is no doubt that Kipling developed, somehow, an extraordinary disjunction from his fellows, which the gang loyalties of a minor public school and later assumption of the life of a sahib did nothing to heal. This is a vice of his sensibility which gives something to the tone of his verse, a sort of aloofness even when he is pretending to be familiar.

Indeed, the tone of false familiarity in much of Kipling's more conversational verse, or verse which pretends to be conversational, is one of its weaknesses. It is particularly noticeable when he is projecting his thoughts through the mouths of the vulgar. No doubt as a journalist in India Kipling mixed a little more freely than an officer or member of the Indian Civil Service would have done, and conversed at times with British Other Ranks and other pariahs. But his view of the British soldier is always that of the outsider. Perhaps he has poked his nose into sergeants' messes, but it is evident that he has never moved at ease in those exclusive circles. With an ear for language, he picked up enough of the manner to impress those who had not been as near as he had, but the view he has of such low life is gathered from the sahib's club from which the other ranks were rigorously excluded.

> We was sick o' bein' punished, an' we let 'em know it, too;
> An' a company-commander up an' 'it us with a sword,
> An' someone shouted, "Ook it!' an' it come to *sove-ki-poo*,
> An' we chucked our rifles from us — O my Gawd![1]

It is not in this tone that troops speak of a mutiny; what we have is the gruesome spectacle of Kipling's puppet being forced to speak of the things he has done as they seem to the officers and

[1] *That Day.*

their ladies talking over his turpitudes. No doubt Kipling picked up the story in the more expensive part of the cantonment.

Some attempt has been made, by T. S. Eliot, to explain Kipling's verse with reference to Dryden. One can understand the point of this approximation, but it is unfair to Dryden who, besides being a much greater poet, was operating in a milieu of much greater solidity and a much more solid civilization. Dryden was at home with the political passions he represented as with the classics out of which he made his translations, and the England of the seventeenth century was a domestic scene, quarrels and all, from which certain sorts of pretension, which became common enough later, were excluded. Kipling's pugnacious world has always about it a phantasmagoric quality which is nearer to the fantasies and brutalities of boyhood than to adult life. This is not to say that it has nothing of adult life in it, or that boyhood is an altogether false prognostication of the future. There is, however, also present, too often, the prefect's tone: Get the little beggars to do this or that—or else—and the little beggars turn out to be, as often as not, the lower orders. There is a strain of unsuccessful authoritarianism about Kipling which is not un-related to the qualities of his verse. He seems to be after the irrefutable prose statement, whether the subject is important or not. The irrefutability, or the anxious search for it, gives his lines a certain weight, though sometimes it is that of the oppressive talker you would escape if you could. He is a little loud, he may disgust you, but he can hardly be said to bore, a qualification rare indeed, it must be admitted, among writers of verse. It was not a small thing Kipling did, whatever it was. About its poetic value questions are raised, and many of the verses no doubt have little enough. But all, or almost all, are the work of a man who is intent on saying something clearly. What he says clearly is not, however, always all he says, and it is these troubling depths, when they are there, which make his work more than the *Barrack-Room Ballads* which, at the outset, they claimed to be.

A comparison somewhat more enlightening than that with Dryden may be made with Thomas Tusser, of whom Kipling was an enthusiastic reader and an edition of whose works he caused to be published. The *Five Hundered Points of Good Husbandry* appeared soon after the middle of the sixteenth century, and for two hundred years or more the book was used as a practical guide by farmers up and down the country. 'What I like about him,' Kipling wrote of Tusser, 'is that he does not seem to have made much of a success of his own job — whereby he came to know what he was writing about.' This comment is interesting because it was to his own failure — on account of defective eyesight — to get into the army that he owed his passionate attention to what he could learn about the life of action. Tusser 'was so dead keen', Kipling goes on — 'to impart his knowledge to his neighbours (I don't think he ever thought much beyond his own country) that he rammed his maxims into metre with a sledgehammer'. It was the same tool that Kipling himself used. The precepts of husbandry are set out as they are to be followed month by month.

> Forget it not,
> fruit brused will rot.
> Light ladder and long
> doth tree least wrong.
> Go gather with skill,
> and gather that will.

Tusser's advice is the patient work which made the countryside, before mechanized excavators and factory building:

> Where stones be too manie, annoieng thy land,
>   make servant come home with a stone in his hand.
> By daily so dooing, have plentie yee shall,
>   both handsome for paving and good for a wall.

There are precepts also for the housewife within doors:

> Make maide to be clenly, or make hir crie creake,
> and teach hir to stirre, when hir mistresse doth speake.

Or this:

> *The first cock croweth.*
> Past five a clock, Holla: maid, sleeping beware,
> *The next cock croweth.*
> Least quickly your Mistres uncover your bare.

Or this:

> New bread is a waster, but mouldie is wurse.

It is difficult for a language which has gone by the ways of
romanticism and journalism to come out as cleanly as that, but it
was something of this sort that Kipling was aiming at. At rare
moments, and as it were involuntarily and by the way, Tusser lets
slip a subtler poetry:

> For time is it selfe but a time for a time,
>   forgotten ful soone, as the tune of a chime.

Kipling too has these aberrations. There are the weird verses from
Puck of Pook's Hill:

> What is a woman that you forsake her,
> And the hearth-fire and the home-acre,
> To go with the old grey Widow-maker?
>
> She has no house to lay a guest in —
> But one chill bed for all to rest in,
> That the pale suns and the stray bergs nest in.[1]

It is as if there was a break for a moment in the strong affirmative
voice. The verse shows it, as also in this:

> 'Have you any news of my boy Jack?'
>   *Not this tide.*
> 'When d'you think that he'll come back?'
>   *Not with this wind blowing, and this tide*[2]

— though that is in Kipling's plainer, ballad vein. Kipling was, of
course, a notable balladist of a kind and in *Danny Deever* — an early
example — he broke the rhythms, which sound like a drum, to let
out the powers of evil.

> 'What are the bugles blowin' for?' said Files-on-Parade.
> 'To turn you out, to turn you out,' the Colour-Sergeant said.
> 'What makes you look so white, so white?' said Files-on-Parade.
> 'I'm dreadin' what I've got to watch,' the Colour-Sergeant said.
>   'For they're hangin' Danny Deever...'

Even in simpler work, such as *The Ballad of East and West*,

---

[1] *The Harp Song of the Dane Women.*
[2] *My Boy Jack.*

Kipling is saying more than is said in the superficial eloquence of Macaulay's ballads. But his real contribution to the verse of the twentieth century is in his plainness. We like it less when the verse is well-worn, and admonitory, but one can hardly deny a minor merit even to

> As it will be in the future, it was at the birth of Man —
> There are only four things certain since Social Progress began: —
> That the Dog returns to his Vomit and the Sow returns to her Mire,
> And the burnt Fool's bandaged finger goes wabbling back to the Fire;
>
> And that after this is accomplished, and the brave new world begins
> When all men are paid for existing and no man must pay for his sins,
> As surely as Water will wet us, as surely as Fire will burn,
> The Gods of the Copybook Headings with terror and slaughter
> return![1]

There is a genuine indignation, unobscured by this prefectorial didacticism, in some of the more unassuming short poems — as this on *A Dead Statesman*:

> I could not dig: I dared not rob:
> Therefore I lied to please the mob.
> Now all my lies are proved untrue
> And I must face the men I slew.
> What tale shall serve me here among
> Mine angry and defrauded young?

And in this:

> If any question why we died,
> Tell them, because our fathers lied.[2]

The statesmen and the fathers continue to lie, however, so useless is poetry.

3

A. E. Housman is, with Hardy and Kipling, a third figure who stands at the turn of the century, his work half in and half out of

---

[1] *The Gods of the Copybook Headings.*

[2] *Common Form.*

the period covered by this history. *A Shropshire Lad* was published in 1896 and *Last Poems* in 1922. Housman was born in 1859, and had he met with the early death he so often contemplated in his poems he would have been grouped with John Davidson, Lionel Johnson and Ernest Dowson. As it was he lived to lecture in Cambridge in 1936. He was born in a Birmingham suburb and his father was in practice as a solicitor. The world of his poetry, with its young ploughmen, its 'men from the barn and the forge and the mill and the fold',[1] and its young red-coated soldiers, was that of a dream. Housman himself was urban, precise and better suited to his final destiny of drinking port at High Table than to rollicking with the lads at Ludlow Fair. His youth was blighted by a homosexual passion, which must have weighed on him and helped to retract him from the world. This is certainly an element in his pessimism; it also gives vividness to his youthful portraits.

From his early years Housman exhibited the enthusiasms of a scholar rather than any which might be thought of as more appropriate to a lyrical poet. While an undergraduate at Oxford, and about the age when Davidson was sending his poems to Swinburne — who did not reply — Housman sent letters to Cambridge to the editor of Lucretius and author of *Criticisms and Elucidations of Catullus*, H. A. J. Munro. He then spent ten years in the Patent Office, where no doubt there is always work for scholars, and emerged as Professor of Latin at University College, London, having accompanied his application with seventeen testimonials and a letter explaining that in 1881 he had 'failed to obtain honours in the Final School of Litterae Humaniores'. At University College he did not distinguish between the faces of his girl students, whom on occasion he reduced to tears. In 1911 he moved to Trinity College, Cambridge, and there spent his remaining twenty-five years. 'A scholar who means to build himself a monument,' he wrote, 'must spend much of his life in acquiring knowledge which for its own sake is not worth having and in reading books which do not in themselves deserve to be read.'[2] He set aside his early work on Propertius in favour of erudite labours on Manilius — 'a facile and frivolous poet,' he said, 'the brightest facet of whose genius was an eminent

---

[1] *A Shropshire Lad*, XXIII.
[2] Quoted by A. S. F. Gow in *A. E. Housman: A Sketch*.

aptitude for doing sums in verse.'[1] H. A. J. Munro, he might have remembered, had expended himself on poets he thought important, which seems sensible. Housman destroyed an essay he had written on Swinburne, not because it was not good but because it was not good enough for him. He also destroyed a drawing of himself by William Rothenstein because he did not like it. He was certainly a man who wished to build a monument for himself, and had some petty notions about what he should build. He was, however, also a poet, and while his passion for meticulous labour was clearly unbounded, he knew that 'poetry is either easy or impossible'.[2]

In his own case it was easy, at certain moments. He has described, in the Leslie Stephen lecture he gave at Cambridge in 1933, how the process worked in his case. It is important to remember that at this time he was seventy-four, and *A Shropshire Lad* had been published in 1896 and *Last Poems*, with no perceptible development of technique or emotion, in 1922. It is therefore as if a member of the Rhymers' Club had been resuscitated to speak, eleven years after *The Waste Land* and three years after Auden's first volume of *Poems*. There is no doubt as to the fidelity of Housman's evidence. He records how, when he is shaving, he has to keep watch over his thoughts 'because, if a line of poetry strays' into his memory, his 'skin bristles so that the razor ceases to act'. Poetry seems to him 'more physical than intellectual' and he describes the process of its manufacture, in his own case, properly pointing out that 'some poetry, and quite good poetry' might be the result of a different process. With Housman composition began with a pint of beer and a walk of two or three hours, and thinking of nothing in particular. Suddenly there would flow into his mind, 'with sudden and unaccountable emotion, sometimes a line or two of verse, sometimes a whole stanza at once, accompanied, not preceded, by a vague notion of the poem which they were destined to form part of. Then there would usually be a lull of an hour or so, then perhaps the spring would bubble up again.' Often there were gaps which had to be filled later. 'I should call it a secretion', he says; 'whether a natural secretion, like turpentine in the fir, or a morbid secretion, like the pearl in the oyster. I think that my own case, though I may not deal with the material so cleverly as the oyster does, is

[1] A. S. F. Gow, *A. E. Housman: A Sketch.*
[2] Quoted by A. S. F. Gow.

the latter.' More generally, he expressed the view that 'the intellect is not the fount of poetry, that it may actually hinder its production', which shows, perhaps, not so much a limited notion of poetry as a limited notion of the intellect, for Housman was no doubt referring to those acrobatics he performed in his work as a scholar. But Housman's view of poetry was limited in a way which would not have been possible to a serious writer whose mind had matured after 1910. He had in 1892 emitted a wish that Shakespeare had brought himself up to the technical standard of Milton and that was, precisely, the point at which he stood in 1933, though he does not say so in so many words. He does, however, treat

Take O take those lips away

as 'nonsense', to make the point that it is not less poetical than

Fear no more the heat o' the sun,

which is sense. This is part of his case against the intellect. Pound, writing in the *Criterion* at the time, commented: 'A. The sample is by no means nonsense. B. The intellect has been in plenary function, Shakespeare being the greatest English technician bar none.' Pound also took issue with Housman on the examples of metric for which Housman expressed the greatest admiration. 'Easier almost to parody than transcribe,' he says, and goes on to parody:

Come, tumtum Greek, Ulysses, come
   Caress these shores with me:
The windblown seas have wet my bum
   And here the beer is free.

Housman did not, in fact, contribute anything to the development of verse in the twentieth century. He practised a superior neatness, with a very high degree of superiority, and the iterations of his feelings had to accommodate themselves to this. It would hardly be too much to say that, when the wells bubbled up, they hit the precise manipulative mind of the scholar and were laid out in a superficial order.

The peculiar quality of Housman's poetry is that the manipula-tive mind did not get the better of the feelings or distort them. It is as if the very limitations of his conscious training, the very limitations of his view of the intellect, preserved him from tampering. The result is verse in which the superficiality and the depth of the man are equally expressed. There are moments when his obsessive concerns are almost transmuted into classical form, which is presumably what he would have aimed at had he not understood too well what his poetry was to allow the censor to control it:

> Here dead lie we because we did not choose
>> To live and shame the land from which we sprung.
> Life, to be sure, is nothing much to lose;
>> But young men think it is, and we were young.[1]

There are poems where the melancholy is almost sunny, he has thrown it so much into light and amenable form, as in

> Loveliest of trees, the cherry now
> Is hung with bloom along the bough[2]

or

> In summertime on Bredon
>> The bells they sound so clear;
> Round both the shires they ring them
>> In steeples far and near,
>> A happy noise to hear.[3]

But it is the lurking demons which give depth to Housman's poetry. It is the young men hanged, shot, saying farewell, getting drunk, giving their brutal lives for the Queen. In a sense all the poems are a single sequence, and if all Housman is present in one short component, the force of it can be understood only by reading the lot. There is no excuse for not reading the lot, and indeed it is difficult to see how anyone who starts can avoid doing so. It is not the cruder facilities of conduct which are expressed in the terrible surrender of the tight-lipped don who wrote:

[1] *More Poems*, XXXVI.
[2] *A Shropshire Lad*, II.
[3] *Bredon Hill*.

Crossing alone the nighted ferry
    With the one coin for fee,
Whom, on the wharf of Lethe waiting,
    Count you to find? Not me.

The brisk fond lackey to fetch and carry,
    The true, sick-hearted slave,
Expect him not in the just city
    And free land of the grave.[1]

[1] *More Poems*, XXIII.

Chapter Three

The influence of prose on verse:
Ford Madox Ford; Walter De La Mare

I

It was one of Ford Madox Ford's stories that he started *The English Review* — in 1908 — to publish a poem of Hardy's which nobody else would print. *A Sunday Morning Tragedy* did in fact appear on the first pages of the first number. Ford, however, made a point about the inaccuracy of his stories and — although it has often been done — there is no reason why anyone should make any other point. He made it early and repeatedly; there is a *locus classicus* in the dedication to *Ancient Lights and Certain New Reflections* (1911). 'Just a word,' he says, 'to make plain the actual nature of this book. It consists of impressions.' He goes on to relate that 'a distinguished critic fell foul of one of the stories' and to explain more or less successfully — according to your appetite for exaggeration and irony — the nature of the misunderstanding. He says 'what I am trying to get at is that, though there have been many things written about these facts, no one has whole-heartedly and thoroughly attempted to get the atmosphere of these twenty-five years' — the twenty-five years of his life which he is thus partially and impressionistically relating. There is no concealment as to the nature of the process.

This book, in short, is full of inaccuracies as to facts, but its accuracy as to impressions is absolute. For the facts, when you have a little time to waste, I should suggest that you go through this book carefully, noting the errors. To the one of you who succeeds in finding the largest number I will cheerfully present a copy of the ninth edition of the *Encyclopaedia Britannica*, so that you may still further perfect yourself in the hunting out of errors.

In case this was not plain enough he adds: 'I don't really deal in facts, I have for facts a most profound contempt.' It is a dangerous doctrine and it would be a foolish one in the hands of anyone less preoccupied than Ford was with the central 'business in life', which he defines as an 'attempt to discover, and to try to let you see, where we stand'. Through all his dazzling impressions Ford

44

was concerned to get to the centre of the mind, and stay there, whether the mind of an individual character, more or less real, more or less fictional, the mind of an age or generation, or that more permanent mind which is that of civilized man, perhaps now on the way to extinction, the man who was recognizably the same anywhere along the Great Trade Route anywhen in the last three thousand years. To be more explicit, the Great Trade Route ran

from China across all Asia to Asia Minor; then along the shores of the Mediterranean as far as Marseilles. There, up the Rhone, it ran inland, by way of Beaucaire and Lyons to Paris; then down the Seine past Rouen to the English Channel, which it crossed at its narrowest, and so away along the south coast of England past Ottery St Mary to the Scilly Isles, where it ended abruptly.[1]

This again is hardly for the reader of encyclopaedias, though assuredly it is not without its truth. 'Taboo ground to taboo ground,' he says, 'at Nijni Novgorod, at Stamboul, at Athens, Marseilles, Beaucaire, Lyons, Paris, Dover, Salisbury, Ottery St Mary.'[2] There is advantage in seeing it as concretely as that, though the type of mind is not fashionable. Ford represents, in the literature of the twentieth century, an immense recall, evocation if you like, of a past which, until recently, was not remembered so poignantly because people still lived in it.

The immediate evocation, in *Ancient Lights and Certain New Reflections*, is of less august memories. They are of Ford's early days in the great Victorian past, which he represents as thronged, perhaps rather more than it was, by Pre-Raphaelites. His mother was a daughter of Ford Madox Brown, and that gave him an entrée, though the historically-minded can discount certain observations on the calculation that Ford was born in 1873. So we have an impression of William Morris hurling a plum-pudding downstairs and of Rossetti surrounding himself 'with anything that he could find that was quaint and bizarre whether of the dead or the live world'. More significantly, we hear of Christina Rossetti as 'the most satisfactory of all the poets of the nineteenth century'. This was an allegiance from which Ford never deviated. Nor, really, did he deviate from the attitude to art and artists imbibed in the Pre-Raphaelite years. This was that

no one who did not produce works of art counted. The laity in fact might not have existed at all. Indeed, even the learned and professional

[1] and [2] *Provence*.

classes were not excluded from the general contempt. An Oxford Don was regarded as a foolish, useless, and academic person, and my grandfather would say for instance, of a doctor; 'Oh, those fellows have nothing better to do than to wash their hands twelve times a day.' It never, I think, entered his head to inquire why a doctor so frequently washed his hands. He regarded it as a kind of foppishness. And I can well remember that I entirely shared his point of view. So that to speak to anyone who made money by commercial pursuits was almost not to speak to a man at all. It was as if one were communicating with one of the lower animals endowed with power of speech.

This attitude, which remained to give the whole vast series of his works a taint of aestheticism, was combined with the more serious passion which gives Ford a crucial place in the history of twentieth-century letters. This was his passion for writing and his curiosity as to how it is done. In the last pages of *Ancient Lights* he compares himself with Hokusai, '*The old man mad about Painting*. So I may humbly write myself down,' he goes on, 'a man getting on for forty, a little mad about good letters.' Twenty-seven years later, in the dedication of *The March of Literature*, he returned to the comparison. 'It is the book of an old man mad about writing—in the sense that Hokusai called himself an old man mad about painting.' In this sheer practicality had at least as much place as aestheticism. He complained that people could not

be practical when it comes to the machinery of the books we produce. We cannot pay any attention to that matter at all. A book has outlines, has ribs, has architecture, has proportion. These things are called in French technique. It is significant that in English there is no word for this. It is significant that in England a person talking about the technique of a book is laughed to scorn. The English theory is that a writer is a writer by the grace of God. He must have a pen, some ink, a piece of paper and a table. Then he must put some vine-leaves in his hair and write. When he has written 75,000 words he has a book.

His interest in these matters was not that of a dilettante who believes that if you learn some tricks you can write. What interested him was technique as a means of conveying an impression —how much, or how little precise statement of detail was required to convey it. The line of influence descends from the Pre-Raphaelites through the nineties. 'When the dust of the *Yellow Book* period died away,' he says in *The English Novel* (1930), 'with the trial and disappearance of Wilde there did nevertheless remain in the public and literary mind some conception that novel-writing was an art and that the novel was a

vehicle by means of which every kind of psychological or scientific truth connected with human life could be very fittingly conveyed.' Not only conveyed but investigated. The process of the novel, as he sees it, is a process of investigation.

It was with writing as a true record of the actual physical body of the life of his day that Ford was concerned. There has never been another English periodical like the *English Review* — under his editorship. Besides Hardy there appeared in its pages, in the course of a few years, Yeats, De La Mare, Wyndham Lewis, D. H. Lawrence and Ezra Pound — reassuring names to a publisher now, but not all of them were so then. Ford was more interested in the prose of the epoch than in its poetry. Except for Hardy, who is more consistently lucid in his verse than in his prose, and whose work was a great individual achievement rather than a technical reform, it was in prose that, in the first decade of the century, the work of paring and refining the language was mainly conducted. Perhaps the more deliberate nature of prose made it easier to correct nineteenth-century excess, and lack of elegance, in that medium. Perhaps also the verse was more rotten than the prose — it generally is. As long as the elements of a language remain — and it is not to be supposed that they are a permanent acquisition — there will always be sensible men who will try to say plainly what they mean, and although this will not secure an exalted literature it will help to preserve the basis on which more refined work can be written. Anyhow there was Conrad — whom Ford claimed to have taught, and to some extent no doubt did teach — George Moore, and Arthur Machen, quite apart from the more revolutionary characters who were beginning to put in an appearance. The series of editorials in the *English Review*, which Ford re-published in 1911 under the title of *The Critical Attitude*, was largely concerned with the manifestations of prose, so far as it was not a general plea for a critical attitude and a general discourse *On the Function of the Arts in the Republic*. At this point in time, the development of prose and verse cannot be considered separately. The common task was the paring of the language, to make it a shapely enough thing to continue in use as a workable tool. Ford himself was, certainly from 1908 until the First World War, an influence indiscriminately on the two media. What has come since is hardly conceivable without the pressure, at this time, of the less exhilarating art on the more exhilarating.

The Critical Attitude does, however, contain a chapter 47

specifically devoted to *Modern Poetry*. It considers 'the case of poetry rather than of the poet', and does not proclaim the existence of great figures. There is some dubious ground in this essay. It notices 'the abolition of the moral standpoint as a factor in modern verse' without meaning by that much more than the passing of the Victorian 'message' which not all poets, after all, took pains to deliver even in those unenlightened days. He is on even more doubtful ground when he says that 'great poetry — poetry with a note of greatness — would seem to demand a simplicity of outlook upon a life not very complex.' Was there ever a life not very complex? Ford's escape from the romanticism of the preceding century was incomplete. 'The poet is a creature of the emotions,' he says, 'and seldom or never is his intellect very powerful or very steady.' He is nearer the truth of the twentieth century when he says that the poet is beginning to write more 'along the lines of his own personality and of his own personal experience' — though these conceptions, too, raise questions, questions which have not yet been given any widely acceptable answer. With a flourish, and establishing perspectives in which virtually all contemporary work disappears, he says that 'the last really great poet working in a really complex age' was Lucretius, but one gets nearer to his real views in his remarks on people nearer at hand. He confesses to liking, of Victorian poetry, 'only a few poems of Browning's and a very considerable number of Christina Rossetti's'. The emphasis is characteristic. In part it is due to revulsion from the great figures of his youth, and his affection for the memory of the woman who wrote on 'the backs of envelopes upon the corner of her bedroom wash-stand', while the great figures 'used up all the clean paper, and chanted very loudly'. In part it is, undoubtedly, due to a preference for writing which is unassuming, and the patient vehicle of a receptive mind, to the rather exhibitionist work of a rumbustious moralist. Ford comments on Kipling, who for all his popularity had not then been regarded with much critical attention, that 'he is to be commended as much for his boldness in the use of the vernacular, as for his skill and his bold- ness, too, in catching the rhythm of popular music, with its quaint and fascinating irregularities'. It would be difficult to put the merits of this author more succinctly. Yeats is also mentioned, but this chapter on *Modern Poetry* contains no other single living name except that of Walter De La Mare. What more deserving figure was there?

De La Mare, born in the same year as Ford (1873), combines the last genuine reverberations of nineteenth-century poetical romanticism with not less genuine intimations of the more personal poetry that was emerging. The combination is perceptible in the *Epitaph* Ford quoted:

Here lies a most beautiful lady,
Light of heart and step was she;
I think she was the most beautiful lady
That ever was in the West Country.
But beauty vanishes, beauty passes,
However rare, rare it be,
And when I crumble who shall remember
The lady of the West Country?

There is a purity of language beyond the reach of the nineties. Grave and a little precious, the lines none the less have the intimate rhythm of speech. De La Mare catches it again and again. They are rather hushed, twilight accents, but of those accents no one is so much a master as he.

'Waiting to...'
'Who is?'
'We are...
Was that the night-owl's cry?
'I heard not. But see! the evening star;
And listen! —the ocean's solacing sigh.'
'You mean the surf at the harbour bar?'
'What did you say?'
'Oh, "waiting".'
' "Waiting?" ' —
'Waiting what for?'
'To die.'[1]

Neither the rhythm nor the emotion seem to be caught when De La Mare ventures beyond his peculiar tract of subjects — those which live on the edge of an affectionate and domesticated dream. But within that range, as Forrest Reid, with an imagination of

[1] *Waiting.*

similar refinement and similar limitations, puts it, there is 'flexibility and subtlety' in the 'rhythms, which linger, rise, drop, following a wavering sinuous course, like the tremulous fall of a snowflake which the wind catches, holds, and releases again'. The impressionistic language is not that of current criticism, but it is not the less exact for that.

Ford himself did not not succeed in finding a similar rhythm in his own verse. In prose, his manner is unmistakable, and can become obsessive. In poetry, his importance is rather as a theorizer than as a performer. He would like to have seen in poetry exactly the kind of reform which he, and some of the other contributors in the *English Review*, were achieving in prose. He wanted to see verse render exactly the life of his day. It may be doubted whether this is, at any time, an adequate objective for a poet. On the other hand, Ford's uneasiness as to the subject-matter of the poetry of his day was undoubtedly justified. 'Is there something about the mere framing of verse,' he asks, in the preface to his poems, collected in 1914, when he was still using the name of Hueffer, 'the mere sound of it in the ear, that must at once throw its practitioner or its devotee into an artificial state of mind? Verse presumably quickens the perceptions of its writer as do hashish or ether. But must it necessarily quicken them to the perception only of the sentimental, the false, the hackneyed aspects of life? Must it make us, because we live in cities, babble incessantly of green fields; or because we live in the twentieth century must we deem nothing poetically good that did not take place before the year 1603?' As to the manner, he wanted to get away from the idea — which is no more than a definition of his own ideals by opposites — 'that all poets must of necessity write affectedly, at great length, with many superfluous words — that poetry, of necessity, was something boring and pretentious'. Pound wrote an essay on Ford in 1914 called *The Prose Tradition in Verse*, and noted the prose training Ford brought to his work. Ford thought that verse was not to be excused from the improvements of prose.

The volume of *Collected Poems* does not contain any single poem which could be said to be of decisive novelty. Indeed, the best of them is probably *The Three Ten*, with its nominally modern subject but perfectly pastoral air, written in a deliciously plain speech but a song rather than a conversation or monologue and using no very abstruse metre:

When in the prime and May Day time dead lovers went a-walking,
How bright the grass in lads' eyes was, how easy poet's talking!
Here were green hills and daffodils, and copses to contain them:
Daisies for floors did front their doors agog for maids to chain them.

It is certainly not solemn, but the irony of it hardly bites into the modern world and the last line is so flat that it may be appalling. The poem can hardly claim to 'render' the age in the way that, say, *The Good Soldier* (1915) did. Yet the triumph of *The Good Soldier* is precisely that it is much more than a series of impressions. It develops a personal subject which Ford had been hatching within himself for ten years or more. It utilizes all that he had learned, technically, about the writing of prose, which was, at the age of forty, more than he ever knew about the writing of verse.

There were returns to verse after the *Collected Poems*, but they still did not succeed in imprisoning in that medium a tenth part of the technical aptitude which Ford again and again displayed in prose. *Mr Bosphorus and the Muses*, which purports to be a short history of poetry in Britain in the form of a variety entertainment in four acts, is amusing enough, and attains at times to a shallowly-ironic elegance, but it does not show that Ford had mastered the art of verse. His most interesting production in verse is, without a doubt, *Buckshee*. It is a sequence of nine poems, first published in 1936—only a few years before his death—and personal in the superficial sense that the subject-matter was found in his own current life as well as in the profounder sense that it was work which could hardly have been done without the years of literary training Ford had given himself. The subject-matter—his new youthful consort and his life with her in Paris and Provence—provided themes at the centre of his long brooding over a certain conception of civilization.

But I like the baked, severe, bare
Hill with the sea below and the great storms sooner or later...

And for me
There is no satisfaction greater
Than the sight of that house-side, silver-grey
And very high
With the single, black cypress against the sky.[1]

[1] *L'Oubli — temps de sécheresse.*

It is the classical outline. Ford is reminding us of certain history, as he had so often done in his reminiscent prose, as much as presenting a scene, though not quite so blatantly, no doubt, as when he talks of the mistral singing 'an infinite number of lays in Latin'. That is a meditative prose rather than poetry; the thoughts have been not quite transmuted. Similarly with the more personal lines:

> Leopard, ounce or ocelot,
> She by turns is cold or hot,
> She is sinuous and black,
> Long of limb and lithe of back.[1]

He is drawing attention to a classic thing, and so stops short of direct experience. It is done better in prose. The forty or more years of preoccupation with the conceptions of *Provence*, and a vast experience of writing, go into this from *The Rash Act:*

Jeanne Becquerel stood in the doorway, leaning back against the doorpost beside the dark girl. Since the light from the upper sky was intense she was not in silhouette and her skin was indeed nacreous as the dark girl said. Like mother of pearl. She stretched out one arm to hold the other door-post so that it cut the doorspace in half, like a straight bar, obscuring St Mandrier. Her head was turned to gaze into the south. The shadows beneath her arms, armpits, breasts and knees reflected the blue of the sky; there was a little pink on the base of the neck, the ribs and the lower limbs. But most of the flesh was rice-white ... A Hellenic figure done in nacre! The dark girl was like a drop of luminous blood!...She would no doubt one day fly away ... Like a scarlet sail before disaster.

It takes more words, of course, and Ford always needed, for his effects, the slow build-up of prose. No paragraph or page can adequately illustrate the peculiar confluence of conscious effect and involuntary motivation which characterizes Ford's best work. *The Rash Act* is a story told, with all the technical mastery of his sixty years, in order to present the author's deepest prepossessions. Verse cannot be used in this way, unless we allow Landor as a case in point. The Tietjens novels are nearer to poetry, and the involuntary ghosts which move in them are more powerful. There are the extraordinary forces which made Ford identify himself with the Anglican Yorkshire squire—Ford who was half German, the son of a music critic, and some kind of lapsed

[1] *Chez nos amis.*

Papist, and who evidently observed as he did because of his rather eccentric position. There is the raging figure of Sylvia Tietjens, who again clearly represents an outrage in his own past. Ford brings all this to an idyllic peace, in the final pages of *Last Post*, which again manages to be a declaration in favour of the now eroded frugalities of French civilization, and a reaching back into an English past profounder than the fevers of the time:

'He whispered:
  "*'Twas the mid o' the night and the barnies grat*
  And the mither beneath the mauld heard that ...
An old song. My nurse sang it ... Never thou let thy child weep for thy sharp tongue to thy good man ... A good man! Groby Great Tree is down ..." He said: "Hold my hand!"'

All this, and more, was waiting to enter the verse of *Buckshee*, but all we get is:

  Tonight the rusty, iron-clappered bell
  Of Richelieu's clock aeons ago strikes one,
  Some hours ago shall strike three, some pulses past
  Jarred twice the drowsy night.[1]

In spite of the relative failure of his verse, Ford remains a profound influence on the poetry as on the prose of the century, for he found English literature poetical and left it spare. Or he so left it, in so far as performance was equal to the taste he had so largely created.

There is a passage in *The English Novel* which sets out succinctly what Ford had learnt about the relationship of the inner urge to create and the discipline of technique. It was written in relation to prose, but anyone who wants to understand the art of verse would do well to reflect upon it: 'You must therefore write as simply as you can — with the extreme of the simplicity that is granted to you, and you must write of subjects that spring at your throat. But why subjects appeal to you you have no means of knowing.'

[1] *Code.*

Chapter Four

Imagism : F. S. Flint ; Richard Aldington ;
T. E. Hulme ;

the verse of James Joyce

I

It is a mistake to attach too much importance to announced literary movements. The proof of the pudding is in the eating, not in the menu. In the end there are only one or two poets, whose work is more or less related, usually less. It is so with imagism. What this movement amounted to has been learnedly discoursed upon by more than one authority; the remains, in terms of work done in accordance with its canons, are slight. There is, however, some point in taking note of what the imagists thought, or said, they were up to because their declarations mark at any rate their sense of the literary vices of the time and the orientation of some of the most intelligent persons writing English verse in the years immediately before the First World War. Their orientation was very much that of Ford Madox Ford, or Hueffer as he then was, and although he did not figure formally as the instigator of the movement he was a large element in the atmospheric influence in which it came about. The value to a provincial like Pound, on his arrival in London, of finding someone twelve years his senior, with the sense Ford had of what needed doing with and to the language of the age, is immeasurable, and Pound has never failed to acknowledge this debt.

The best and most accessible statement of what imagism was about is to be found in *A Stray Document* which Pound reprinted in *Make it New*:

1. Direct treatment of the 'thing' whether subjective or objective.
2. To use absolutely no word that does not contribute to the presentation.
3. As regarding rhythm: to compose in the sequence of the musical phrase, not in sequence of a metronome.

These are little else than the rules of good writing. The minds of the authors — H. D., Richard Aldington, and Pound himself — were still at work on the Augean stable of nineteenth-century prolixity. They were, also, expressing their approval of the broken rhythms which had long been emerging from the ruin of a previously fashionable prosody. The bleak commandments, or resolutions, give little indication of the positive intentions of the imagists. No doubt those intentions were various. What unified the group, and what they encouraged one another with, was a rejection. That makes as good a common starting point as any. Even Pound's definition of the 'image' does not take one very far:

An 'Image' is that which present an intellectual and emotional complexs in an instant of time. I use the term 'complex' rather in the technical sense employed by the newer psychologists, such as Hart [a good touch, that, for an advertising manager], though we might not agree absolutely in our application.
It is the presentation of such a 'complex' instantaneously which gives that sense of sudden liberation; that sense of freedom from time limits and space limits; that sense of sudden growth, which we experience in the presence of the greatest works of art.[1]

It is a fallible statement. One does not easily reconcile this instantaneous image with the time sequence which is the essence of verse. Nor can it have been precise to drag in the alleged effects of 'the greatest works of art' to explain the modest performances which were being exhibited. It was more to the point to say: 'Don't use such an expression as "dim lands *of peace*". It dulls the image. It mixes an abstraction with the concrete. It comes from the writer's not realizing that the natural object is always the *adequate* symbol.'[2] It is with extreme difficulty that such precepts are followed for any length of time, and the typical imagist poem was, consequently, short to the point of approaching the instantaneous. The very brevity of the exercise was beneficial. Attention was invited to the *mot juste* and the rhythmic phrase, and if that was wrong it was all wrong, as Richard Aldington said in another connection. It was this concentration on the elements of writing which made it not altogether absurd for Pound to claim, as he did in a note published in 1912: 'As for the future, *Les Imagistes*, the descendants of the forgotten school of 1909, have that in their keeping.'[3]

[1] and [2] *A Stray Document.*
[3] Appendix to *Ripostes.*

One of the most interesting, and no doubt authoritative, accounts of the imagist school is given by F. S. Flint in a *Verse Chronicle* he contributed to *The Criterion* in January 1932:

> Like most inventors, Pound did not create out of the void. The 'image' he took from T. E. Hulme's table talk. The 'ism' was suggested to him by the notes on contemporary French poetry which I wrote for Harold Monro's *Poetry Review*. The collocation of 'image' with 'ism' came to Pound after I had told him about Fernand Divoire's essays on 'stratégie littéraire'. Pound devised a 'stratégie littéraire'. It succeeded, and swept the American continent... In this country, Imagism was treated either as a lunacy or a joke.

The 'traditions of this country are deeply rooted,' Flint adds without approval, meaning perhaps that the reign of many versifiers omitted from this history was for many years unimpaired. Anyway, the imagists had made a technical adjustment to the language which could not be disregarded by a serious writer after their day, and that is more important than the argument about who invented the 'image' and who added the 'ist' and the 'ism'.

This bit of literary history has been extensively written up by Glenn Hughes in *Imagism and the Imagists* (1931), Hughes then being Professor of English in the University of Washington. For what it is worth, he records that it was at the Poets' Club founded by T. E. Hulme in 1908, 'that the first experimental imagist poems were read and discussed', although 'none of the poets who became officially the imagists were members of this early group'. Then Hulme met Flint, who was already an advocate of *vers libre*, and there was play with Japanese verse forms, which should at least in theory have encouraged a certain concentration. After that Pound turned up, and added an 'isme', which afterwards became anglicized. Pound abandoned the movement after the publication of *Des Imagistes: An Anthology* early in 1914. To this anthology there were eleven contributors, including Aldington, H.D., Flint, William Carlos Williams, James Joyce, Hueffer, Pound and Amy Lowell. It was Amy Lowell who organized the three later anthologies, called *Some Imagist Poets*, of 1915, 1916, and 1917, to which there were seven contributors: Aldington, H.D., John Gould Fletcher, F. S. Flint, D. H. Lawrence and herself. This rich, dynastic lady also organized the imagists themselves, and their historian records that she dined them on

Hors d'Oeuvres Norvégienne
Consommé Sarah Bernhardt
Bisque de Homards
Filets de sole Lucullus
Cailles en Gelée aux Muscats
Selle d'Agneau Richelieu
Canetons d'Aylesbury à l'Anglaise
Petits Pois aux Laitues
Jambon d'York au Champagne
Haricots Verts Maître d'Hôtel
Bombe Moka Friandises Dessert
Café

The profession of poet was not entirely unrewarding.

2

F. S. Flint was not evidently predestined to eat such a meal. He
was born in London, the son of an unprosperous commercial
traveller, and left school in 1899 at the age of thirteen and a half.
He had various odd jobs, in a warehouse and elsewhere, until the
age of nineteen when he entered upon his career by becoming a
typist in the Civil Service. He went to night-school, where he
picked up French and Latin. Meanwhile there were the second-
hand book-stalls — the twopenny box, no doubt. He married at the
age of twenty-four, had two children to support and did in fact
support them. He discovered that he was a remarkable linguist
and before he had finished he could read ten or more languages. It
should be recorded that this poet rose to a respectable position in
the Statistics Division of the Ministry of Labour, and spent his
time compiling overseas information which was probably of no
value to anyone. He was never a hardened character — the reverse,
rather. Ford called him 'one of the greatest men and one of the
beautiful spirits of the country'.[1] Glenn Hughes, meeting him
after he had given up writing poetry, speaks of him as 'torn
between reality and dream, between this world and another
world' and says that he had 'wearied of trying to express in
poetry this never-ending conflict'.

The interest of Flint's work is more than merely technical,
but he certainly had an unusual technical flair. He made his own
way to literature because he needed to, and at twenty-four he had

[1] Quoted by Glenn Hughes in *Imagism and the Imagists*.

already appeared in the *English Review* and the *New Age* and was publishing his first volume of poems, *In the Net of the Stars*, to which he added a prefatory note:

> This book is one poem.
> I have, as the mood dictated, filled a form or created one. I have used assonance for the charm of it, and not rhymed where there was no need to. In all, I have followed my ear and my heart, which may be false. I hope not.

He was unassuming and ingenuous to the point of originality. The book itself, some fifty poems divided into four groups, reflects, under the romantic language, the clerk and his girl, under the shadow of a London which is still unmistakably close to that of John Davidson and his *Thirty Bob a Week*. There is a veil of gentle aspiration over all, as if Flint was already the man of whom Glenn Hughes was to write that 'the poet in him was defeated — partly by the difficulty of earning a living for himself and his family; partly by a peculiarity of his nature, a tendency towards self-disparagement, which not only cuts off his creative powers, but which also prevents him from impressing his work on the public.' So in his early twenties

> My heart is bitter with this barren desolation —
> Dead trees, grey skies, gaunt streets, smoke, grime, and squalor of
> London.[1]

It is no ingenuity but a feeling for the physical sense of words which produces such — admittedly trifling — novelties as

> Along the road the wind is blowing red
> Rose petals and they wed
> The brown-grey sand.
> The roses of my hope and heart dispart[2]

— where in the first line the insulation of 'red' from its noun gives it momentarily an adverbial flavour and colours the wind, before it becomes joined to the 'rose' to which it belongs, and where in the last line the unexpected internal rhyme gives a sudden emphasis to the final word. And there are queer colloca-

[1] *Sunday in London.*
[2] *Monody.*

tions in this, which evoke the passing female crowd of the shabby world:

> Old women, young, dull-eyed, of sordid flesh,
> Caught, coiled and crushed.[1]

Absurdity does not hold him back from setting down what he feels:

> would she have understood
> My wistful mood
> Had I told
> It was not she
> I would have kissed in her, but me,
> And for my friend's sake only she?[2]

He can even dare a shaming *Simplicity*:

> I am a follower of Jesus Christ

—and to explain what he means:

> He would have taken me,
> I think, for I have lain with buried head
> Sideways among long grasses.

There is here a poetic personality — that is, a personality expressing itself in poetry — of unusual quality and of no little force. If somehow it failed to ripen entirely, as we must admit that it did, all the more reason to treat with respect these early gleanings.

Glenn Hughes sets side by side two poems, one of which was a revision of the other, to show what Flint's evolution was and what imagism did for him. The comparison is indeed instructive. *A Swan Song* in *In the Net of the Stars* begins:

> Among the lily leaves the swan,
> The pale, cold lily leaves, the swan,
> With mirrored neck, a silver streak
> Tipped with a tarnished copper beak,
> Towards the dark arch floats slowly on;
> The water is deep and black beneath the arches...

[1] and [2] *A Mood and Its Images.*

The second version, published in *Des Imagistes* (1914), contains the lines:

> Over the green cold leaves
> and the rippled silver
> and the tarnished copper
> of its neck and beak,
> towards the deep black water
> beneath the arches,
> the swan floats slowly.

The rhythm has gone; the emotion has gone. One is almost tempted to say that Flint, the poet, was killed by imagism. At any rate the comparison may cause one to reflect on the extreme danger of literary theories which are supposed to bind the poet who, after all, if he is a poet, knows better.

3

Richard Aldington was a less vulnerable character, and also a coarser one — not perhaps that that is necessarily a bad thing, though the progress from his early Hellenism to the rather silly denigration of his betters in his lecture on Pound and Eliot is not edifying. He was the son of a solicitor in Portsmouth, where he was born in 1892, and attended preparatory schools, Dover College and, for a year, London University. For his reaction against this environment, and more generally for indications of the atmosphere — what is called the intellectual atmosphere, meaning that which prevails in the tracts between literature and fornication — of his pre-war London, as well as for the impact of the First World War on such a young man, his novel, *Death of a Hero*, may still be read with profit. Aldington was a moderate and self-seeking rebel, of considerable intelligence, reading and literary talent. It is of historical interest that *Death of a Hero*, published in 1929, has stars for the rude words, but one should not conclude from that that life was then unduly inhibited.

Aldington's contribution to the literature of the century was in his attempt to cultivate a small renaissance of his own, and like Ford and Flint he turned on to the rather soggy atmosphere of his day a stream of French, or more generally Latin influences. Like the others, he picked up the thread of tradition from the Paris movement which included Rémy de Gourmont, Charles

Maurras and Jean Moréas, who provided a link with the more remote sources. Moréas, it will be remembered, was a Greek, born in Athens in 1856. The names of Moréas and Maurras do not, to my knowledge, appear explicitly among Aldington's sources, but the kinship is clear, and carried one back to other latinizers and hellenizers, Verlaine and Andre Chénier, and so to Ronsard, Du Bellay and the Renaissance proper. There is a long call to the past in such verses as these from *Les Stances* of Moréas:

Palinure au grand coeur, le pilote d'Enée
    Qui, prudent, d'un fort bras
Guidait le gouvernail, subit la destinée
    Que l'on n'évite pas.

Instrument de la haine, un repos exécrable
    Lui vint tromper les yeux,
Et, déjà près du port, il périt, misérable,
    Dans les flots tortueux.

Aldington published prose versions of *Anyte of Tegea* in 1915, of *Latin Poets of the Renaissance* in 1916 and of *Meleager* and *Anacreontica* in 1919 — the last 'entirely a "war work", as it was started in a camp and finished, after a long interval, in the village of Taintignies near Tournai'. The prose, if less translucent than that of Forrest Reid's *Poems from the Greek Anthology*, is elegant and a trifle nostalgic. There is no doubt that application to such tasks was of immense value to Aldington as a poet. The other side of the French line of influence was less valuable, and may in the end have proved too seductive. The intellectual libertism of Rémy de Gourmont proved to be a dead end, though it is almost impossible to over-rate the importance of Gourmont, at a certain stage, to a young man seeking his way out of the Anglo-Saxon morass and into certain Gallic lucidities. Aldington later (in 1928) published a volume of selections from Gourmont, and prefixed to it an introduction in which he presented his author as 'the Individualist, always opposed to the Christian theory of repression'. 'Let us make no mistake about it,' he says in the introduction,

Gourmont's art and thought are profoundly revolutionary, not in the conventional, Moscow, barbarous way, but in the subtle, acute, elegant, delicately graduated way of a highly-civilized, over-civilized, thinker. He is the greatest of the intellectual Nihilists foretold by Nietzsche, after whom there is —what? Gourmont is the unfailing champion of Individualism —of Egotism if you like —and the one clue to his multiple and complex personality is a recognition of this uncompromising Individualism. He is the defender of liberty of expression, liberty of morals, liberty of action. Perhaps he claimed the impossible, but only the efforts of these uncompromising Individualists have saved us so far from a new Middle Ages of dreary collective tyranny.

After Gourmont Aldington took to Voltaire.

Aldington's history, like many other writers', is of development from an initial tongue-tiedness to a repetitive facility. Only continued difficulties, and a developing process of thought, can assure the continued interest of a man's work, and in Aldington's case the resources were not there. His early productions, however, are of considerable interest. The contents of the first volume, *Images* (1915), were written from 1910 onwards —they are very much a young man's work, therefore. The technical skill of these hellenizing verses is considerable:

> Cold lips that sing no more, and withered wreaths,
> Regretful eyes, and drooping breasts and wings —
> Symbols of ancient songs,
> Mournfully passing
> Down to the great white surges,
> Watched of none
> Save the frail sea-birds
> And the lithe pale girls,
> Daughters of Oceanus.[1]

Some of the short poems in *Images of Desire* (1919) are better. They have —to quote the epigraph he takes from Rémy de Gourmont—less the air of 'des pensées déjà exhalées'. The rhythm is tighter and encloses the image with which it is loaded:

> Your mouth is fragrant as an orange-grove
> In April, and your lips are hyacinths,
> Dark, dew-wet, folded, petalled hyacinths
> Which my tongue pierces like an amorous bee.[2]

or

[1] *Choricoo.*
[2] *Epigram.*

62

Your body is whiter than the moon-white sea,
More white than foam upon a rocky shore,
Whiter than that white goddess born of foam.[1]

Or this:

The scarlet that stains your lips and breast-points —
Let it be my blood that dyes them,
My very blood so gladly yielded.[2]

These are small things, instantaneous productions no doubt. The casual versifier should reflect on how much training went to the making of them.

Once or twice, in later life, Aldington found a subject to which he managed to bring enough of himself to write a poem of some duration. It was the recollection of war that so moved him. The sixteen lines *In Memory of Wilfrid Owen* (1931) are of respectable gravity:

But I have never quite forgotten, never forgotten
All you who lie there so lonely, and never stir
When the hired buglers call unheeded to you,
Whom the sun shall never warm nor the frost chill.

There is the *Epilogue to 'Death of a Hero'* (1929):

Eleven years after the fall of Troy,
We, the old men — some of us nearly forty —
Met and talked on the sunny rampart
Over our wine, while the lizards scuttled
In dusty grass, and the crickets chirred.

He watches a boy of twenty

Say petulantly to a girl, seizing her arm:
'Oh, come away; why do you stand there
Listening open-mouthed to the talk of old men?
Haven't you heard enough of Troy and Achilles?'

[1] *Epigram.*
[2] *Images of Desire.*

There is a real evocation of more than one past:

> And I thought of the graves by desolate Troy
> And the beauty of many young men now dust,
> And the long agony, and how useless it all was.
> And the talk still clashed about me
> Like the meeting of blade and blade.

4

A much more powerful figure of the renascence loosely connected with imagism, an instigator indeed of that as of much else, was T. E. Hulme. It is hardly too much to say that Hulme has been, in this country, one of the dominant minds of the century. Certainly there can be no understanding of the literature of the age without some grasp of what he stood for. Hulme had his sources, like another man, and I am not suggesting that everything which shows signs of the change of temper Hulme represents has his personal mark upon it. It is evident that Wyndham Lewis, in particular—a much greater figure and one whose influence is still far from having been fully absorbed—arrived by his own intuitions at related positions. Hulme, however, because of his short life and limited scope, stands as a monument at a certain point reached in the century. One may say that Hardy, Shaw and Kipling were incurably pre-Hulme, whereas Eliot and Pound were post-.

Hulme, born in 1883—within a year of Lewis, therefore—was in his way as deeply rooted in the traditional life of this country as Hardy, or as nearly so as a man born more than forty years after him could be. He had his inheritance, however, from the industrial as well as from the rural life of the country, coming from a land-owning family which had taken to manufacturing in Stoke-on-Trent. His father seems to have lived the life of a sort of squire, but without pretensions which required his son to be educated anywhere but at the village school and later at the High School at Newcastle-under-Lyme. Hulme went up to Cambridge on the strength of a County Council Scholarship. He was large, argumentative and some say offensive. He was certainly impatient of authority, having had enough of his father's. He was sent down from Cambridge, for crimes no longer clearly determinable, and later pursued some further studies at University College, London. He wanted to do philosophy, but that was 'no use at all—in Staffordshire'. His father then thought he should try for the Civil

Service, but he said he would rather live on bread and cheese and went to Canada where he worked with his hands. When he came back — apparently with a few pounds in the bank but working his passage — he soon went off to Brussels to improve his French and to learn German. It was in 1908 — at the age of twenty-five — that he returned to London to begin his noticeable career, in which he was supported by an allowance said to be small, but still it was an allowance.

Hulme became associated with A. R. Orage and the *New Age*, on which such thinking about society as was then going on in London was centred. The contributors, who were not paid, included Shaw, Belloc, Wells, Arnold Bennett and Havelock Ellis as well as Aldington, Middleton Murry, Katherine Mansfield and Herbert Read. Ezra Pound was the music critic. Hulme was not left to sharpen his wits alone. Nor was he sexually deprived. Wyndham Lewis's *Blasting and Bombardiering* contains some information about his 'abstruse devotions to Venus'. He was anyhow 'very fond of the girls'. His title to fame rests on a volume of essays and notes, published seven years after his death, and a few very short poems. He was killed while serving with his battery in 1917.

The water-shed Hulme represents is indicated in the essay on 'Humanism and the Religious Attitude' which stands first in the volume of *Speculations* (1924). The underlying notion is the rejection of the principle of *continuity*, the 'elaboration and universal application' of which was 'one of the main achievements of the nineteenth century' while 'the destruction of this conception' was 'an urgent necessity of the present'. The nineteenth-century doctrine — still widely held now, of course — was that there are no breaks in reality, that it is all of the same kind. The 'popular conception of evolution' is an obvious illustration of the idea. The point is, however, that 'continuity' is a preconception, not a conclusion drawn from reality, but it is so prevalent a notion that it is thought of not as a notion but as if it were reality itself. 'We now absorb it unconsciously,' says Hulme, 'from an environment already completely soaked in it; so we regard it not as a principle in the light of which certain regions of fact can be conveniently ordered, but as an inevitable constituent of reality itself. When any fact seems to contradict this principle, we are inclined to deny that the fact really exists. We constantly tend to think that the discontinuities in nature are only *apparent*, and that a fuller investigation would reveal the underlying continuity. This shrinking from a gap or jump in nature has developed to a degree which paralyses any objective perception.' Against this Hulme set the conception of an absolute discontinuity, a chasm, between the various zones of reality. Thus one might assume a division into '(1) the inorganic world, of mathematical and physical science, (2) the organic world, dealt with by biology, psychology and history, and (3) the world of ethical and religious values'. The division between (1) and (2) is still fairly generally recognized — though it could be said that the recognition of the difference has faded a little since Hulme's day — because it 'falls easily into line with humanism', which is the superstition of the Renaissance, while the division between (2) and (3) 'breaks with the whole Renaissance tradition'. It was this break which Hulme was seeking to get people to understand. For Hulme 'the *divine* is not *life* at its intensest. It contains in a way an almost *anti-vital* element; quite different of course from the non-vital character of the outside physical region.' The art he was concerned to recommend was inhuman and geometrical. The cosy world of sentiment and progress was left behind. There is no need to insist on the kinship of this view with the formalizing inventions of the visual art of the period, and in particular with the work of Wyndham Lewis.

In its application to literature, Hulme's view meant that 'after a hundred years of romanticism, we are in for a classical revival', and that, for the purposes of this revolution, 'fancy will be superior to imagination'. He recommended 'the dry hardness which you get in the classics', and which was 'absolutely repugnant' to most people, to whom 'poetry that isn't damp isn't poetry at all.' It was a limited and definite poetry he wanted to see, something that would do without the 'strange light' of romanticism, which had the effect of a drug. It is a programme which defines, despite some deviations, the main movement of English poetry in the twentieth century. Hulme was himself an uncompromising practitioner of the art he recommended, no doubt because his theories were of a piece with his impulses. He had a brain which he could use in verse.

The *Complete Poetical Works* of T. E. Hulme, consisting of five poems, were first printed as an appendix to Ezra Pound's *Ripostes* (1912), and reprinted in Hulme's posthumous *Speculations* (1924). The five poems were not quite all, however. A couple of dozen poems, and some fragments, with a textual introduction for good measure, are to be found in *The Life and Opinions of Thomas Ernest Hulme* (1960) by Alun R. Jones. It would be a service if some publisher would give this tiny collection a little volume on its own. It would be of impressive weight for its size. The success of the word imagism has been such that it is generally taken that the interest of the poems is simply as illustrating this dead movement. On the contrary, the verse has intellectual and rhythmic qualities not found elsewhere in English verse. The images are there, of course:

> The lark crawls on the cloud
> Like a flea on a white body.[1]

Or, from the *Complete Poetical Works* published by Pound:

> Above the quiet dock in midnight,
> Tangled in the tall mast's corded height,
> Hangs the moon. What seemed so far away
> Is but a child's balloon, forgotten after play.[2]

The verse has the throw-away rhythm of talk and — unless it is in the 'forgotten after play' which however is also part of the visual impression — there is no concession to sentiment. There is such concentration that one feels one has the complete content of the mind at the moment of the poem. As in this, called *Susan Ann and Immortality*:

> Her head hung down
> Gazed at earth, fixedly keen,
> As the rabbit at the stoat
> Till the earth was sky,
> Sky that was green,
> And brown clouds past,
> Like chestnut leaves arching the ground.

In *A Tall Woman* we have such a combination of sensual absorption with the disjunction of the intellectual man as is hardly to be paralleled since Donne:

[1] *Images.*
[2] *Above the Dock.*

67

The same promise to many eyes.
Yet when she forward leans, in a room,
And by seeming accident her breasts brush against me,
Then is the axle of the world twisted.

Each poem of Hulme is a sort of instantaneous carving cut out of
reality with a knife. If there is a contemporary parallel, it is with
certain work of Gaudier-Brzeska rather than with that of the
official imagists. But a line of verse can carry with it a world of
thoughts as a drawing cannot:

A rough wind rises, dark cliffs stare down.
Sour-faced Calvin — art thou whining still?[1]

A man walking on the sea-shore has to have something in his
head. The romantic is, so to speak, a holiday-maker, with vague
thoughts of luxurious beauty. The classic is a man no less serious
than the fisherman mending his nets. His preoccupations do not
leave him. He does not turn aside for beauty. No good writer
does. In a sense Hulme's distinction between 'classic' and
'romantic' is merely the distinction between good writing and bad.

5

It is not entirely beside the point to conclude this chapter with a
reference to the verse of James Joyce, which has properly been
over-shadowed by his prose. *Chamber Music*, first published in
1907, when Joyce was twenty-five, in no way suggests that a
decisive new mind had put in an appearance. These poems are the
skilful songs of a man who had read — and sung — the madrigalists
as well as acquainted himself with the poets of the nineties.

Gentle lady, do not sing
Sad songs about the end of love;
Lay aside sadness and sing
How love that passes is enough.[2]

Let no mere follower of fashion sneer at that; it takes more skill
than he supposes. Still, *Chamber Music* is a man singing a tradi-

[1] *A Sudden Secret.*
[2] Untitled poem.

tional tune in one corner of his mind. But as early as 1904 Joyce had written verse of much greater originality.

> He travels after a winter sun,
> Urging the cattle along a cold red road,
> Calling to them, a voice they know,
> He drives his beasts above Cabra.[1]

This he kept back, no doubt as out of tune with the rest of his early verses, for publication in *Pomes Penyeach*. That small volume contains among its thirteen poems several which catch a personal rhythm, though none which contains the intellect of the author in the way that Hulme's poems do. Nothing could more completely demonstrate the involuntary nature of poetry than the inability of so inventive a man as Joyce, who clearly desired to write verse, to put more than a fraction of his thought into it. The most sophisticated poem in the volume is a failure. *A Memory of the Players in a Mirror at Midnight* is intended poetry — verse with a misplaced deliberation.

> They mouth love's language. Gnash
> The thirteen teeth
> Your lean jaws grin with. Lash
> Your itch and quailing, nude greed of the flesh.

The small triumphs are in simple emotions:

> Rain on Rahoon falls softly, softly falling,
> Where my dark lover lies.
> Sad is his voice that calls me, sadly calling,
> At grey moonrise.[2]

Perhaps best of all, *On the Beach at Fontana*:

> Wind whines and whines the shingle,
> The crazy pierstakes groan;
> A senile sea numbers each single
> Slimesilvered stone.
>
> From whining wind and colder
> Grey sea I wrap him warm

[1] *Tilly.*
[2] *She Weeps Over Rahoon.*

69

And touch his trembling fineboned shoulder
And boyish arm.

Around us fear, descending
Darkness of fear above
And in my heart how deep unending
Ache of love!

apples and snails were.' The exultation is unmistakably akin to that felt by Thomas Traherne. Few, as the years of boyhood went on, can have made more than Edward Thomas did of the commons and odd scattered fields of South London. He went to the local board school, and then to Battersea Grammar School, and somehow managed to finish with a short spell at St Paul's. He was a boy of parts, and by the time he was seventeen bits of his descriptive writing had appeared in the *Speaker* and the *New Age*. By the time he was nineteen his first book was published — *The Woodland Life*. Meanwhile, he had already attached himself firmly to the girl who was to become his wife, Helen, the daughter of a writer and journalist, Edward Noble. There was still argument about Thomas's future. His father wanted to hound him into the Civil Service. He himself wanted to go to Oxford, and in the end he did go, passing there, undoubtedly, the time of his life when he was nearest to ease and luxury. For his own pleasure he read the poets and naturalists; for his degree, which was mediocre, modern history. The idea of going into the Civil Service, no doubt with better prospects than before, was presented to him again, with the same reaction as before. Edward Thomas managed his own affairs, and felt no desire to manage other people's. He had proposed to himself two things: to marry Helen and to write. The marriage had taken place and his first child been born while he was still at Oxford. When he came down, he took his wife and baby from his parents' house, where they were living, to a squalid half-house with a dirty backyard. His connections with editors and publishers were, for so young a man, already of long standing, but he did not find it easy to get the work he wanted. No one was ever less of a showman than Edward Thomas. If it was possible to give the putting-off answer to someone who might employ him he seems to have given it. Nevinson, on the *Daily Chronicle*, was intelligent enough not to be put off, and gave him books to review. After that book-reviewing became a main source of income — a depressive and miserable occupation for a man of Thomas's temperament, and one which certainly gave him a profound contempt for the poetry of the day, for he did not take poetry lightly. About this time he managed to move into the first of his houses in the country, and he was never more than a visitor to the town thereafter. This first house was near Maidstone. It was no beauty, apparently, but it gave Thomas access to a Kentish countryside more at peace then than it now is. When he was not working he wandered about. As a boy he had already walked many miles in Wiltshire and elsewhere; roads, lanes and fields were a natural habitat and going on foot his ordinary means of progression. It is difficult, in a world ravaged by the internal combustion engine, to understand the nearness to the ground these habits can give. A nearness to the past, too, it may be added, for this is how people lived until technology insulated them. Thomas's walks were long or short, a few hours or days and weeks at a time. Often he did not know the name of the village he was passing through. It was not that which interested him. He was interested in the anonymous life of the country, animal or human, and the weather and vegetation which belonged to the same nature. He was not a refugee from town, but someone exploring the country because it gave him life. There were successive homes — for a time on the Weald near Sevenoaks and then, in order to be able to educate the children in an enlightenment Helen Thomas approved of, in Hampshire near Bedales. Ideas of enlightenment, as of reaction, were far from Thomas's mind. He was too close to reality for that. He had thought nothing of Helen's officially intellectual friends earlier; he thought nothing of progressivism. He was without perceptible ambition but he wrote his books and did his reviews, moving steadily from the influence of Oxford and Walter Pater to a prose without airs and graces, and all the time under the tuition of the reality presented to him by natural objects, including his wife and children. He seems intermittently to have wandered off, partly for the pleasure of wandering, partly to get material for his books, and partly because he felt the strain of domestic affections. At least once he loaded a revolver and went out to shoot himself. He suffered a good deal of real poverty, which it is easy to do with three children. He had difficulties with editors and publishers and wrote an immense number of books with, apparently, very modest financial results. His books were mainly either critical or topographical. He was a good workman, but it cannot be said that these books are profoundly exciting, or that much would have been lost if they had disappeared, though, as from such a man they must, they contain much that is sensible and pleasing as well as occasional turns of phrase and rhythms which pre-figure the poetry. But for Thomas's own development the books no doubt had a great importance. When the time came for poetry there was an immense, unheated experience of words to draw on.

There are few stranger things in the history of modern poetry than Thomas's sudden outburst. From the point of view of the ordinary literary man, the extraordinary thing is that Thomas had kept silent for so long. All the talents were there, and an intimate knowledge of poetry to give him his technical starting point. Perhaps he had too high a view of poetry to think it proper for him to try. When he started the atmosphere was troubled by war, uncertainty about his own future, and perhaps more strain than usual in his domestic arrangements. More simply, he met Robert Frost, who told him to write verse, and he did so. The meeting with Frost was no doubt fortunate. Thomas was probably better equipped than any man to understand what the American was doing. The low tone, the attentiveness to people, the straightforward language, were such as Thomas could take to naturally. It is more than likely that Frost's suggestion was a mark of confidence Thomas needed, and he could respect it from that source if from few others. When he started to write verse he found it came easily; he had only to be unbound in order to be able to walk. He was thirty-seven, at what might have seemed the *mezzo del cammin*, though in fact he was at the end. He wrote therefore out of no ill-informed ecstasy but as one who had brooded on the inside of life as well as watched the changes of natural phenomena. It is the poetry of thirty-seven or thirty-nine years, not of two, which is packed into Thomas's two hundred pages of verse. The stimulus which occasions a poem does not overwhelm him; it rattles a chain of connections which take him back into the depths of his history. It is to be recorded that, with the gift of verse and his engagement as an effective soldier, Thomas's melancholy cleared. He seems to have been a good officer and his death, very likely, was what he wanted.

It is difficult to speak too highly of the rhythmic variety and aptitude of Thomas's verse. The break into cadences which are virtually those of speech at its most poised and sensitive, which seems in retrospect to have been the aspiration of the poetry of the nineties as of the imagists, was achieved instantaneously. The workmanship is completed by an extraordinary tact with external reality. The physical concomitant of what Thomas has to say is never absent; the wind rustles as he speaks of it. When he enters a wood one enters with him:

I have come to the borders of sleep,
The unfathomable deep

Forest where all must lose
Their way, however straight,
Or winding, soon or late;
They cannot choose.[1]

One is physically present at the occasions he chooses to remember:

And I can only wonder how much hereafter
She will remember, with that bitter scent,
Of garden rows, and ancient damson trees
Topping a hedge, a bent path to a door,
A low thick bush beside the door, and me
Forbidding her to pick.[2]

It would be a shallow judgment on such verses to think of
Thomas as the poet of country places, as if that meant some easy
evocation of agreeable scenes. He is touched to the quick by the
human relationships he has known, and one function of the
natural background is to reduce people to a tempo in which they
can be observed. All passion for the truth is revolutionary and
Thomas's work is a critique of what the world thinks of itself,
and of its methods of thought:

To-day I think
Only with scents...

Odours that rise
When the spade wounds the root of tree,
Rose, currant, raspberry, or goutweed,
Rhubarb or celery;

The smoke's smell, too,
Flowing from where a bonfire burns
The dead, the waste, the dangerous,
And all to sweetness turns.[3]

Thomas's impressions are vivid to the point that his own mind
gives before the reality, and he evokes what he remembers with
marvellous clarity:

[1] *Lights Out.*
[2] *Old Man.*
[3] *Digging.*

> I never knew a voice,
> Man, beast or bird, better than this. I told
> The naturalists; but neither had they heard
> Anything like the notes that did so haunt me
> I had them clear by heart and have them still.
> Four years, or five, have made no difference.[1]

All his years are in the poems in which past and present meet together. It is work grown from a rich deposit:

> the dead that never
> More than half hidden lie[2]

—as in *Celandine*

> the flowers were not true,
> Until I stooped to pluck from the grass there
> One of five petals and I smelt the juice
> Which made me sigh, remembering she was no more,
> Gone like a never perfectly recalled air.

Life and death come together as if even the trace of a dried carcase was not yet extinction:

> But now that he is gone
> Out of most memories
> Still lingers on,
> A stoat of his,
>
> But one, shrivelled and green,
> And with no scent at all,
> And barely seen
> On this shed wall.[3]

Thomas went to the war without regret, above all without fuss. Towards the end of 1914 he wrote: 'I have been thinking a good deal from time to time, trying to decide whether to enlist or not. I

[1] *The Unknown Bird.*
[2] *Two Houses.*
[3] *Under the Woods.*

don't want to: only I feel that it is the only thing to do if a man is able-bodied and has nothing else to do.'[1]

> Now all roads lead to France
> And heavy is the tread
> Of the living; but the dead
> Returning lightly dance.[2]

He did not care about causes, or what the newspapers said. It was 'no case of petty right or wrong'.

> But with the best and meanest Englishmen
> I am one in crying, God save England, lest
> We lose what never slaves or cattle blessed.
> The ages made her that made us from dust:
> She is all we know and live by, and we trust
> She is good and must endure, loving her so:
> And as we love ourselves we hate her foe.[3]

It was Thomas's nearest approach to political poetry, and he had as much right to the words as anyone could have. But his real world is below these clamours, with a profound humanity based on an intense physical apprehension.

> Then past his dark white cottage front
> A labourer went along, his tread
> Slow, half with weariness, half with ease;
> And, through the silence, from his shed
> The sound of sawing rounded all
> That silence said.[4]

Or the shepherd's widow:

> And I think that even if I could lose my deafness
> The cuckoo's note would be drowned by the voice of my dead.[5]

[1] Letter to Miss Townsend, November 1914.
[2] *Roads*.
[3] *This is No Case of Petty Right Or Wrong*.
[4] *Home*.
[5] *The Cuckoo*.

He praises a man whom the common talk of respectable people had dismissed as worthless, because a gipsy praised him for having paid up his half-crown when her daughter had a baby. The ordinary perspectives are nothing to Thomas, except in so far as he has himself felt their reality. The animal world is as present to him as the world of people:

> Boys knew them not,
> Whatever jays and squirrels may have done.[1]

Or this:

> But far more ancient and dark
> The Combe looks since they killed the badger there.[2]

It was himself Thomas was pursuing in this terrible but beautiful world of scents, rain, thunder, sunshine and death. There is a poem, *The Other*, in which he becomes explicit about the pursuit:

> The forest ended. Glad I was
> To feel the light, and hear the hum
> Of bees, and smell the drying grass
> And the sweet mint, because I had come
> To an end of forest, and because
> Here was both road and inn, the sum
> Of what's not forest. But 'twas here
> They asked me if I did not pass
> Yesterday this way. 'Not you? Queer.'
> 'Who then? and slept here?' I felt fear.

He follows the other until once, in a tap-room, the other derisively asks for him. Then he flees.

> And now I dare not follow after
> Too close. I try to keep in sight,
> Dreading his frown and worse his laughter.
> I steal out of the wood to light;
> I see the swift shoot from the rafter
> By the inn door: ere I alight

---

[1] *Birds' Nests.*

[2] *The Combe.*

I wait and hear the starlings wheeze
And nibble like ducks: I wait his flight.
He goes: I follow: no release
Until he ceases. Then I also shall cease.

In another poem, *The Long Small Room*, Thomas records
how

When I look back I am like moon, sparrow, and mouse
That witnessed what they could never understand
Or alter or prevent in the dark house.

It is his own house he is speaking of.

Walter De La Mare claimed for Edward Thomas in 1920
that 'when the noise of the present is silenced … his voice will be
heard far more clearly.'[1] I would say that fifty years have not yet
given him his rightful place. He is, without doubt, one of the most
profound poets of the century. What did he say? He said what is
in the poems, and there is no message beyond them. But he
belonged to the underside of the world, from which renewal
must come, and he speaks with conviction of matters which may
be touched and felt. The irregularity and straggling rhythms of
his verse, and the happy invention of his language, are far beyond
what was achieved by more explicit innovators. And he understood as well as Ford Madox Ford or Pound that no poem could
be good at all that contained definite purple patches.

2

There has always been war, but there have certainly not always
been 'war poets', in the sense in which we use that journalistic
phrase. The author of Chevy Chase was not a war poet, although
he described how Sir Richard Witherington fought on his knees
when his feet had been cut off. Nor for that matter was Homer,
who composed a poem about a war in Troy, the reality of which
is now more believed in than it used to be. The 'war poet', in our
sense of the term, is an invention of the events of 1914–18, and
there was a determined attempt to resuscitate the idea in the
second war of the century. It does not, really, refer to the work

[1] From the foreword to Thomas's *Collected Poems*.

even of all the combatant poets of the periods in question. Thus it is only by an extension of the general usage that the term could be applied to Edward Thomas, although his work fell wholly within the period of the war, and mostly during the time of his military service. Not only did he fail to describe the combatant scene; his whole attitude to war was wrong. For him war was only an incident in the life on which he was soberly brooding. The war poet, in the popular conception, has to do better than that. He should regard war as apocalyptic. It is not enough to think that there is in any case life and death, but that some men die in battle. That would be to place, relatively, too high a value on the ordinary life of man. The 'war poet' must reflect popular sentiment about war — whether the initial enthusiasm or the sated disgust. He must, moreover, send back reports from the front, for the benefit of civilians, though one can see this role being taken over by the television camera and by commentators, so much more lyrical than any poet would be.

Wilfred Owen was a war poet if ever there was one. There was one solid reason, if there had been no other, which fitted him for this role better than Thomas. He was, when he went to the front, a much younger man. He was only twenty-two when he joined the Artists' Rifles in 1915, and only twenty-five when he was killed on the bank of the Sambre-Oise Canal. The production of profound poetry is not, despite a popular prejudice to the contrary, statistically a characteristic of extreme youth. It is, moreover, the case that the young poet is apt to be dominated by his immediate experiences. No doubt to be overwhelmed and not to die of it is a condition of being a poet at all, but it does not follow that whatever overwhelms one is the fittest subject for one's poetry. The reactions which make the final article are very complicated. Whatever sort of poet Owen might have been, circumstances conspired to make him a war poet, and however little one may believe in the seriousness of the genre, it is worth considering him in that light because the public demand for a poetry as big as the event is not unrelated to some of the prominent literary vices of the age.

Owen is one of those poets about whom biographical information is plentiful. According to the editors of his letters — of which a volume of six hundred large pages has been published — his mother and his sister Mary 'were perfect squirrels in the way in which they hid and hoarded all manner of objects and forgot where they were' and his mother 'kept every word written to her by her eldest son from his early childhood'. He also had the good fortune—if that is what it is—to have had a younger brother of a literary turn of mind. Harold Owen, one of the editors of the letters, has extensively written up the memoirs of the family. We even know what Harold saw in the school lavatory, a literary touch, that, which goes back to Jean-Jacques Rousseau. One would have to have a very hearty appetite for the historical sub-structure of poetry to regret now, as Edmund Blunden more understandably did when he wrote his memoir of Owen in 1931, that Wilfred had once given his mother a sack full of papers to burn, with strict orders 'not to reserve a sheet'. The extracts from the family photograph album, which have been made public by the editors of the letters, include one showing Plas Wilmot, Oswestry, the house where Wilfred was born, on—one feels one should give the full date—18 March 1893. It is a pleasant house, with large windows and a greenhouse. A sketch done a few years earlier by Wilfred's mother—whose birthplace it also was—shows it to have been a sizeable establishment, agreeably surrounded by trees and shrubs. Here the family lived until the death of Mrs Owen's father, which happened when Wilfred was four, after which Mr Owen was never able to keep his wife in the manner to which she had been accustomed. He was a minor official on the railways. At first he had aimed at a career in India, where no doubt he would have been more dignified and better remunerated, but he had come home, after a few years, for wholly creditable domestic reasons. For ten years from 1897 the Owen family lived in Birkenhead, in circumstances which brought Wilfred into contact with some rather rough boys, though he was educated from the age of eight at a somewhat superior school, the Birkenhead Institute. His formal education ended at the age of eighteen, after four years or so at the Technical School at Shrewsbury, where the family had moved in pursuit of Mr Owen's livelihood. After that Wilfred had jobs as a pupil-teacher and as some sort of lay assistant to the vicar of a parish near Reading. In 1913 he went to Bordeaux as a teacher of English for the Berlitz School of Languages, and that and various tutorial jobs saw him through until he returned to England and joined the army. He saw his full share of fighting and was awarded the M.C.

The *Poems* of Wilfred Owen were published posthumously—in 1920—with an introduction by Siegfried Sassoon, a writer with some notoriety as a war poet whom he had met during a spell at a military hospital near Edinburgh. A considerably enlarged edition, with a sympathetic memoir by Edmund Blunden, which remains the best introduction to this poet, was published in 1931. This edition has been frequently reprinted. In 1963 there was an edition with an introduction by the present Poet Laureate, who calls Owen 'a major poet'; it is not indicated by what standards.

There is no doubt that Owen is one of those writers whose work is so implicated in the social sentiments of the age that judgment of its durable value is delayed. The nature of his implication is clear from the jottings he made towards a preface to a volume of poems which, as Blunden says, was 'to strike at the conscience of England in regard to the continuance of the war'.

This book is not about heroes. English poetry is not yet fit to speak of them.
Nor is it about deeds, or lands, nor anything about glory, honour, might, majesty, dominion, or power, except War.
Above all I am not concerned with Poetry.
My subject is War, and the pity of War.
The Poetry is in the pity.

It is an embarrassing statement. On the one hand, it communicates a sentiment which cannot be disregarded, coming from a young man who expresses it after undergoing great hardship, and exhibiting great courage, in the appalling conditions of the Western Front which are now almost forgotten. On the other hand, it contains so many unresolved perplexities that it comes near to being absolute rubbish. The sentence about English poetry not yet being fit to speak of heroes connotes an ill-placed progressivism. Were there any grounds for thinking that the language of Chaucer and Shakespeare was taking a turn for the better, so that one day, if it continued to get good reports, it would be able to speak of matters which were above the heads of those beginners? The sentence about 'might, majesty, dominion or power' is a sort of promise of the truth at last, a journalistic trick which never fails to leave a good deal not accounted for. The assertion that the author is 'above all ... not concerned with Poetry' has more than a touch of Mrs Owen's puritanism about it. Poetry

goes the same way as 'might, majesty, dominion and power' and other Prayer Book trash; none of these things is serious compared with what Wilfred is going to say.

Anyway, what right has a poet to say that he is not concerned with poetry? If his work is not that, it can only be some inferior form of literature. But no, 'the poetry is in the pity' — presumably the meaning is that if you look after the pity the poetry will look after itself. Owen means in some way to establish the primacy of pity, a difficult conception which promises, at best, a very limited kind of poetry and, at worst, a relapse into sentimentality. Of course Owen is not at his best in such statements. He had neither the intellectual training nor, it would seem, curiosity, for such formulations, and he was outside the movements of thought which might have instructed him. He was, moreover, emotionally immature, still wrapped psychologically in his mother's embrace and apparently, at twenty-five, still unvisited by that Eros which, for all but a few chosen natures, is a preliminary of any more diffused love of humanity. Quite simply, he was a bit of a prig.

It is certainly on a handful of war poems that Owen's title to consideration rests. There are sketches in which imagination and observation are simultaneously trained upon the scene:

Halted against the shade of a last hill,
They fed, and, lying easy, were at ease
And, finding comfortable chests and knees,
Carelessly slept. But many there stood still
To face the stark, blank sky beyond the ridge,
Knowing their feet had come to the end of the world.[1]

These are moderate, discrete words, and sober rhythms. It is the language of a man brought up in the poetic of the nineteenth century and who is beginning to find his own tone and a new directness of speech. The traditional music sounds skilfully through Owen's verse:

Red lips are not so red
As the stained stones kissed by the English dead.[2]

The passion of Owen's reading had been Keats, and it has been claimed that there is a profound affinity between the two poets.

[1] *Spring Offensive.*
[2] *Greater Love.*

Certainly there is a resemblance, in the manner of their feeling for language and in the way in which some of their work is disfigured by a youthful bad taste. It is impossible, however, on the evidence of Owen's volume, to give him more than a shadowy place beside his genial predecessor. Keats was, even early, going back to the language of the Elizabethans in order to refresh the poetic idiom of his time. The basis of Owen's language remains that of a century of predecessors. But the eloquence of his speech is unquestionable:

> Happy are men who yet before they are killed
> Can let their veins run cold.
> Whom no compassion fleers
> Or makes their feet
> Sore on the alleys cobbled with their brothers.[1]

It is, often, in subject-matter rather than in manner that the novelty of Owen's work consists, and there is no doubt that he and other war poets contributed to the development of modern poetry by their urgency to introduce into it the material which was pressed so vividly upon them. It was a long time since English poets had come face to face with such brutal circumstances; indeed, one might say that there is no historical parallel to the mass immersion of literate young men in the conditions of the Western Front. But the new material, if it could be presented at all, needed a profound linguistic invention. Owen was no Wyndham Lewis. For the most part his language, at its best, still has the romantic glow, and the adaptations to an unromantic subject-matter are for the most part superficial:

> If in some smothering dreams, you too could pace
> Behind the waggon that we flung him in,
> And watch the white eyes writhing in his face,
> His hanging face, like a devil's sick of sin.[2]

Here indeed the subject has been turned into a romantic grotesque. If Owen escapes from the romantic it is, most often, into the trivial and the conventionally not quite nice:

[1] *Insensibility.*

[2] *Dulce et Decorum Est.*

Next day I heard the Doc's well-whiskied laugh:
'That scum you sent last night soon died. Hooray.'[1]

It is unpleasant and tasteless. It is the voice of protest, but
protesting against an attitude no adequate mind would defend.
This is the worst element in Owen's work, and certainly below the
level of literature.

Despite its romanticism Owen's work has a certain technical
interest, in particular in its use of half-rhymes. D. S. R. Welland,
in his critical study of Owen, has made the interesting suggestion
that Owen might have come to this device through an acquaintance with the work of Jules Romains. There is some reason to
believe that Owen's reading in France may have been rather more
sophisticated than his reading in England. He met Laurent
Tailhade—a pacifist, incidentally—and he no doubt had some
tips on what to read of the literature of the day. The possibility
that Owen was acquainted with *La Vie Unanime* has an interest
which extends beyond rhyme-schemes. It is clear, anyhow, that
Owen did not feel his way blindly to the half-rhyme, as Edward
Thomas occasionally did. There is evidence of a consistent
practice which could have come only with deliberation.

> Has your soul sipped
>   Of the sweetness of all sweets?
> Has it well supped
>   But yet hungers and sweats?[2]

—and Owen continues to ring similar changes through nearly
fifty lines of otherwise rather ninety-ish verse. However he
became attracted to this device, he learned to use it with sombre
effect. *Strange Meeting*, Owen's best-known and best poem, is
much cruder in conception than the meeting Thomas describes in
The Other. It is the enemy he killed that Owen meets, and
identification is obvious enough.

> 'Strange friend,' I said, 'here is no cause to mourn.'
> 'None,' said the other, 'save the undone years,
> The hopelessness. Whatever hope is yours
> Was my life also; I went hunting wild

[1] *The Dead-beat.*
[2] Fragment quoted in C. Day Lewis's introduction to *Collected Poems.*

After the wildest beauty in the world,
Which lies not calm in eyes, or braided hair,
But mocks the steady running of the hour,
And if it grieves, grieves richlier than here.'

The half-rhyme lends a new tone to the still Keatsian language.
It is in the opening lines that there is the greatest novelty of
effect, and it is an effect which could not have been achieved
without this aid. The lines are otherwise unremarkable iambic
pentameters!

It seemed that out of battle I escaped
Down some profound dull tunnel, long since scooped
Through granites which titanic wars had groined.
Yet also there encumbered sleepers groaned
Too fast in thought or death to be bestirred.
Then, as I probed them, one sprang up, and stared.

Owen recurrently aspires to the purple patch against which the
other innovators of the day had set their faces, and there is a
certain inebriation of language which is tolerable only so long as
one succumbs to the emotional pressure:

To miss the march of the retreating world
Into vain citadels that are not walled.

Owen is the last of a long line of magicians.

3

Isaac Rosenberg is a poet of a very different kind. Born three
years before Owen—in 1890—he was killed on the Western
Front in 1918, but there the resemblance ends. If Owen's circumstances were mediocre, Rosenberg's would by almost any
standards be considered poor. He was the son of Russian Jews
and lived for most of his life in what was then firmly called the
East End of London, though in fact he had been born, and spent
his first seven years, in Bristol. The poverty of his family no
doubt precluded many indulgences, but his career was by no
means without its good fortune. The headmaster of the Stepney
Board School had the intelligence, rare enough in academic

establishments, to allow Rosenberg, towards the end of his schooling, to spend all his time in drawing and writing. He had to leave at the age of fourteen, and was apprenticed, in conditions apparently none too healthy, to a firm in Fleet Street, to learn the trade of preparing blocks for the press. This he hated, but he managed to go on writing and to attend evening classes at the Birkbeck College of Art. By 1911 he had found three ladies, of his own community, who were willing to pay for him to go to the Slade. At the age of twenty-one, therefore, at the latest, he was well placed to acquaint himself with what was going on in the world of art and, no doubt, literature. Of course he was still short of money, but one way and another he was early acquainted not only with Keats but with Hardy, Donne and Crashaw. He also read F. S. Flint, which shows he kept his ears open, and his comments on him are authoritative: 'I suppose Flint's poems gave me pleasure because of their newness to me. They don't seem to be ambitious, they seem to me just experiments in versification except some, which are more natural; and I think those are the ones I like best.'[1] Rosenberg remained at the Slade until 1914, and by late 1915 he had joined the army. There are some side-lights on this event in his letters to Edward Marsh, the civil servant and poetical impresario, with whom he conducted a considerable correspondence. 'I have managed to persuade my mother,' he wrote, 'that I am for home service only though of course I have signed on for general service. I left without saying anything because I was afraid it would kill my mother or I would be too weak and not go.'[2] A little later:

I never joined the army from patriotic reasons. Nothing can justify war. I suppose we must all fight to get the trouble over. Anyway before the war I helped at home when I could and I did other things which helped to keep things going. I thought if I'd join there would be the separation allowance for my mother. At Whitehall it was fixed up that 16/6 would be given including the 3/6 a week deducted from my 7/-.[3]

The pay of a soldier was then a shilling a day, it will be remembered. He went to France in 1916 and was killed in action on 1 April 1918.

Rosenberg had two poems in *Poetry* (Chicago), in 1916. Otherwise his verse appeared during his life time only in little

[1] Undated letter to Miss Seaton.
[2] and [3] Undated letters.

pamphlets he had printed by I. Narodiczky, Printer, in the Mile End Road, or the Paragon Printing Works, Ocean Street, Stepney Green. The first of these was *Night and Day* (1912). Rosenberg was already doing remarkable work. The Argument of the title poem opens with:

The Poet wanders through the night and questions of the stars but receives no answer. He walks through the crowds of the streets, and asks himself whether he is the scapegoat to bear the sins of humanity upon himself, and to waste his life to discover the secrets of God, for all.

It is evident at once that this is no technical juggler, but a man with a subject. The voice of Jewish antiquity is immediately audible. The verse is varied and muscular, and ideas and images come in a torrent. Rosenberg was bursting with things to say, as Flint, or Aldington, or even Pound could scarcely be said to be. The tension of Rosenberg's verse arises directly from his fullness with his subject.

> Sudden the night blazed open at my feet.
> Like splintered crystal tangled with gold dust
> Blared on my ear and eye the populous street.[1]

There is in this early work an occasional echo of Pre-Raphaelite language — 'these do lute my litanies' — but it is only occasional. The main impression is of a new and individual force.

> My Maker shunneth me.
> Even as a wretch stricken with leprosy
> So hold I pestilent supremacy.[2]

Rosenberg was dominated by the notion of an evil, vindictive God, whom it was a satisfaction to cheat. This was not a conception thought up to scandalize and astonish. There is nothing merely silly about it. It represents a profound struggle in Rosenberg's mind, and the contortions of his language express it. In the second pamphlet, *Youth* (1915), we have *God made blind*:

> It were a proud God-guiling, to allure
> And flatter, by some cheat of ill, our Fate
> To hold back the perfect crookedness its hate
> Devised, and keep it poor,

[1] *Night.*
88 [2] *Spiritual Isolation.*

And ignorant of our joy —
Masked in a giant wrong of cruel annoy,
That stands as some bleak hut to frost and night,
While hidden in bed is warmth and mad delight.

The presentation is more powerful in the third pamphlet, *Moses: A Play* (1916). Rosenberg says of God:

In his malodorous brain what slugs and mire,
Lanthorned in his oblique eyes, guttering burned!
His body lodged a rat where men nursed souls.
The world flashed grape-green eyes of a foiled cat
To him. On fragments of an old shrunk power,
On shy and maimed, on women wrung awry,
He lay, a bullying hulk, to crush them more.
But when one, fearless, turned and clawed like bronze,
Cringing was easy to blunt these stern paws,
And he would weigh the heavier on those after.

The final stage direction of the play itself evokes a world of violence and agony supposed, by Englishmen before 1914 — and since! — to have been superseded. Moses 'places his hand on the unsuspecting Egyptian's head and gently pulls his hair back (caressingly), until his chin is above his forehead, and holds him so till he is suffocated'. Rosenberg carried in him the unerased memory of former times, which are also the future, while the world of such a writer as Rupert Brooke is merely Georgian, or Edwardian. It is a mark of Rosenberg's potential as a poet that the experience he sought to present was not merely a reportage of his personal life but an apprehension of the complexity of a wide universe. For this he found drama a natural medium. So, at twenty-five or six, he can speak for an 'old Hebrew';

I am broken and grey, have seen much in my time,
And all this gay grotesque of childish man
Long passed. Half blind, half deaf, I only grumble
I am not blind or deaf enough for peace.[1]

Yet he can also speak for himself:

[1] *Moses.*

I did not pluck at all,
And I am sorry now,
The garden is not barred,
But the boughs are heavy with snow,
The flake-blossoms thickly fall,
And the hid roots sigh, 'How long will our flowers be marred?'[1]

Fragments apparently written well before the printing of the *Moses* pamphlet show that Rosenberg had mastered what the imagists could teach:

Amber eyes with ever such little red fires,
Face as vague and white as a swan in shadow.

Other fragments show a neat, epigrammatic turn, which must owe something to Blake:

A flea whose body shone like bead
Gave me delight as I gave heed.

A spider whose legs like stiff thread
Made me think quaintly as I read...

But the flea crawled too near —
His blood the smattered wall doth smear

And the spider being too brave
No doctor now can him save.

Or this:

In all Love's heady valour and bold pains
Is the wide storehouse for your female gains.

There are times, especially in the earlier poems, when the syntax is tumbled, but there is never an affectation of obscurity nor are words used merely for their beautiful sounds. Rosenberg is always thinking—a painful process—and it is always towards clarity that he is striving. What he had to say was important enough for him to want, desperately, to make it clear. His order of priorities—unlike that of the imagists, one might think—was, something to say, then a way of saying it clearly. 'You know how

[1] *First Fruit.*

earnestly one must wait on ideas,' he wrote to Marsh, who perhaps did not know; '(you cannot coax real ones to you) and let as it were a skin grow naturally round and through them. If you are not free'—and the qualification seems to relate at once to the bondage of the idea and to the fact that he was writing from the army in France—'you can only, when the ideas come hot, seize them with the skin in tatters raw, crude, in some parts beautiful and in others monstrous. Why print it then? Because these rare parts must not be lost. I work more and more as I write into more depth and lucidity, I am sure....If I could get a few months after the war...'. He has a sense of the profound mystery of his craft. 'You can talk about life, but you can only talk round literature.' He aims at a poem 'as simple as ordinary talk'[1] but the matters he had to talk about were often high and difficult.

The poems Rosenberg wrote from the trenches, or on his way there, show a concern for the visual aspects of the war as well as for the subcutaneous suffering. The poetry is not all in the pity. On board *The Troop Ship*:

Grotesque and queerly huddled
Contortionists to twist
The sleepy soul to a sleep,
We lie all sorts of ways
And cannot sleep.
The wet wind is so cold,
And the lurching men so careless,
That, should you drop to a doze,
Winds' fumble or men's feet
Are on your face.

Or, in the grimmer *Break of Day in the Trenches*,

Poppies whose roots are in man's veins
Drop, and are ever dropping;
But mine in my ear is safe,
Just a little white with the dust.

Lice are the occasion of a lurid pantomime (*Louse Hunting*):

[1] Letter to Edward Marsh, 4 August 1916.

Then we all sprang up and stript
To hunt the verminous brood.
Soon like a demons' pantomime
The place was raging.
See the silhouettes agape,
See the gibbering shadows
Mixed with the battled arms on the wall.
See the gargantuan hooked fingers.

It is the painter's eye. Rosenberg is far from any attempt to whip
up the emotions; in the most desperate scenes he tends towards a
contemplative gravity — not, one may suspect, because he is not
touched but because he is touched so profoundly:

We heard his weak scream,
We heard his very last sound,
And our wheels grazed his dead face.[1]

For nearly a year before his death Rosenberg 'worked intermittently', as his editors say, at a play called *The Unicorn*. The
work might well be intermittent for he was, of course, composing
as he moved in and out of the trenches. The design never became
entirely clear. He was still working it out, not as an entertainer
might think up the scenario of a film or a novel, but writing 'into
more depth and lucidity', without the shape having ever emerged
satisfactorily from the creative darkness. The theme is clear
enough. 'It's a kind of "Rape of the Sabine Women" idea,' he
told Edward Marsh; 'some strange race of wanderers have settled
in some wild place and are perishing out for lack of women. The
prince of these explores some country near where the women are
most fair. But the natives will not hear of foreign marriages; and
he plots another Rape of the Sabines, but is trapped in the act.'[2]
One thinks of Gaudier's drawings of a procession of women being
carried off. The central subject is not new to Rosenberg. In the
Youth pamphlet we have:

O lust! when you lie ravished,
Broken in the dust,
We will call for love in vain,
Finding love was lust.

[1] *Dead Man's Dump.*
92   [2] Undated letter to Edward Marsh.

In *The Unicorn* the exploration is far more profound, and more agonized. By what was, obviously, a natural trick of Rosenberg's mind, as he moved into deeper water the purely personal note disappeared and he took to a dramatic form to give objectivity to his expression. It is a human situation, not particularly his own, that he is exploring. Nothing so convinces one that a major poet was lost in Rosenberg as this drive towards universality of expression. That the drive is powered by his own suffering merely assures the reality of what he depicts. One may detect in this subject the massive deprivation of the soldiery. One may suspect that, when Lilith says

> He tugged the wheels,
> The mules foamed, straining, straining,
> Sudden they went

it is a lurching gun-carriage Rosenberg sees. A 'black naked host' riding on various animals threatens the settled community. Tel, their leader, who rides the unicorn, is 'a black naked giant'. Saul, Lilith's husband, speaks:

> God riding with
> A mortal would absorb him.
> He touched my hand, here is my hand the same.
> Sure I am whirled in some dark fantasy —
> A dizzying cloven wink, the beast, the black,
> And I ride now...ride, ride, the way I know
> That rushing terror...I shudder yet.
> The haughty contours of a swift white horse
> And on its brows a tree, a branching tree,
> And on its back a golden girl bound fast.
> It glittered by
> And all the phantoms wailing.

Lilith, who is to be carried off by Tel, is fascinated. Moreover, she understands the aesthetic purpose of the rape, though at the final approach she shrieks in terror. She says:

> Beauty is music's secret soul,
> Creeping about man's senses.
> He cannot hold it or know it ever,

But yearns and yearns to hold it once.
Ah! when he yearns not shall he not wither?
For music then will have no place
In the world's ear, but mix in windless darkness.

TEL: Am I gone blind?
I swim in a white haze.
What shakes my life to golden tremors...?
I have no life at all...I am a crazed shadow
From a golden body
That melts my iron flesh, I flow from it.

In the final stage direction of the last fragment the host is seen riding away, 'on various animals, the Unicorn leading. A woman is clasped on every one, some are frantic, others white or unconscious, some nestle laughing.'

4

A poet of the generation, almost of the age, of Edward Thomas, who should not be overlooked is Harold Monro. Born in 1879, his childhood was divided between Brussels and Wells, in Somerset. He went to Radley and to Cambridge, where he studied horse-racing, and then mooched around, reading for the bar a bit, then keeping chickens in Ireland, and mixed with socialists and vegetarians, including the Russells, in Surrey. The full history is more miscellaneous than that. What must not be omitted is that in 1913 he opened the Poetry Bookshop, off Theobald's Road. There books of verse were sold or displayed on the shelves, poets or 'poets' read their poetry or their rubbish. For a short time T. E. Hulme lived over the shop. But Monro was not a man of literary schools, nor certainly of instantaneous discrimination. He was, however, honest — several friends testify to the fact — in 'a milieu where honesty, in the degree he possessed it, is by no means a matter of course'. That is from Ezra Pound, in the excellent obituary essay published in *The Criterion* after Monro's death in 1932, and reprinted in *Polite Essays*. There are also, in *The Collected Poems* (1933), a biographical sketch by F. S. Flint and a critical note by T. S. Eliot. One cannot really add to this tryptich.

Monro published a number of volumes of verse from 1906 onwards. They reflected, to some extent, the changes of poetical fashion during his life time. But Monro was no mere fashion-monger. He was too slow to re-act, for the best of reasons, because he was, all the time, trying to eject something that lay at the bottom of his own mind. There is a development in his work which can be followed, and it is the development of the man. The interest, therefore, is authentic. There are encounters with people, presented in such of their simple truth as he saw, whatever the awkwardness. There is the pleasure of weekends in the country, to which it was then customary to escape by train. There are the houses and trees which at moments filled his mind. In 1916 we get:

I want nothing but your fireside now.
Friend, you are sitting there alone I know,
And quiet flames are licking up the soot,
Or crackling out of some enormous root:
All the logs on your hearth are four feet long.[1]

It is solid and satisfactory verse. At the end of Monro's career as a poet the words come from a deeper interior. He was at once disintegrating and learning:

How many many words may pass
Before one ever makes a friend
And all that conversation prove, alas,
However subtle, nothing in the end.[2]

He had the merit of striving for expression to the end — the poetic equivalent of holding out to the last round, like Yeats and unlike Wordsworth. *Bitter Sanctuary*, one of his last poems, concludes with the lines:

How do they leave who once are in those rooms?
Some may be found, they say, deeply asleep
In ruined tombs.
Some in white beds, with faces round them. Some
Wander the world, and never find a home.

[1] *Hearthstone.*
[2] *The One, Faithful.*

95

Chapter Six

Ezra Pound

I

To pick one's way among the work of Ezra Pound is to go back deep in the history of the century, to the nineties of the last century indeed, and to follow a course which touches Hueffer, Hulme and Flint—even Rosenberg—and so to Eliot and to Yeats who lived to be influenced by the man twenty years his junior who, in the first place, had been influenced by him. After that, the influence, or the give and take, is less patent, as well it might be, except in the case of some professional post-Poundians, but probably no one writing serious verse since the First World War has not undergone the influence of this technician in a manner which has essentially affected his performance. It is not likely to be forgotten that Eliot addressed him as *il miglior fabbro*, and there is no one now writing who can afford to take that compliment lightly, however much fashion and the direction of literary innuendo may change.

Pound emerged in London in the first decade of the century. What he emerged from can be understood only dimly by a native Englishman, who is apt to see him simply in the crude category of the American abroad, a role which he has played throughout his life with dramatic panache, often no doubt to the irritation of less exuberant members of the category. It could even be contended that the further he has got from his base, or the longer he has been away from it, the more outrageously he has affected his role, rather as Englishmen living abroad sometimes end up as caricatures of an animal which is well known, but non-existent. Only an American could trace this figure convincingly to its originals, or fully separate the melodramatic element from the sober heritage of the native hearth. There is no doubt that the hearth has been of profound meaning to Pound. He retained the closest connection with his parents until their death. He has, more generally, always had his eye on the *patria* and no doubt recognition in that quarter is more to him than what other people can offer. His local relationships, so far as they can be described, are sufficiently marked by the characteristics of the New World. Hailey, on the Big Wood River in south central Idaho, was, when Pound was born there in 1885, a single street, with forty-seven saloons, a newspaper, and one hotel without locks on the doors. It was not 'incorporated as a village', whatever that may mean, until nearly twenty years afterwards. The population was about two thousand. It is safe to say that whatever liberty reigned there was different in kind from what was known, at that date, in any English collectivity of similar or indeed any other size. The house where Pound was born was a pleasant building, with three bed-rooms and three reception rooms, as estate agents call them, one of them a 'music room' which one supposes to be a usual middle-class appurtenance of the time. Pound's father was a government employee in Hailey, running the local Land Office, and miners came from up to two hundred miles to this administrative centre to file their claims. He became a skilled assayer, and four years after Ezra's birth, assistant assayer of the United States Mint, in Philadelphia, and it was there that Pound grew up. Ezra describes his father as 'the naïvest man who ever possessed good sense'. Homer Pound was presumably, less a demon of energy than either his son or his father — Ezra's grandfather — Thaddeus, who had made money with enterprise out of lumberjacking, railways and mines — pursuits proper to the time — and apparently lost most of it. Thaddeus was also three times elected to Congress, as a Republican. Through his paternal grandmother Pound claims to be descended from horse-thieves. Altogether one might presume him to be of good American stock. His immediate family was well enough off for his youth not to be regarded as straitened. As a boy he had a trip to North Africa and Italy with a great-aunt and he later accompanied his father on a visit to the Mint in London. At the University of Pennsylvania he became acquainted with William Carlos Williams, who was qualified to be an admirer. He also had the opportunity of falling in love with Hilda Doolittle. Altogether he seems not to have suffered from isolation. He studied Romanics and had a fellowship which took him for a period of study in Madrid. He also went to France, Italy and Germany. He therefore had every opportunity to equip himself for his work as a poet, and he was not the man to waste such opportunities. In 1907 he started to teach Spanish and French

97

at an establishment called Wabash College in Crawfordsville, Indiana, 'a most Godforsakenest area of the Middle West', but was dismissed after six months because a girl was found occupying his bed. He had apparently been feeding her, not sleeping with her, in case that is thought relevant to a history of poetry. It may be that some other incident would have ended Pound's career as an academic, if that one had not. He was, however, only at the beginning of his passionate career as a pedagogue, in which he had to make do without the salaries accorded to less useful professors.

How the new expatriate's beard was trimmed, and what were the colour of the suits he wore as he walked down Kensington Church Street, are not matters which will be pursued here. It is, however, of interest to know how his native land appeared to him, as he receded from it. There is evidence of this in his articles serialized in the *New Age* in 1912 and not published in book form[1] until 1950, the American publisher having mislaid the manuscript for thirty-seven years. America is described as 'almost a continent and hardly yet a nation', the idea being that it had not yet acquired 'a city to which all roads lead', which would unify it as Madrid had unified the provinces of Spain, or Paris caused the disappearance of the constituent kingdoms of France. It may be observed that, by these standards, England must rank as a very old nation indeed, given the date at which, first, the heptarchy disappeared and next, the rule of London and Westminster asserted itself, more or less. As for America, Pound said, 'one cannot soundly consider it as older than 1870.' There is no doubt that, at this date, Pound was favourably impressed by the social arrangements he found obtaining in London. His view is not a very profound one, being evidently based on the impressions of a foreigner who had been well received and entertained by the well-to-do. He speaks of the clubs, where men could entertain without introducing people into their homes, or luncheon parties to which wives could invite you without bothering their husbands, who must be presumed — though Pound does not say so — to be meanwhile making money in the city. As he looks back on the strange people of the land of his birth one cannot help feeling that he is comparing the natural confusion of a land about which he knew quite a lot, in the indiscriminate but organized way in which

[1] As *Patria Mia.*

one does know the country in which one is brought up, with the superficial order of a favoured group in a capital in which he had done the rounds. He is, however, seeking to define civilization, which one most easily does by contrasting it with everything one knows best. He seems to confuse the general problem of civilization with the qualifications of an élite. 'Nine out of every ten Americans,' he says — and one wonders why he stops at Americans — 'have sold their souls for a quotation. They have wrapped themselves about a formula of words instead of about their own centres…They will not judge for themselves. They will pretend to do so. They will hold an opinion.' He sees his compatriots as a race who think they know what they want, and go after it without thought. 'Among them understanding is of no repute.' It is, after all, the general condition of mankind. But there is no doubt of the affection he feels amidst all this abuse. It is a crack at the English when he says that the American is a 'man of the Midi', which to the student of Romanics is a compliment. The Englishman thinks 'that the United States, once a set of his colonies' — there is the indelible rub — 'is by race Anglo-Saxon'. This is of course precisely what the Englishman did think, still would, perhaps, if he had not meanwhile forbidden himself to think in racial categories, if at all. It is not without interest to compare Pound's distant prospect of the United States with the view of an accredited Englishman who visited the country only a few years earlier and dedicated his findings, with a fine bit of residual Latin, *Aluredo Baroni Northcliffe* — a nobleman who was presumably not without some appreciation of the benefits to be derived from American customs. Charles Whibley did not hesitate to speak of the Americans with all the authority of an elder brother.

It is an irony of experience that the inhabitants of the United States are wont to describe themselves as a young people. They delight to excuse their extravagances on the ground of youth. When they grow older (they tell you) they will take another view of politics and of conduct. And the truth is that old age long ago overtook them. America is not, never was, young. She sprang, ready-made, from the head of a Pilgrim Father, the oldest of God's creatures. Being an old man's daughter, she has escaped the virtues and vices of an irresponsible childhood. In the primitive history of the land her ancestors took no part. They did not play with flint knives and set up dolmens where New York now stands. They did not adorn themselves with woad and feathers. The Prince Albert coat (or its equivalent) was always more appropriate to their ambition. In vain will you search the United States for the signs of youth. Wherever you cast your eye you will find the signal proof of an eager, grasping age.[1]

The crucial point of Pound's complaint, which is not out of line with Whibley's rather supercilious talk, is that the American's sources are not where he was born, and that 'the few dynamic people who really know good from bad' still live near those sources. 'If you have any vital interest in art and letters, and happen to like talking about them, you sooner or later leave the country.' It is only fair to say that Pound left England for Paris, after the First World War, for much the same reasons.

There was certainly no political tergiversation in these early travels of Pound. 'It would,' he says, 'be about as easy for an American to become a Chinaman or a Hindoo as for him to acquire an Englishness, or a Frenchness, or a European-ness that is more than a skin deep.' He went in pursuit of his own particular game, which was no doubt partly frivolous — the 'happen to like talking' — but was mainly the serious business of searching for the roots of the civilization which not only Pilgrim Fathers but Italians, French, Germans and even Chinese had, for better or worse, planted on the North American continent. He was, precisely, in the role of the Renaissance scholar from Northern Europe who sought Italy, no longer primarily as the home of the Papal See but as the point of directest contact with the antiquity which was seen as the source of civilization. Pound's travels were an intellectual search to discover 'what sort of things endure, and what sort of things are transient', and he did in fact look for some kind of American renaissance as a result of such inquiries as his own. He was part of a necessary search party. American poetry was bad, 'not for lack of impulse, but because almost no one in that country knows true from false, good from bad'. It is instructive that, at this time, Pound found even Oxford dons who understood this distinction. There was an old gentleman who unhesitatingly condemned *The Hound of Heaven* because of the superfluous adjectives. The level of literary culture in England has taken several downward turns since Pound wrote *Patria Mia*, and one can feel a greater sympathy with the objectives of his search party than, perhaps, he might have found in the London of 1912. The difference is that there is now nowhere for the search party to go — a conclusion which Pound may himself well have reached meanwhile.

[1] *American Sketches*, 1908.

The tendency Pound had to identify himself with an élite — or even to pose as a one-man élite — did not lessen as time went on. Instead, he extended the notion from the field of literature, where he had a certain right to it, to the dangerous ground of public affairs. Believing with Hueffer, from whom perhaps he learnt it, that there is a Function of the Arts in the Republic, he came to see the language as inflated and softened by usury, as it probably is. At any rate he was not mistaken in seeing literature in this age, as in none before it, bludgeoned down by various forms of profit-taking which had the effect of ousting good work in favour of the bad. This process has not been reversed, nor is it likely to be in the time of anybody now living. There is no doubt, moreover, that he was profoundly affected by the disappearance of several brilliant talents — Gaudier and Hulme in particular — on the Western Front in the First World War. The performance of England in that war impressed him, but he was even more impressed by her inability, and that of the Allies altogether, to make anything of the peace. These sentiments were certainly not peculiar to him. He saw the tangle of debts, and the inability of the victorious nations to make use of the resources at their command, which he attributed, with a show of reason, to the financial system. Since everybody now agrees that the obsession with gold and the restriction of credit in the inter-war years was collective lunacy, it could not be said that Pound's targets were wholly illusory. The detail of his analysis is more doubtful and less creditable. There is no doubt, however, that it was a right sequence of thought to proceed from the mismanagement of the system of credit by private interest to an examination of the conduct of governments. In the course of these inquiries he was driven back into the American past, for if the cultural past of the United States was in Europe his own country at least had a political past going back to the eighteenth century. He summarized American history in thirty lines of quotation. The summary, originally produced ten years earlier, appeared in a pamphlet published in Venice in 1944 under the title of *L'America, Roosevelt e le cause della guerra presente.* The first quotation was from John Adams, to the effect that 'all the perplexities, confusion, and distress in America' arose 'not from defects in their Constitution or confederation, not from want of honor or virtue, so much as from downright ignorance of the nature of coin, credit, and circulation'. The second was from Thomas Jefferson proposing, in 1816, a scheme for the issue of 'national bills' guaranteed by future taxes and issued free of interest 'because they would answer to every one the purposes of the metallic money withdrawn and replaced by them'. The third quotation was from Abraham Lincoln, who spoke of giving the people of the Republic 'the greatest blessing they ever had—their own paper to pay their own debts'. Last of all, Pound displayed an extract from Article I of the Constitution of the United States: 'The Congress shall have Power…to coin Money, regulate the Value thereof…' It is a mark of Pound's ingenuousness that he seems to have been under the impression that such generalities, repeated often enough, with enough passion, and with a wealth of historical illustration, would somehow change the course of history. The transition from generalization to practice completely eluded him, and since the whole agony of practical affairs is in that transition, the gap was a pretty serious one. The pamphlet starts with statements which belong to this simplified world: 'This war was not caused by any caprice on Mussolini's part, nor on Hitler's. This war is part of the secular war between usurers and peasants, between the usurocracy and whomever does an honest day's work with his own brain or hands.' Anyone with the remotest grip on the reality of affairs would realize that, in wartime, no one would read beyond the first of those two sentences and that, if they did, it would be assumed that Germany and Italy bore arms on behalf of the virtuous peasant and England and the United States on behalf of the wicked usurers. That was, no doubt, at times exactly what Pound did mean and it was, to say the least, a somewhat incomplete view of the matter.

Pound's residence in Italy, uninterned, during the Second World War, was itself enough to raise doubts as to his loyalty. The broadcasts he gave over the Italian radio naturally made matters worse. At the opening of the broadcasts, an announcer stated:

The Italian radio, acting in accordance with the Fascist policy of intellectual freedom and free expression of opinion by those who are qualified to hold it, following the tradition of Italian hospitality, has offered Dr Ezra Pound the use of the microphone twice a week. It is understood that he will not be asked to say anything whatsoever that goes against his conscience, or anything incompatible with his duties as a citizen of the United States of America.

It is a pretty speech, and if Pound misunderstood the sense of it his studies of the Italian renaissance must have brought him less light than he supposed. To judge by the texts of such as have been made publicly available, the broadcasts themselves were poor stuff enough, from any point of view. At times Pound seems to have been fighting again the American Civil War. 'The control of the national credit, control of the national currency, the national purchasing power, passes right away from the people and right out of the control of the national and responsible government.' The references to Roosevelt were hardly tactful, given that he was the best president the Americans had at the time: 'any man who submits to Roosevelt's treason to the public commits breach of citizen's duty.' Pound certainly seems to have wanted to make clear that America as she was was not fit to win the war: 'When a nation's inner life is so palpably made up of the economic aggression of one class or group against the whole rest of the population, it is very difficult for any foreigner, or indeed for anyone not carried away by political heat of the moment, to see why that particular nation should be entrusted with the latch key of any other.' Common sense should have led the author of such words to expect a charge of treason. The best one can say is what Pound himself said in an interview published in the *Paris Review* in 1962: 'Oh, it was paranoia to think one could argue against the usurpations, against the folks who got the war started to get America into it. Yet I hate the idea of obedience to something which is wrong.' Pound's fondness for his own opinion had got the better of the *carità del natio loco*, a fault which is not peculiar to his side of the political and economic argument.

2

The Spirit of Romance (1910), Pound's first critical collection, contains the dictum that 'all ages are contemporaneous'. The idea, of large and uncertain meaning, or rather of a collection of meanings, hangs over several of the characteristic literary produc- tions of the twentieth century — *The Waste Land, Ulysses*, the *Cantos* themselves. To some extent it is the product of the regurgitation of information which the luxury of technical aids has made possible. To some extent it represents the break down of the narrownesses perceptible, once they are past, in settled societies which drink deeply of their most evident sources rather than sip here and there. It seems to make a promise, which is obviously absurd, of a sort of egalitarian treatment for all past ages, though evidently our knowledge of them is fragmentary in widely varying degrees and, in the case of the periods we know best, infinitesimal compared with the reality to which our ideas attempt to correspond. For the youthful Pound, however, the dictum had a simple, practical meaning. 'What we need,' he said, 'is a literary scholarship, which will weigh Theocritus and Mr Yeats with one balance, and which will judge dull dead men as inexorably as dull writers of today, and will, with equity, give praise to beauty before referring to an almanack.' Of course one can claim too much for this method. Writers of all past ages are not in fact equally accessible to one, as the ups and downs of literary reputations show. The virtual disappearance of Donne in the eighteenth and nineteenth centuries, and his re-emergence in our own day, does not mean that we are suddenly intelligent compared with those stupid centuries. Nor was Samuel Johnson less discriminating than his successors who did not share his view of correctness. If one fails to enjoy work which was held in high esteem by the good judges of other ages, it is reasonable to ask whether it is not the reader, rather than the author, who is dull, or at any rate ill-equipped to appreciate a certain range of beauties. On the other hand, the freshness of approach Pound recommends has everything to recommend it as compared with the academic custom with which he was in combat, of preferring the scholarship before the work. Useful scholarship, that of the rare great commentator, such as Robinson Ellis, the expositor of Catullus, brings one within reach of regarding a long dead poet as a contemporary. In the end it is the impulse to be got from the work that counts, and one may sometimes have to abandon a great poet, even someone so near as Milton, as inaccessible for the time being.

It is the great merit of Pound's critical work that he declares unashamedly what does not interest him, and searches out, sometimes in unlikely corners, work which is capable of contributing to the pleasure and the poetics of his own time. *The Spirit of Romance*, his first critical book, is the spoil of his first onrush into Romance literature. The sub-title, *An attempt to define somewhat the charm of the pre-Renaissance literature of Latin Europe*, is exact. Pound was perfectly aware of the rashness of his attempt, and there is a pleasing acknowledgement to Ernest Rhys, to whom, he says, 'some stigma will doubtless attach' for instigating the volume. Pound was, if not covering, at least rooting around in a vast field. 'The book treats only of such mediaeval works as still possess an interest other than archaeological for the contemporary reader who is not a specialist.' This twenty-five-year-old scholar has zest. He has, also, the much rarer gift of knowing exactly what mediaeval work will contribute to the lucidity he is trying to introduce or re-introduce into the language of his day, an absolute sureness of touch, within his limits, which is his inestimable contribution to literature. 'Good art,' he says, 'never bores one. By that I mean that it is the business of the artist to prevent ennui; in the literary art, to relieve, refresh, revive the mind of the reader—at reasonable intervals—with some form of ecstasy, by some splendour of thought, some presentation of sheer beauty, some lightning turn of phrase—for laughter, especially the laughter of the mind, is no mean form of ecstasy. Good art begins with an escape from dullness.' To some extent Pound's hunting among the literature of the past is that of a technician. His eye is always open for some clarity he might be able to use himself. But he has more than the technician's eye, and indeed it may be said that no one is any sort of hand as a technician in the art of literature who has not more than that. As he passes, in this aboriginal Poundian survey, from the *Pervigilium Veneris* to Arnaut Daniel, Dante, or Lope de Vega, his eye is on the man as well as on his works, secondary though he regards mere biographical informations as being. His commendation of Montcorbier, *alias* Villon, is characteristic: 'Villon never forgets his fascinating, revolting self. If, however, he sings the song of himself he is, thank God, free from that horrible air of rectitude with which Whitman rejoices in being Whitman.' He quotes some lines of Whitman—'Lo, behold, I eat water melons, etc.'—and then says: 'They call it optimism, and breadth of vision. There is, in the poetry of François Villon, neither optimism nor breadth of vision…Villon paints himself, as Rembrandt painted his own hideous face'; and that is why 'his few poems drive themselves into one in a way unapproached by the delicate art of a Daniel or a Baudelaire.' In Pound's 'drive themselves into one' one has, succinctly, both the man and the technique, the cutting edge of the words, and the plainness.

The critical work of Pound is in the full sense exploratory. He really is looking for himself, as if no one had ever looked before, and he is looking for whatever will help him to give full intelligibility to what he has to say. For this purpose 'all ages are contemporaneous'. The attraction of Rémy de Gourmont was less for his 'enlightenment'—which was the main attraction for

Aldington — though Pound feels that too, than for the assistance he can give in the art of communication. He was a man who 'would have known what you were driving at' in a way that the admirable Yeats and the admirable Hardy would not, and he was 'an artist of the nude...concerned with hardly more than the permanent human elements'. This was Pound in 1918 (in the *Little Review*, reprinted in *Make it New*), still working up to his maximum efficiency as a writer and still actively seeking for means of expression. His early excursions into Chinese and Japanese were similarly motivated. No doubt he could not, in relatively few years, master all the languages in which he sought for methodologies and techniques. But whatever inaccuracies experts may detect, it would be a presumptuous critic who would make light of the many and varied labours represented by these linguistic enterprises. The encounter with the work of Ernest Fenellosa was decisive. One can see the attraction for Pound of this man who went to Japan as a professor of economics and ended as Imperial Commissioner of Arts. But it was Fenellosa's illuminating explanation of the 'The Chinese Written Character', the unfinished essay which Pound edited in 1918, which gave a new dimension to Pound's thought. He found in it the exposition of a process which enabled the mind, even in the most abstruse fields, to follow directly the movements of perceptible reality. 'In reading Chinese,' says Fenellosa, 'we do not seem to be juggling mental counters, but to be watching *things* work out their own fate.' Here was a possibility of a speech more direct than Villon's. The worn abstractions of our much-used language could be discarded, and Pound, having mastered the thought processes of the ideograph, might hope to renew the language by packing it fuller of things. Fenellosa showed the relationship between metaphor and the Chinese mode of writing. In Chinese the 'accumulation of metaphor into structures of language and into systems of thought' remained visible. Pound was delighted to find that Gaudier-Brzeska could read some Chinese characters on sight, so acute was his appreciation of the meaning hidden in line. 'Poetry is finer than prose,' Fenellosa says, 'because it gives us more concrete truth in the same compass of words.' And 'the Chinese written language has not only absorbed the poetic substance of nature and built with it a second work of metaphor, but has, through its very pictorial visibility, been able to retain its original creative poetry with far more vigor and vividness than any phonetic tongue.'

These Chinese studies of Pound's were an aid to concentration of language, and in *Cathay* (1915), in the composition of which he made use of Fenellosa's notes 'and the decipherings of the Professors Mori and Ariga', he attempted to see what of this methodology could be carried back into English speech, as he had attempted to carry over the music of Arnaut Daniel in his exercises from the Provençal.

Pound was never tired of trying to impart the discoveries he had made for himself in his pursuit of clarity. His crucial didactic works are essential for anyone who wants to understand the aims of his poetry and the nature of his contribution to the literature of the century. Pound has attempted to set out a programme of reading which would acquaint the student, in short space, with the technical discoveries necessary for the production of efficient writing. There is some absurdity about this, but only if one imagines that he is offering a comprehensive programme of reading matter, or that he supposes that a man without a natural impulse towards literature could benefit by it. Of course the adolescent's first flounderings will be among whatever plausible writing comes first to hand. He will, moreover, have to make some progress in discriminating among the classics of his own language before he can make much use of the eclectic programme Pound offers. But there can be no doubt of the value, at an appropriate moment, of the succinct report Pound gives of his explorations. As one moves, perhaps over a long series of years, in the various directions he has indicated, one has to admit that his tips are all good ones. And once more, the technical interest is not merely technical; it is united, as in any serious writer it must be, with vital concerns which are beyond letters. 'It appears to me quite tenable,' he says in *How to Read* (1931), 'that the function of literature as a generated prize-worthy force is precisely that it does incite humanity to continue living; that it eases the mind of strain, and feeds it, I mean definitely as *nutrition of impulse.*' He classifies writers into six groups, starting with the inventors who discover particular processes, and the masters who, besides themselves contributing to the sum of inventions 'assimilate and co-ordinate a large number of preceding inventions, and so through the more or less worthy diluters and those who write in the fashion of a period to the purveyors of belles lettres and the starters of crazes'. As a framework for critical assessments, these classifications certainly bear thinking about. Pound then divides poetry into three kinds: melopoeia, which has a musical quality, phano-poeia, which operates on the visual imagination, and logopoeia, 'the dance of the intellect among words', including the play of irony. These again are classifications which repay reflection. The 'minimum basis for a sound liberal education in letters', according to *How to Read*, includes Confucius (the French version by Paulthier is allowed—Pound's own Confucian translations came later); Homer; Ovid, Catullus and Propertius; Dante and Villon; Stendhal, and Flaubert; Gautier, Corbière and Rimbaud. Pound quite rightly rates the first-class translation above most so-called original work, and anyone who has been sent by him to Golding's *Metamorphoses* or Gavin Douglas's *Eneados* —which Pound calls 'better than the original'—will see what he means.

The method of *How to Read* was elaborated and illustrated in the *ABC of Reading* (1934). 'The proper method for studying poetry and good letters,' it is explained in Chapter One, 'is the method of contemporary biologists, that is careful first-hand examination of the matter, and the continual COMPARISON of one "slide" or specimen with another.' And in Chapter Four: 'Great literature is simply language charged with meaning to the utmost possible degree.' Pound's idea is in no sense to discourage the reading and enjoyment of secondary work. But he holds that until you know certain master-works you will not be able to see clearly what you are reading. The original and the derivative sort themselves out as one's knowledge expands. It could be argued—though Pound does not explicitly argue it—that an age which believes that self-expression is a simple matter is ill placed to grasp this truth. People think that there is something sacred about an individual opinion, however ill-informed. A young man anxious to persuade will imagine he is emitting 'his own ideas' when it is evident to any instructed bystander that those ideas have a history going back for two hundred or some other number of years. It is the same with poetry. The simple soul pouring out his heart is almost certain to be pouring out literary methodologies of traceable recent ancestry: the German critic E. R. Curtius should be consulted on this point. The unadven-turous reader of a few books, especially if they are mostly con-temporary ones, has simply not understood what a rigorous world he has entered upon, in taking literature for his province. To

absorb any substantial part of the Poundian programme of reading

—one might say simply, to absorb *any* part of it—is to have your perspectives changed in an objective way. That is to say, once you have seen the point of the inclusion of, say, Villon or Gavin Douglas in the programme, a great mass of respected writing looks comparatively soggy and can never be rated so highly again.

The second section of the *ABC* is a collection of exhibits in illustration of the recommended method. It is of course limited by space and the gaps are filled by peremptory indications which are not of a kind to win over the unsympathetic reader, though he had better get used to them if he wants to learn. Thus we are told that 'the poetic bunk of the preceding centuries gave way to the new prose' of Flaubert and Stendhal, and that 'poetry then remained the inferior art until it caught up with the prose of these two writers'. The sentence is, in fact, a key to the verse literature of the century, and the catching up, so far as this country is concerned, took place largely through the agency of Ford Madox Ford. Once again, there is no trace of the delusion that there is such a thing as a mere technical mastery which will operate on its own to instruct the understanding or to improve a writer's own performance. 'No man,' says Pound, 'understands a deep book, until he has seen and lived at least part of its contents.' There is in Pound a close attachment to experience in books as in life; the two are not really separable. What Pound does discourage is a brute attachment to experience, as if it were legitimate for a human being to wallow in his sensations without using his brains. The comparisons here recommended put Villon beside Chaucer, Shakespeare beside Dante, and the mere collocation helps a good deal more in the understanding of these masters than a great many volumes of exegesis. Directness, above all, is the quality Pound's examples recommend. That is why he gets 'more pleasure from the Bishop of Dunkeld' (Gavin Douglas) 'than from the original highly cultured but non-seafaring author'. No doubt this comparison ignores other qualities in which Virgil is certainly Douglas's superior, but Pound's statement is instructive as far as it goes. Of Golding's Ovid Pound says that he does not 'honestly think that anyone can know anything about the art of lucid narrative in English, or let us say about the history of the development of English narrative-writing (verse or prose), without seeing the whole of the volume', and the reader who has followed this tip will be unlikely to disagree. Pound is at his best in these recommendations which are, as he says, of writers 'all intent on what they are saying, they are all conscious of having something to tell the reader, something he does not *already know*, and their main effort is spent in telling him'. The next part of the book is concerned with 'authors who are gradually more and more concerned with the way they are saying it'. The exhibits include Marlowe and Donne, Rochester, Waller and Pope, Crabbe and Landor. The choice is idiosyncratic, and once again the pointing omits to draw attention to qualities as valuable as those that are pointed to. But there is no extract which does not offer matter for reflection and indeed delight, and the collocations are mutually illuminating. The *ABC* as a whole is only the sketch of a method, but it is a method which a qualified reader will continue to develop for himself, with more or less consciousness, once he has seen what Pound is after.

3

Of his early poems Pound has said, in his foreword to the 1965 edition of *A Lume Spento*: 'A collection of stale creampuffs. "Chocolate puffs, who hath forgotten you?"' Of the reprint. 'No lessons to be learned save the depth of ignorance, or rather the superficiality of non-perception—neither eye nor ear. Ignorance that didn't know the meaning of "Wardour Street".' Certainly at this early stage Pound was given to taking the short cut to beauty through the use of what must have seemed to him at the time aesthetically pleasing language. It is a curious speech, even by the standards of Butcher and Lang. It is not simply what the tourist might take for the language of the Old World; it is contorted by an attempt at thought, a genuine attempt to approach genuine thought, of which the young man has detected the presence, without yet being able to feel its outline clearly. The *Note precedent to 'La Fraisne'*, in *A Lume Spento*, exhibits these tendencies more clearly than the language of the verse itself. 'When the soul is exhausted in fire, then doth the spirit return unto its primal nature and there is upon it a peace great and of the woodland

" *magna pax et silvestris*".'

Even more contorted: 'Also has Mr Yeats in his *Celtic Twilight* treated of such, and I because in such a mood, feeling myself divided between myself corporal and a self aetherial, "a dweller by streams and in woodland", eternal because simple in elements

"Aeternus quia simplex naturae."'

One can understand the revulsion of the eighty-year-old poet from this abuse of speech, yet it contains evidence enough of a genuine youthful feeling for language. Pound was not more than twenty-three at the time, and the comparison one must make is with the contemporary work of Arthur Machen or F. S. Flint, not with the later work of Pound himself or with the work of young men of a later date who had the use of a language purified by Eliot, Lewis, Joyce and Pound himself. Yet such anti-quarianism was not, even at this time, obligatory. One has only to think of Kipling, or of the way in which Hardy had, years before, gone straight to his subject. Pound was a little mesmerized by his medium, and if the mesmerism left him he remained, none the less, a man for whom the medium, as much as the subject, was an object of consciousness.

Even those for whom bibliography is not more important than poetry may find a certain interest in the manner of Pound's early publications. *A Lume Spento* was printed in Venice in 1908 in an edition of a hundred copies. A further volume, *A Quinzaine for This Yule*, was printed in London, later in the same year — twice, indeed, by different publishers, each time in an edition of a hundred copies. Whatever the economics of such productions were, they were different from those which obtain in our own time. It is of interest, too, that the first publication should have been in Venice. One is, with Pound, very much in the presence of the American for whom European countries seem, reasonably enough — though the perspective is odd if one is born here — to be merely so many mediaeval provinces. It is with this air of the *grand* democratic *seigneur* that Pound regards the literatures of the world. The attitude is not unrelated to the peculiar metempsychosis he describes, rather flatly, in the early poem *Histrion* — from *A Quinzaine for This Yule* — and which remains significant for his later work, in particular for the *Cantos*:

> Thus am I Dante for a space and am
> One François Villon, ballad-lord and thief,
> Or am such holy ones I may not write
> Lest blasphemy be writ against my name;
> This for an instant and the flame is gone.

He describes how these assumed figures take possession of the central 'I'

And as the clear space is not if a form's
Imposed thereon,
So cease we from all being for the time,
And these, the Masters of the Soul, live on.

A young man under an influence is the commonest of literary
spectacles. Pound is under a number, and he is, as it were,
admitting them one by one, and consciously. There are traces of
his reading in French, Italian and Provençal. There is—most
pervasive and perhaps not fully conscious—the rather tired
aestheticism of the nineties. There is also a deliberate play, as in
an effort to get away from too easy a beauty, with the manner of
Robert Browning.

Aye you're a man that! ye old mesmeriser,
Tyin' your meanin' in seventy swadelin's.[1]

There is even a *Beddoesque,* though the hope of striking new fire
from the particular variant of romanticism represented by Thomas
Lovell Beddoes must have seemed a little faint, even then. One
feels that Pound's heart is most in his echoes of the nineties, as
The Decadence.

Tarnished we! Tarnished! Wastrels all!
And yet the art goes on, goes on.
Broken our strength, yea as crushed reeds we fall,
And yet the art, the *art* goes on.

This is the true starting-point, though it is far from the best
manner of the early volumes. The best is where, with an ortho-
doxly 'poetic' theme, he is trying his hand at escaping from too
obvious a rhythm, though he is not, at this point in his development,
escaping very far:

Though thou does wish me ill,
    Audiart, Audiart,
Where thy bodice laces start
As ivy fingers clutching through
Its crevices,
    Audiart, Audiart.[2]

[1] *Mesmerism.*
[2] *Na Audiart.*

If, in 1909, one had got hold of Flint's *In the Net of the Stars*, together with Pound's volume issued only the year before, one would not have had much doubt which had the more nervous control of language, even though one might have thought Flint expressed a more authentic emotion. There is nothing in *A Lume Spento* or the *Quinzaine* to indicate with any sureness the course Pound was to run or the quality to be achieved in his best work. But there is plenty to show the presence of a talent with a restless interest in the art of verse.

It seems that the volumes published in 1908 did not contain all the best of Pound's verse written before that date. There is, for example, *In Durance* (1907) which, if ninetyish in subject-matter, is remarkable for the way it holds a rhythmic sequence through some fifty lines and, some poeticisms apart, for its genuine spoken tone.

I am homesick after mine own kind,
Oh I know that there are folk about me, friendly faces,
But I am homesick after mine own kind.

'These sell our pictures'! Oh well,
They reach me not, touch me some edge or that...

But Pound's verse develops decisively with *Ripostes*. The variety of this volume is remarkable. There is an assurance not hitherto attained in epigrammatic writing, as in *Quies*:

This is another of our ancient loves.
Pass and be silent, Rullus, for the day
Hath lacked a something since this lady passed;
Hath lacked a something. 'Twas but marginal.

That of course bears evidence of Latin studies. But there is also the now well-known version of the Anglo-Saxon *Seafarer*, in which Pound is testing to see what holds good of the extinct rhythm of the rather more muscular language that preceded our own. The experiment gave his verse a new resource, which can be traced here and there among the many elements of the *Cantos*. It re-established, for his successors as well as for himself, connections which had long been severed. The mood of the Anglo-Saxon comes over with the rhythm, the heavy yet athletic brooding, the sense of doom without abandon, which are still central to the English character.

> There I heard naught save the harsh sea
> And ice-cold wave, at whiles the swan cries,
> Did for my games the gannet's clamour,
> Sea-fowls' loudness was for me laughter,
> The mews' singing all my mead-drink.[1]

Or this:

> The blade is layed low.
> Earthly glory ageth and seareth.
> No man at all going the earth's gait,
> But age fares against him, his face paleth,
> Grey-haired he groaneth, knows gone companions,
> Lordly men, are to earth o'ergiven,
> Nor may he then the flesh-cover, whose life ceaseth,
> Nor eat the sweet nor feel the sorry,
> Nor stir hand nor think in mid heart.[2]

It is a new tone in the verse of the twentieth century. One does not think of Kipling as within Pound's sphere of influence, but one might ask whether the poem quoted on p. 37, with its two-part line, marked by two heavy stresses,

> What is a woman that you forsake her[3]

would have been written without this *Seafarer*. The *Ripostes* volume also contains *A Girl*, in sinuous verse of another kind — a remarkable absorption of the Ovidian metamorphosis in a lyrical impulse:

> The tree has entered my hands,
> The sap has ascended my arms,
> The tree has grown in my breast —
> Downward.
> The branches grow out of me, like arms.[4]

[1] and [2] *The Seafarer.*
[3] *The Harp Song of the Dane Women.*
[4] *A Girl.*

The sharpening of Pound's weapons went on in *Lustra*. The poems are often mannered, the attitude of the writer supercilious. If one were to single out one influence, on a mind that had undergone so many, it would be that of Rémy de Gourmont. It is the alliance of intelligence and sensuality, with the conviction that this makes for liberty, as within narrow limits perhaps it does. There is a rather raw assumption of superiority to virgins and other uneducated persons. Altogether this world is as unreal as, say, Watteau's. Pound had not arrived at the art of, as he says of Rembrandt, 'painting his own hideous face'; he paints himself as he likes to think he is—intelligent, precise, masterful. His folly even extends to asserting that 'the female is ductile'. There is a touch of ordinary Edwardian posing about all this. What saves these verses is the verse itself. The lines are as taut as pieces of a mainspring.

> Will they be touched with the verisimilitude**s**?
>   Their virgin stupidity is untemptable,
> I beg you, my friendly critics,
> Do not set about to procure me an audience.[1]

A witty neatness, a deliberate *logopoeia*, in Pound's terminology, is part of this epigrammatic style:

> Four and forty lovers had Agathas in the old days,
> All of whom she refused;
> And now she turns to me seeking love,
> And her hair is also turning.[2]

Trivial in a sense, no doubt, but such lines will not be dismissed as merely trivial by anyone who understand what differentiates literature from the unformed speech of the world at large. It is this neatness and propriety of words to thought which is the very nature of literature, and however quickly such lines are done they are the result of hours and years of attention to cadence of words. Beside these epigrams, with their rather formal wit, there are short poems which bear evidence of more precise social observation:

[1] *Tenzone.*
[2] *Ladies.*

All the while they were talking the new morality
Her eyes explored me.
And when I rose to go
Her fingers were like the tissue
Of a Japanese paper napkin.[1]

—where the last two lines, with their sudden sense of touch, save the poem from what might have been a rather abstract commonplace. There are also the imagist poems, as

The apparition of these faces in the crowd;
Petals on a wet, black bough[2]

—which is said to have been rendered down from a considerably longer draft. There are also short poems which contain lyrical bursts of the kind which from time to time emerge to refresh the reader of the *Cantos*:

Empty are the ways of this land
    Where Ione
Walked once, and now does not walk
But seems like a person just gone.[3]

There is also the Browningesque *Near Périgord*, and there are other echoes of the Provençal. Pound works by reference to others, because he *works*, not pours 'himself' out as if the self could be poured into a vessel without shape.

The great accretion to Pound's range during these years is in the versions from the Chinese in *Cathay*. This is a new injection into his impulses, as were his experiments with the Anglo-Saxon in the *Seafarer*, but different in kind. With the *Seafarer*, the weight and texture of the language itself were affected, because he was dealing with native roots. With the Chinese, the influence could only be visual, or on the succession of ideas. But just as one cannot have much awareness of what the English language is like until one has some acquaintance with a Latin and a purely Germanic language, so to have a sense of the identity of the

[1] *The Encounter.*
[2] *In a Station of the Metro.*
[3] *Ione, Dead the Long Year.*

Indo-Germanic group of languages one must have ventured beyond that into some field not covered by the group. There is no doubt that Pound's excursions into the Chinese and Japanese brought him this sort of awareness. There is no doubt, also, that these studies — and one should recall Fenellosa's essay in this connection — helped him further towards an English in which the unpoetical, and as it were unphysical, interstices were reduced to a minimum. That is the technical moral of such lines as these from Rihaku:

Ko-Jin goes west from Ko-kaku-ro,
The smoke-flowers are blurred over the river.
His lone sail blots the far sky.
And now I see only the river.
    The long Kiang, reaching heaven.[1]

Finally, there is the *Homage to Sextus Propertius* (1919), which Eliot made more mysterious by praising and keeping out of his edition of Pound's *Selected Poems*. The scandalization of classical scholars need not detain us, for any version in the end lives or dies on the strength of its own readability. Eliot thought that 'the uninstructed reader who is not a classical scholar' would 'make nothing of it'. That is overstated, for the difficulty of the poem is only an extreme case of the difficulty which faces more and more people as Latin fades from the curriculum, and a whole tone is missed over a wide range of English poetry. No doubt there are obscure allusions, but readers are perhaps more willing than they were to 'enjoy' what they do not 'understand', if only because they have learned that a lot of painting does not 'mean' anything. The more common weakness now is that people are not puzzled enough. But there is in the *Homage* irony that can be understood without learning, parallels which are only too easy for the uninstructed reader to draw:

Annalists will continue to record Roman reputations,
Celebrities from the Trans-Caucasus will belaud Roman celebrities
And expound the distentions of Empire,

But for something to read in normal circumstances?
For a few pages brought down from the forked hill unsullied?

[1] *Separation on the River Kiang.*

The *Homage* is part of Pound's preparation for the *Cantos*. It can hardly be recommended to the reader for this purpose. But if one goes first to the *Cantos*, and finds pleasure in their rhythms and allusiveness, one will certainly want to come back to the *Homage* which is, indeed, a test of one's tolerance of Pound.

4

Hugh Selwyn Mauberley is a much weightier and more decisive work. It is, without doubt, one of the essential poems of the twentieth century, as Marvell's *Horatian Ode* is of the seventeenth. In it many currents meet. All Pound's work hitherto is implicated in it, but it has an urgency and a seriousness not found so consistently in any comparable stretch of his writing, and rarely indeed found anywhere. A note in the American collected edition of the shorter poems (*Personae*, 1926), describes *Mauberley* as 'a farewell to London', and this is a key to the superficies of it. Pound is summing up his career before he departs to the banks of the Seine and a new phase of development. The work dates from 1919–20. Pound was therefore at the same fruitful age as Edward Thomas was when he began to write verse, or as Dante when he began the *Comedia*. Pound suddenly found a major subject worthy of the technical skill derived from so many practices. The mild shocks he occasionally administered, one might say for amusement, to a departing Victorian morality, were never a central preoccupation. Nor was he, as he says in a poem published in *Blast* (1914), one of those who

> Still sigh over established and natural fact
> Long since fully discussed by Ovid.[1]

His concern has been with his art, the proper use of words and what goes with it. It is here that one has to look for the core of his moral conviction, and he speaks of what he knows. *Life and Contacts* is the sub-title of *Mauberley*, and it is because he is looking at the age from his point of view as a persistent craftsman, who cares for good work more than for anything, that his poem has the seriousness it has. He is old enough to have seen the play of the world on his craft, and intelligent enough to put two and two together. All his preoccupations, down to his political troubles of a

[1] *Fratres Minores.*

later date, stem from this. At the point of writing *Mauberley* the tensions were right. He could express himself with measure and without excess.

One striking thing about the technique of *Mauberley*, when one comes to it from his earlier verse or indeed from the *Cantos*, is the prominence, not of regular metre but of recognizable slight variations from standard forms. The development is in parallel with that of Eliot in rhymed four-lined stanzas of the same date, but in Pound, who at his best has distinctly the better of the comparison, his matter has, after all, burst the agreed bounds. The poem opens with the superb *E. P. Ode pour l'élection de son sépulchre* :

> For three years, out of key with his time,
> He strove to resuscitate the dead art
> Of poetry; to maintain 'the sublime'
> In the old sense. Wrong from the start —

This is a variant — and what a variant — of the 'form' of Gray's *Elegy*, which only shows how superficial such notions of 'form' must be. Every word is in its place in this opening ode, and the rhythm is as stirring and memorable as that of any lines written this century. The ode describes the aesthetic preoccupations of the poet's early years, and how he 'passed from men's memory' with an evocation of Villon. The second poem of the sequence is a general characterization of the age, from the point of view of the serious workman :

> The 'age demanded' chiefly a mould in plaster,
> Made with no loss of time,
> A prose kinema, not, not assuredly, alabaster
> Or the 'sculpture' of rhyme.

The notions of profitability which have now become a national religion are meticulously illustrated and exhibited, and the consequences pointed to :

> We have the Press for wafer;
> Franchise for circumcision.

The fourth and fifth poems express indignation at the war in which several of Pound's brilliant associates, Gaudier and Hulme among them, had been killed, as part of the

> Daring as never before, wastage as never before.
> Young blood and high blood,
> fair cheeks, and fine bodies.

The nascent political Pound appears in the

> home to old lies and new infamy;
> usury age-old and age-thick
> and liars in public places.

Then Pound returns to his aesthetic themes. The Pre-Raphaelites and the Rhymers' Club are recalled and there are splendid if unconventional lines of elegy for Lionel Johnson and for Dowson, who in a sense are Pound's beginning. Ford Madox Ford, then at a low point of his career but gestating the Tietjens books, is evoked, and there is perhaps a reference to Henry James. There is a withering designation of Fleet Street, the squalor of which has not since lessened, and further definitions of the predicament of the man whose 'fundamental passion' is

> The urge to convey the relation
> Of eye-lid and cheek-bone
> By verbal manifestations,

and of whom the age requires a kind of agility for which

> chance found
> Him of all men, unfit
> As the red-beaked steeds of
> The Cytheraean for a chain bit.

Some critics, headed by F. R. Leavis, one of whose most useful enterprises was to draw attention to the importance of *Mauberley*, have been so impressed by the weight of Pound's performance, and perhaps still more that of his subject, in this poem, that they are inclined to make light of everything that precedes and follows it. This, however, is grossly to misunderstand the merits of *Mauberley* itself. For the very tautness which gives *Mauberley* its enduring value is a characteristic of Pound's writing as a whole, in the best of his prose as well as in his verse, and to ignore the great treasure-trove of the *Cantos* because the treasures are not equally valuable on every page is grotesque.

The opening *Canto*, at any rate, is unlikely to repel anyone who has any sense of verse at all.

And then went down to the ship,
Set keel to breakers, forth on the godly sea, and
We set up mast and sail on that swart ship...

What is evoked? Odysseus, no doubt, whether in the wine-dark sea of Butcher and Lang, or some other medium and, for the reader of Pound, the Anglo-Saxon seafarer. But more importantly, since so much is made of allusion in Pound, the sea itself, and the sense of land-bred men going down to it with their craft which has not been entirely lost even in the twentieth century. It is not merely history, still less merely literary allusions, that Pound evokes with his admittedly sometimes heavily-literate verse. He writes — and this is the sense in particular of the *Cantos* — with a profound feeling of the identity of mood and interest of civilized man in whatever quarter of the world and whatever epoch. No doubt this centres, as it must for Europeans, on the Mediterranean of antiquity, but the sweep is from China to the founding fathers of the American Republic. It is an important note in a technological world, in which the popular mind is so bemused by change that the more permanent elements of society are lost sight of. There is, in the *Cantos*, a more emphatic imagination playing on the themes which are central to the work of Ford Madox Ford and explicit in such later productions as *The Great Trade Route*, *Provence*, and *The Rash Act*. In the ancient world Pound evokes he gives a perhaps involuntary prominence to the religious elements. There are the libations to the dead:

Dark blood flowed in the fosse,
Souls out of Erebus, cadaverous dead, of brides,
Of youths and of the old who had borne much;
Souls stained with recent tears, girls tender,
Men many, mauled with bronze lance heads,
Battle spoil, bearing yet dreary arms,
These many crowded about me.

The invocation is an essential preliminary to the voyage of the *Cantos*; from these depths the shallowness of the merely contemporary world can be judged. The first lines of the second canto plunge one into the jumble of allusions from all times and places which is the characteristic kaleidoscope of this poem — Robert Browning, Picasso, China, Homer again, Golding's Ovid. It is better not to stop for them, but to read on, as it is easy to do, giving way without inhibition to the rhythms, a source of excitement in themselves. The allusions will not, unless for the reader who is on the look-out for pedantry, swamp the physical evocation of scenes and creatures:

> The gulls broad out their wings,
>   nipping between the splay feathers.

It is worth remembering that one reason Pound gives for preferring Gavin Douglas to Virgil is that 'Douglas had heard of the sea'. Whether fair or not, the comment reminds us that Pound's aim is to render the world directly. The lumber is there because the mind of man, at this late date, is filled with lumber, and the attempt to render the world without a sense of its past is an illusion as well as an impiety.

There are many splendid beginnings, in the *Cantos*, as in IX:

> One year floods arose,
> One year they fought in the snows,
> One year hail fell, breaking the trees and walls.
> Down here in the marsh they trapped him
>   in one year
> And he stood in the water up to his neck
>   to keep the hounds off him,
> And he floundered about in the marsh
>   and came in after three days,
> That was...

—and so on. Sigismundo Malatesta gets a good deal of space to himself, but he is only part of the kaleidoscope. The reader who has a feeling of being foiled when an introduction breaks off and the scene shifts should consider what sort of continuation would be possible in a modern poem. The poet, even of this sort of work which bears so many marks of conscious craftsmanship, cannot choose, in any wilful sense. Various schemes have been given for the *Cantos*, which lend themselves to proliferation in this kind. Pound himself must have emitted several, but his irritation at having them talked back at him is exhibited in a letter in which he says: 'Damn that paragraph of Yeats'—a reference, presumably, to the *Packet for Ezra Pound* in which a scheme of musical structure, with recurrent themes, is indicated. A straight narrative is hardly thinkable now as the structure of a long poem, because there is no generally received narrative round which the matter for a poem could crystallize, as happens in epical ages. Nor is a theological frame-work such as that of the *Divine Comedy* available, because there is no theology with either definition or acceptability enough for the purpose. The satisfactory long poem is, of course, a rarity in any age. *The Faerie Queene* is hardly one, although its readability and the lucidity of its language are much greater than is now commonly supposed; and anyway it is unfinished. Chaucer's *Troilus and Cressida* is probably the most successful long poem in the language, and that is a straight narrative. But the *Cantos* should be thought of as a sequence rather than as an entity of that kind, and the reader should shift on, from one scene to another, without imagining an abstract pattern that he 'ought' to be able to follow. Whatever plans Pound may from time to time have had—and no man could give so many years of his life to such a work without elaborating excuses—the *Cantos* have obviously in time become a vast repository, the form of his thought in verse, and the unity is that of the composing mind. As the work has moved on through time, events have obtruded themselves on the composition. Sometimes, one suspects, books read by chance, a line of study of interest at the time, have reflected the deeper course. More often the reading or events of the moment have been carried on the general stream, or have become the strands on which the matter held in the deep solution has crystallized. And indeed with a thoughtful man, writing the work of his maturity, and meeting with crucial ideas or events, the case could hardly be different.

Pisan Cantos (LXXIV–LXXXIV)—the last to be published in the period covered by this history—were written in captivity. It was in Pisa that the United States military authorities incarcerated the sixty-year-old poet in a cage on a suspicion of treason. Such an event could hardly fail to shake Pound to the core, and, however broken he may have been, it is hardly too much to say that, as a poet, he was refreshed. There is a new life in the verse, after the solid historical cantos LII–LXXI dealing with China from the First Dynasty to the eighteenth century, with Japan, and with John Adams. There are lyrical passages of great beauty, and echoes which go back to the beginning of this long work and presumably, for the poet, to happier days. The lynxes and leopards of the second canto re-emerge:

Here are lynxes   Here are lynxes
Is there a sound in the forest
        of pard or of bassarid
or crotale   or of leaves moving?

        Cythera, here are lynxes

We are in the depths of the poet's mind, and what should one find in such a situation except images?

If one had to name a single subject for the diverse material of the *Cantos*, it would be — all technicalities apart — usury. What is here exposed, against a background of civilizations and myths which establish its perspective in the history of mankind, is the monstrous aberration of a world in which reality is distorted, down to a detail never so comprehensively implicated before, by the pull of a fictitious money. It is a noble subject and, when one reflects on it, may well be the only possible one for a long poem in our age. The interest of the subject is not likely to diminish, as the age recedes and its characteristics come more clearly into view.

Chapter Seven

T. S. Eliot

I

T. S. Eliot was born in St Louis, Missouri, in 1888. He was the seventh child of Henry Ware Eliot, to whom *The Sacred Wood* was dedicated, posthumously, with the epigraph *tacuit et fecit.* What Henry Ware Eliot did — the *fecit* — was to be secretary, and ultimately chairman, of the Hydraulic-Press Brick Company, in which he made quite a lot of money, providing an affluent home for his children and benefactions for cultural and other institutions in St Louis. What he was silent about will never be known; perhaps the *tacuit* was Tom's translation of 'too much pudding chokes the dog', which is reported to have been his comment on the suggestion that he should go into the Unitarian ministry. The Eliots were a notable Unitarian family. H. W.'s father — T.S.'s grandfather — was a figure in St Louis : Unitarian preacher, civic mover, perhaps saint, and finally he became Chancellor of the University, with the foundation of which he had been associated.[1] He was evidently a man of ability and charm. A friend speaks of his 'sweet plain-speaking' and calls him 'calm, quiet, kindly and sincere in his reproofs'. He must have contributed significantly to his grandson's heredity. Moreover, although he died before Tom was born, his ghost was powerful in the family. William Greenleaf Eliot had come from New England for the enlightenment of the Middle West, and it must have been as if Tom had grown up in the shade of a sort of Unitarian Clapham Sect. Good works, the perfectibility of man, and a distrust of ritual, must have hovered over the household. Charlotte Eliot, the poet's mother, was the daughter of 'a commission shoe merchant' who became a partner in the trading firm of Stearns and Bailey — her father was the Stearns. She was intelligent, well-educated,

---

[1] See Herbert Howarth, *Notes on Some Figures behind T. S. Eliot* —a title which, incidentally, recalls the mannerism of the master's prose style.

and a performer of good works. Her influence must have reinforced and continued that of William Greenleaf Eliot, whose
biography she wrote. A Protestant piety surrounded Tom's
cradle, and a serious literacy awaited him as he came to the age
for it. Charlotte Eliot, who lived not only to see *The Waste Land*
but to receive the dedication of *For Lancelot Andrewes*, followed
her son's literary career with sympathy and hope. She was herself
a poet, in the pages of *The Unitarian*, *The Christian Register*, and
Our Best Words, and towards the end of her life her 'dramatic
poem', *Savonarola*, was published in London by Cobden-
Sanderson, with a preface by T. S. Eliot. She thus attained at
least a vicarious distinction as a woman of letters.

Tom was at Smith Academy, St Louis, and at this establishment,
on Graduation Day, 1905, when he was seventeen, he recited a
poem of his own composition in which he looked into 'the future
years' and saw

> Great duties call – the twentieth century
> More grandly dowered than those which came before.

He added, fairly enough, that

> If this century is to be more great
> Than those before, her sons must make her so
> And we are of her sons.

The recital must have been very pleasing to Tom's mother and to
the headmaster. This 'queen of schools', as the poet called her,
was to close down a few years later for lack of pupils, but Tom
could not foresee this and, apostrophizing her, proclaimed:

> Thou does not die – for each succeeding year
> Thy honor and thy fame shall but increase
> Forever.

After this Tom went to Harvard, and at the age of twenty-two
(Harvard Class Day, 1910) that establishment also was graced
with an *Ode*:

> For the hour that is left us Fair Harvard, with thee,
> Ere we face the importunate years,

In thy shadow we wait, while thy presence dispels
    Our vain hesitations and fears...

concluding with:

And only the years that efface and destroy
    Give us also the vision to see
What we owe for the future, the present, and past,
    Fair Harvard, to thine and to thee.

But by this time Eliot had also written, and published in *The Harvard Advocate*, mannered verses after Laforgue, which are interesting not only as showing how early this influence came to him but also that the manner, and even 'cats in the alley', came to him before the poetry.

At Harvard Eliot studied Greek and Latin, attended a course on Dante, did some French and German and some philosophy. After taking his master's degree in 1910 he spent a year in Paris. He then returned to Harvard and enrolled himself for a doctorate. By now his mind was turned resolutely to the study of philosophy — the philosophy not only of Europe but of India — and in 1911 he was enrolled for a course of Indic Philology. His preparation for his future mission, whatever it was to be, was as deliberate as Milton's. It looked at this time, however, as if his mission was to be not a poet but a Harvard philosopher. In 1914 he was in Marburg; it was the war which brought him back to London and to Oxford. He completed his doctoral thesis at Merton College. It was published nearly fifty years later: *Knowledge and Experience in the philosophy of F. H. Bradley*. It is as if Eliot would not yield to the muse until he had tested all that rationality could do for him — a disposition unusual enough in the poets of this or perhaps of any other age. Eliot came in time to think that he had no gift for abstract thought, and no doubt he was no Berkeley or Coleridge, in whom such expression touched the roots of the mind. He was an able, acute, immensely conscientious man, whose training set him to work things out with the sort of thoroughness which gives merit to the work of, say, a James Fitzjames Stephen. The solid, evangelical background probably counted for something in the matter, as well as a genuine diffidence before, and respect for, minds of another cast than his own. There is no doubt that this was of great value to him; Harold Joachim, under whom he studied at Merton, understood what his pupil wanted to say and 'how to say it'. But looking back towards the end of his life, Eliot found himself 'unable to think in the terminology' of his doctoral thesis, and there is little doubt that had he continued with his 'academic philosophizing' he would have left his real springs untapped.

Oxford provided the best teachers for Eliot's immediate purpose, but one may wonder whether it was the best initial point of contact for an American who wanted to understand this country. It must certainly have had limitations for the young man who had come from what Dreiser characterized as the 'newly manufactured exclusiveness' of the well-to-do quarters of St Louis and the self-conscious superiority of Harvard. From Oxford Eliot went for a year as a teacher at the Highgate Junior School; he was later employed in a bank. Meanwhile, he had not merely drifted into the London of Pound, but, more discreetly, as a no doubt acceptable recruit, into the world of the Spenders — before Stephen had pulled more than an apron-string — of the Gosses, the Garvins, and the Sitwells. There were still drawing-rooms in Mayfair during Eliot's first years in London. When in 1922 he founded *The Criterion*, the money was put up by Lady Rothermere. When she failed him, there was Geoffrey Faber and, fruitful and profitable though that association was, one cannot but wonder whether the emanations of distinguished upper-middle-class Victorian family were exactly what Eliot needed. A sensitive ear cocked for the conversation of the lower orders never quite made up for the lack of immediate roots in this country, and Eliot became the imitation Englishman as Pound became the imitation American.

2

The position of a young American in London during the latter part of the First World War must have been odd. Most of the young natives had gone off to the trenches, and many of them were killed. In 1917 Eliot, aged twenty-nine, took over the editorship of *The Egoist* from Aldington, aged twenty-five, when the latter in his turn went to France. There are no direct traces in Eliot's work of this sort of situation, but it must have left its mark on him. His social success cannot have been altogether unaccompanied by a growing sense of isolation from his contemporaries. There is an element of pre-vision in poetry, to the extent that it may uncover elements which have not yet begun to operate in the conscious life of the poet, but will do so in time, and *The Love Song of J. Alfred Prufrock*, which was brought to London in 1914 by Conrad Aiken, before the poet himself appeared, designates profoundly certain aspects of Eliot's situation in the late teens of the century. No doubt Eliot had contemplated London from St Louis, through the eyes of what he came to regard as the decadent genius of Dickens, and Dickens remained with him, distorting as well as sharpening his vision. He has told us that he was, between the ages of sixteen and twenty, a reader of John Davidson, and there are lines in *Prufrock* which could well have come straight from *Thirty Bob a Week*.

> And time for all the works and days of hands
> That lift and drop a question on your plate

is both the mood and rhythm of Davidson. So is this, with the characteristic eleven syllables packed into the line:

> To have bitten off the matter with a smile.

It was an attempt to reach beyond the prim circumference of a well-protected youth. But there are other elements in *Prufrock*, of a more directly autobiographical kind:

> Deferential, glad to be of use,
> Politic, cautious, and meticulous.

The footman who held Eliot's coat as he made his first forays into Mayfair no doubt partook of 'the Eternal Footman', and no doubt he 'snickered'. The polish which must have recommended the young American was a protection.

> There will be time to murder and create

means, perhaps, time to dawdle in ratiocinations about F. H. Bradley, time to finish the thesis, before giving way to the subterranean and insistent muse.

One can see, from *Conversation galante* in the *Prufrock* volume of 1917, as well as from several of the poems published in the

Harvard Advocate in 1909–10, the value to Eliot of French poetry, and of Laforgue in particular, as an aid to standing apart from the American scene and, more important, as an aid to speaking in something different from the current Anglo-Saxon tone. There is a note of irony which makes the casual reader — and must above all have made the first readers who were surprised by the poem amidst the oceans of diluted Shelley and Keats — think that he is in the presence of the self-conscious wit of ordinary clever conversation. But not at all : the irony of Laforgue has been a lever, a crowbar to heave out of the way the literary preconceptions of the time, so that the poetry can spring from deeper wells. *Prufrock* is an intensely confessional poem, and what hope would there have been of using the language of John Drinkwater to pour out the apprehensions of this taut, acute mind which had been seeking for truth in Bradley and Bosanquet, Moore and Russell, McTaggart and Meinong, to say nothing of the Vedas? Under the transparent mask is the cerebral young man, whose experience is not equal to his intellect, looking with longing, not least, at the ordinary mysteries of youth.

> Arms that are braceleted and white and bare
> (But in the lamplight, downed with light brown hair!)

If he has 'known the arms already, known them all', it is in the appalled imagination which sees the end before it arrives at the beginning. Always, as long as Eliot is developing, there is this acute spreading of antennae towards the future, as when in the first poem of *Ash Wednesday*, not yet forty-five, he is the 'aged eagle' who no longer has motive to 'stretch its wings'. *The Portrait of a Lady*, the second poem in the *Prufrock* volume, is in the same strain. The poet is pretending to a sophistication which he possesses only intellectually. His airs of superiority to the lady portrayed are, patently, the nerves of a young man wishing to begin, but held by complicated strands.

> I smile, of course,
> And go on drinking tea.

What else would the young academic philosopher, from a highly disciplined family presided over by the ghost of William Greenleaf Eliot, attempt? Or even think it best to do? Nor should it be thought, by some idiotic dogmatist of the permissive, that that was not in fact the best thing for him to do. It was a complicated ball of string that the young Eliot was unwinding. In the charming, if slight, *Figlia che piange* — the subject of which is a statue — his considerations reach a momentary stasis. The other two important poems in the volume are *Preludes* and *Rhapsody on a Windy Night*, in which the lonely young man finds his 'objective co-relative' in the scenes of the streets he has wandered in at night.

> You had such a vision of the street
> As the street hardly understands[1]

are words addressed to a feminine *persona*, but there is little doubt that the poet is also, and more particularly, addressing himself. He is

> moved by fancies that are curled
> Around these images, and cling:
> The notion of some infinitely gentle
> Infinitely suffering thing.[2]

Precisely, and the sputtering street-lamps, the cat which 'devours a morsel of rancid butter', and *la lune* which *ne garde aucune rancune*, are there to conceal the need. There are, throughout this volume, hauntings which become more explicit later, the London scene of *The Waste Land*, the lilacs matching the hyacinth garden, just as Christ the tiger appears already in *Gerontion*, before the poet knows who has taken possession of him.

    Gerontion is by far the best poem in the next, the 1920, volume. The epigraph now is from *Measure for Measure*, not from the grandiloquent *Jew of Malta*, which lends itself to dramatic attitudes, and the versification is now firmly modelled on that of the Jacobean dramatists. It could be maintained that *The Love Song of J. Alfred Prufrock* is the more original poem. There is in *Gerontion*, for all its magnificence, a touch of writing up, in a Shakespearian manner, the hesitations and misgivings more rawly confessed in *Prufrock*. This is true particularly of the crucial paragraph beginning

[1] and [2] *Preludes*.

which, however, ends with a sudden release from the depth of the poet's own mind:

These tears are shaken from the wrath-bearing tree.

'As to the problem of knowledge, we have found that it does not exist', as the doctoral thesis on Bradley says. The ratiocinations are the evasions. Where Eliot hesitates and reasons, he does so in order not to be lost, but he recognizes the vanity of the exercise, without concluding that we can or should give it up, the human race being what it is. It is this honest duplicity which makes it quite beside the mark to compare Eliot's intellectualism disadvantageously with, say, an alleged natural directness in D. H. Lawrence. Eliot has absorbed his civilization, not forgotten the apes. The rhymed quatrains of the 1920 volume — the counterpart of Pound's approximations to regular verse in *Mauberley* — are brilliant and, so to speak, suppress some powerful impulses, but despite a certain novelty of tone, a cleverness long absent from English verse, they do little to advance what Eliot has to say nor do they do much to liberate the language for new expression. The poetic triumphs of the poems are at bottom conventional:

The nightingales are singing near
The Convent of the Sacred Heart,

And sang within the bloody wood
When Agamemnon cried aloud,
And let their liquid siftings fall
To stain the stiff dishonoured shroud.[1]

There is, in Eliot, an ever-present disposition to retreat, and the bastions of the quatrain, within which Pound could not contain himself, proved almost morbidly attractive to the slightly younger man.

3

The Waste Land represents an immense advance. It is, above all Eliot's works, probably the one to which one can confidently

[1] *Sweeney Among the Nightingales.*

apply the analysis of the process of composition given in *The Use of Poetry and the Use of Criticism*,

that some forms of ill-health, debility or anaemia, may (if other circumstances are favourable) produce an efflux of poetry in a way approaching the condition of automatic writing – though, in contrast to the claims sometimes made for the latter, the material has obviously been incubating within the poet ... it seems that at these moments, which are characterised by the sudden lifting of the burden of anxiety and fear which presses upon our daily life so steadily that we are unaware of it, what happens is something *negative*: that is to say, not 'inspiration' as we commonly think of it, but the breaking down of strong habitual barriers – which tend to reform very quickly ...

The poem was written at a time when Eliot had some sort of breakdown.

As is now well known, the original manuscript was sold in 1922 – the year of the poem's first publication in *The Criterion* – to the American collector John Quinn, and came to light only in 1968 when the New York Public Library announced that it was in their possession. The original chaos is therefore now emerging; the poem as published had undergone various excisions and revisions which left it a more impersonal monument than it might otherwise have been. There is, however, no question of the discovery at last of the whole of an original poem out of which the published version was carved. It may not explain how large the original work was. It is clear, however, even from the fragments reproduced with Donald Gallup's article on the manuscript in *The Times Literary Supplement* in November 1968, that the editing in 1922 – in which Ezra Pound played an important part – took the reader a little further from the poet's mind, a proceeding of which Eliot probably thoroughly approved. His defences were further strengthened by the addition to the printed volume of the Notes, which had a certain scandalous value of their own. They carried a suggestion that poetry could be erudite, a notion which seemed strange to a generation brought up on the Georgians, and ranked as a novelty or even an aberration. The careless reader was apt to think that erudition was impersonal. In fact, Eliot was able to make poetry out of *From Ritual to Romance* because his own sexual preoccupations gave life to the world of fertility ritual and legend. The ancient cities that fell about his ears did so because, as he walked through London, he was conscious of the sharpness of his own desires. The notes contain references to Ovid,

Shakespeare, Baudelaire, Dante and others, as clues to some of the allusions or quotations in his text. This pointed Eliot's by no means novel practice of drawing on other poets and could be read as a sort of defiance of current notions that poetry was inspirational lark-song. Curtius had not yet revealed that most of the expressions in which the romantic poets claimed to pour out their souls had already appeared in late classical times as themes for academic exercises in rhetoric.

The decisive novelty of *The Waste Land* went far beyond these superficialities. The kaleidoscopic effect produced by the succession of contrasting scenes was no doubt enhanced by Pound's editorial aid; it might be expected from the man who was to pour his mind into the *Cantos*. But an ebb and flow of themes, and unexpected juxtapositions, are an original feature of *The Waste Land* as of the *Cantos* and indeed of much of the visual art of the century. The real proof of originality, however — if any could be said to be needed after *Prufrock* — was in the rhythm, where indeed it is always to be looked for in poetry. The opening of the first section, *The Burial of the Dead*, is superb:

> April is the cruellest month, breeding
> Lilacs out of the dead land, mixing
> Memory and desire, stirring
> Dull roots with spring rain.
> Winter kept us warm ...

It is a drum-beat never exactly heard before. The whole section is triumphant in its masterly dawdlings, hurryings, alterations of pace. Eliot had a regurgitating mind, and he uses here not only Ezekiel, Webster, Baudelaire and Dante but his own earlier work. *The Death of Saint Narcissus*, which probably belongs to the period 1911–15, contains the lines

> Come under the shadow of this gray rock —
> Come in under the shadow of this gray rock,
> And I will show you something different from either
> Your shadow sprawling over the sand at daybreak, or
> Your shadow leaping behind the fire against the red rock:
> I will show you his bloody cloth and limbs
> And the gray shadow on his lips.

The version in the *The Burial of the Dead* is tauter, and the conclusion of the passage immeasurably more powerful:

> There is a shadow under this red rock,
> (Come in under the shadow of this red rock),
> And I will show you something different from either
> Your shadow at morning striding behind you
> Or your shadow at evening rising to meet you;
> I will show you fear in a handful of dust.

The opening section of *The Waste Land*, besides announcing in ringing lines the theme of fertility and death, adumbrates the London which is, in a sense, the scene of the whole poem because it was Eliot's scene at the time of writing, and one which he was still exploring with sympathy and horror.

> Unreal city,
> Under the brown fog of a winter dawn,
> A crowd flowed over London Bridge, so many
> I had not thought death had undone so many.

It is the hell of the commuter, that type figure of the unanimous crowds drifting around the over-populated world. Odd personages stick out of Eliot's London crowds. There is the cosmopolitan detritus — Madame Sosotris, or, in the third section of the poem, Mr Eugenides, the Smyrna merchant. There are other figures of low life, with whom Eliot appears to have a different relationship. Those in the second section:

> When Lil's husband got demobbed, I said

— are almost certainly figures from eavesdropped conversations, in pubs or elsewhere. One imagines the young Eliot with a powerful longing to acquaint himself with the cockney world to which Dickens had long ago introduced his imagination. Among the passages struck out of the published version of *The Burial of the Dead* is one of some length which recalls a world which must be that of *Sweeney Agonistes*. One has the impression — it can be no more — of being in the presence of something more than the fruits of eavesdropping, perhaps an incursion into an unaccustomed

135

milieu, with the poet something between a participant and a listener on the fringe.

> First we had a couple of feelers down at Tom's place,
> There was old Tom, boiled to the eyes, blind,
> (Don't you remember that time after a dance,
> Top hats and all, we and Silk Hat Harry,
> And old Tom took us behind, brought out a bottle of fizz...)

There is the brothel, which is surely akin to the scene of *Sweeney Agonistes*:

> I turned up an hour later down at Myrtle's place,
> 'What d'y' mean,' she says, 'at two o'clock in the morning,
> I'm not in business here for guys like you.'

The mention of a cabman 'who read George Meredith' perhaps indicates the autobiographical nature of this recollection; that is the sort of detail one does not invent.

The next section is *A Game of Chess*, labelled in the manuscript 'HE DO THE POLICE IN DIFFERENT VOICES, Pt. II'—a sub-title which points to the synthesis Eliot made of the underworld of Dickens and his own listening-in to demotic conversations. Lil and her husband fill the latter part of the section, with an episode which Pound thought too long for the quality of the verse but which Eliot perhaps preferred to the episode with Myrtle and Silk Hat Harry, in which he may have felt more implicated. There is a good deal of evidence in this section that Pound did not have it all his own way, *il miglior fabbro* though he might be.

> The wind under the door

is annotated in the margin with what looks like a warning: 'Beddoes.' Pound also seems to have had some objection to 'inviolable' voice, though one cannot believe that Eliot was wrong to retain the adjective. No doubt, however, he meditated deeply all the exceptions of his so highly qualified reader.

The third section of the poem is explicity concerned, almost throughout, with the London scene. It was a sleight-of-hand characteristic of Eliot to call it *The Fire Sermon* from the allusion to Buddha near the end. The London is the London of history and imagination as well as of current reality, which of course is thought of as more sordid. There is the quotation from Spenser—

Sweet Thames, run softly till I end my song

—and the reference to Elizabeth and Leicester, looming larger on the London stage for a newly-arrived American, perhaps, than for the native. Eliot's own brief experience of an office where he had no business is in

the violet hour, when the eyes and back
Turn upward from the desk, when the human engine waits
Like a taxi throbbing waiting.

Others beside the typist had felt that at the end of long, unwelcome hours in the bank. There is autobiography woven into the texture of the whole section. The bundle in the New York Public Library even contains hotel bills from Margate.

The fourth section, *Death by Water*, is apparently one of those which underwent important excisions. The surviving brief lines, which of course translate Eliot's own French poem, *Dans le Restaurant*, from the 1920 volume—

Phlébas, le Phénicien, pendant quinze jours noyé

—were preceded by a much longer episode describing the voyage and shipwreck of a fishing schooner sailing past Dry Salvages to the eastern Banks.

So the men pulled the nets, and laughed, and thought
Of home, and dollars, and the pleasant violin
At Maron Brown's joint, and the girls and gin.
I laughed not.

The personal voice of Eliot the observer is unmistakably in those last three words, which come with sudden force. Eliot's recollections of the sea are implicated with Conrad and perhaps Coleridge, even more than his London scenes are with Dickens. No doubt his actual acquaintance of the sea was slight. For a poet a very slight experience may suffice.

> For an unfamiliar gust
> Laid us down.

The schooner moves to shipwreck through a visionary horror. A quotation from *The Heart of Darkness*—'The horror! the horror!'—was to have been used as epigraph for *The Waste Land*, but Pound persuaded Eliot that it was not 'weighty enough to stand the citation'. Eliot did, however, go to the same source in Conrad in 1925 for the epigraph to *The Hollow Men*. The schooner passed 'the furthest northern islands'

> So no one spoke again. We ate slept drank
> Hot coffee, and kept watch, and no one dared
> To look into another's face, or speak
> In the horror of the illimitable scream
> Of a whole world about us.

One element in the vision is, unmistakably, a puritan apprehension at a first sexual encounter—whether in reality or dream—though it is not only that which is expressed by the 'three women' in the schooner's 'fore cross-trees'

> who sang above the wind
> A song that charmed my senses while I was
> Frightened beyond fear.

The schooner breaks on an iceberg with bears on it.

The fifth and final section of the poem, *What the Thunder Said*, is portentously annotated by the author: 'three themes are employed'—the word *employed* conveys a pretension to deliberation which is characteristic in the Eliot of this period, and doubtless deceptive—'the journey to Emmaus, the approach to the Chapel Perilous (see Miss Weston's book) and the present decay of Eastern Europe'. A welter of memories and scraps from Eliot's wide-ranging studies fills the section. F. H. Bradley, the subject of the doctoral thesis, is there, and the Vedic studies. The whole does convey, powerfully, a groping after a vision to set against the squalor of contemporary London:

Falling towers
Jerusalem Athens Alexandria
Vienna London
Unreal

—as he says in one of the more contrived parts of the section. The greatness of the poem, however, is in the very failure to present a coherent alternative. *The Waste Land* is a *Blick ins Chaos* — Eliot's most profound and veridical statement of his position.

4

The prestige of *The Waste Land* was immense in the twenties and thirties, not the less so for being, at first, the taste of a few which spread more slowly than might be imagined by the generations to whom Eliot has always seemed to be part of the English syllabus. The achievement of this distinction was painful and contested. It was likewise eight years — 1920 to 1928 — before what has certainly been the most influential book of literary criticism of the century, *The Sacred Wood*, exhausted its small first edition and went into a second. The prestige of *The Waste Land* was not, as Auden remarked in his broadcast at the time of Eliot's death, accompanied by a comparable direct influence. 'When reading a poet who found his own voice after 1922,' Auden said, 'I often come across a cadence or a trick of diction which makes me say "Oh, he's read Hardy, or Yeats, or Rilke," but seldom, if ever, can I detect an immediate, direct influence from Eliot.'[1] The influence of Eliot before the Second World War was, above all, that of the man, as it became clear that this prestigious writer, *the* poet of the age as Pope was of the first half of the eighteenth century, had attitudes which the common prejudice of literary men or more generally of intellectuals, had long ago assumed could not be those of the poet or, indeed, of any intelligent and enlightened person. The razor-cut of the verse, in its wit and rhythm, were not to be denied, but surely the scholarly seriousness of the prose might be called in question. When, in the preface to *For Lancelot Andrewes* in 1928, Eliot made what he afterwards thought to be

[1] *A Tribute* (broadcast 4 January 1965).

the injudicious summary of his position in politics, religion and literature, the ripple of scandal and derision so started ran on over many years. It was a measure of the extreme ingenuousness, not to say ignorance, of the professionals of the intelligence in those years. The publication of T. E. Hulme's *Speculations*, in 1924, should have helped for those who came across it. At least that book made clear that a simple progressivism was not the only possible point of view. More generally, the slow pressure of *The Criterion*, from 1922 onwards, must have increased the general awareness of European currents of thought and, belatedly, brought some notions of Péguy, Sorel and Maurras into at any rate a marginal currency. Before these could do their work, however, they were overwhelmed by the liberal-marxist exclusiveness of the thirties, which discredited Eliot's ideas before they had been understood.

Particular definitions apart, the general atmosphere between the two wars was hostile to an appreciation of the matter-of-factness of Eliot's more sombre mood, because it was assumed that reality must be otherwise and that Eliot was a *poseur*. Alternatively, he was just a poet and whatever he *said*, his critics knew better, as if what was said in poetry was not what the poet meant, but something with a special quality of doubtfulness. Eliot himself perhaps contributed to this confusion by bandying words with I. A. Richards about poetry and belief, in his essay on *Dante* (1929). Up to and including *The Waste Land*, the satirical note was sufficiently prominent for everything to be pardoned. It could be held that if Eliot introduced a more solemn note, it was only to make fun of it. With *The Hollow Men* (1925) the situation changed. There is nothing very funny about that poem, unless you so account 'the prickly pear' or the world ending 'not with a bang but a whimper'. In some sense these apparent trivia did enable the poem to be swallowed, and concealed as much as they revealed its true nature. It was hoped this might be a joke poem after all. It was thought evident that it must have some kind of social reference. *The Hollow Men* would be some sort of characterization of the age, as well as being a prank of the poet, exhibiting a yet more *outré* pose. The thought that men might be hollow, and that the poet might feel this as a matter of fact, about himself and others, was hardly digestible. Yet what Eliot was feeling his way towards was an attitude many generations had thought normal, and taken for granted as corresponding to the world they knew. The perfectionist hope, in which Eliot himself had been brought up, had eaten too deeply into Anglo-Saxondom for such gropings to seem other than extraordinary. There was another kind of silliness current in the twenties, which may be illustrated by Edith Sitwell's note in *Bucolic Comedies*: 'We are accused of triviality; but poetry is no longer a just and terrible Judgment Day—a world of remorseless and clear light.' But poetry had not changed; it was merely that there were, as always, people about who were trying to make out that the trivial is important. It is sobering, looking back over the poetry of the century, to see how soon the Judgment Day has come, for how many gaudy figures. It does not take much of the 'remorseless and clear light' of time. *The Hollow Men* survives in this light, not least because it is an incomplete expression, a groping which proved to be preliminary to a Christian discovery, in whatever sense Eliot came upon one. It is a poem of holding back—which had always been a natural attitude with Eliot—but with a new, uncertain awareness as to what he was holding back from.

> Let me be no nearer
> In death's dream kingdom
> Let me also wear
> Such deliberate disguises
> Rat's coat, crowskin, crossed staves
> In a field
> Behaving as the wind behaves
> No nearer —
>
> Not that final meeting
> In the twilight kingdom...

He is in the 'dead land', the 'cactus land'—characteristic images of drought—but with an intense longing, which never quite attains its objective or even recognizes it:

> Waking alone
> At the hour when we are
> Trembling with tenderness
> Lips that would kiss
> Form prayers to broken stone.

The faint, interrupted echo of the Lord's Prayer—'For Thine is 141 the Kingdom' is no more than an echo, perhaps, or it may be a beginning.

By the time we come to *Ash Wednesday* (1930), Eliot had decided that it was a beginning. This poem is crucial for Eliot's subsequent development. The break with the tone of the earlier poems is now complete. A whole element has been subtracted. The moral duty to be ironical, which hangs over the earlier poems, is no longer recognized. It is as if the native earnestness had reasserted itself, and this time completely. What Eliot most wants he says he renounces. It is difficult to speak of the poem without entering rudely upon the man's inner integrity, which one cannot know. But all criticism involves this presumption. One ought not to put the question quite in the form of whether Eliot in fact accepted the Christian faith as he hoped he did, for that would be to assume that one knows what the manifestation of such acceptance would look like. The question for the critic is whether we have in *Ash Wednesday* an expression of belief that carries us with it. There is the impediment offered by

> Consequently I rejoice, having to construct something
> Upon which to rejoice

and the question what that construction amounts to, how *wilful* it is, for poetry is not wilful. An immense and difficult step has been taken. Has it been taken successfully? Certain traditional expressions of the Christian faith are used without irony:

> Pray for us now and at the hour of our death.

In what sense is this expression used? Directly, as Donne when he says:

> Batter my heart, three person'd God;

or in some way dramatically?

The second poem of the sequence is more successful, for the poet gives himself up to images — the 'three white leopards' and the Lady 'in a white gown'. The three white leopards convince us, because we do not understand them, and feel that perhaps the poet does not, completely. The Lady is identifiable with the

Virgin, easily enough, but there is an ambiguity about this figure, not merely because of our unsleeping sexuality but because of the historical confusions with the pagan Venus which are unmistakable in the Latin world. This air of dubiety gives authenticity to the figure, in the poem, for we distrust any pretension to an unmixed adoration.

> End of the endless
> Journey to no end
> Conclusion of all that
> Is inconclusible

also has enough of doubt in it to convince that we are hearing the poet's voice, and not the voice he would like to have. The third poem, also, with its images of the stairway, and the pagan scene through the slotted window —

> The broadbacked figure drest in blue and green
> Enchanted the may-time with an antique flute

—likewise holds our attention, for it is an admission of the flickering world we know. With

> Lord, I am not worthy

the poetry seems to fall. The poet is again trying to case himself in a liturgical expression. The words are used by Christians approaching the Sacrament, from duty or habit, but that is life. It does not follow that the poet has a right to use them here, in his poem, and the poem does not really comprehend them. In the fourth poem, too, we may catch our breath at the images — the 'blue of larkspur',

> The silent sister veiled in white and blue
> Between the yews, behind the garden god,
> Whose flute is breathless

—but the success of the attempt at a theological connotation is less certain. Has Eliot really restored

With a new verse the ancient rhyme?

One does not feel certain, and the

> Redeem
> The time

has the inadmissable effort of construction about it. The opening
of the fifth poem, with its echoes of Andrewes's *Sermons*, is also
dangerous ground. For Andrewes the case was different. He was
expounding what was accepted. We are looking for an apprehension. What is the place of ratiocination in this dilemma? It is
uncertain, but Eliot was always inclined to take refuge in it. No
doubt he was conscious of being one of the

> children at the gate
> Who will not go away and cannot pray,

one of those who

> are terrified and cannot surrender

—in a situation not unrelated to that of *Prufrock* or of the
narrator in *Portrait of a Lady*. The final poem elaborates the
same situation. How far does Eliot succeed in giving it a theological context? The question is not unrelated to one's view of the
success of a poem, as a poem. For if he does not succeed, then the
glimpses of 'the dream-crossed twilight', 'the empty forms between
the ivory gates' are lyrical moments held together by wilful
manipulations. The literary skill of the operation is, of course,
immense.

5

A poem of a very different character, which of course pre-dates
Ash Wednesday, is *Sweeney Agonistes*. This is a crucial poem, the
importance of which has to some extent been obscured by the
later plays. The best introduction to it is probably the notes, which
must have been written not far from the date of its composition,
which Eliot prefixed to the Cobden-Sanderson edition of his
mother's *Savonarola* (1926):

Dramatic form may occur at various points along a line the termini of which are liturgy and realism; at one extreme the arrow-dance of the Todas and at the other Sir Arthur Pinero — or at least the ideal Pinero of Mr William Archer, who has abundantly proved, in attempting to prove the contrary, the complete futility of complete realism. In genuine drama the form is determined by the point on the line at which a tension between liturgy and realism takes place.

This is, evidently, the germinal thought from which the whole of Eliot's dramatic development springs. The next step the drama had to take was clearly to be in the direction Pinero did not take. At the same time, Eliot saw — as Charlotte Eliot could hardly be expected to do — that 'the recognized forms of speech-verse are not as efficient as they should be'. He added that 'probably a new form will be devised out of colloquial speech', coyly not admitting that that was exactly what he was then up to himself. Eliot probably approached his task in a very tentative and sceptical manner, uncertain what would come. He was to use Seneca as a model, no doubt in order to escape from the over-bearing influence of the Elizabethan and Jacobean drama — in the origins of which, however, Seneca also had his place. It was the London scene of *The Waste Land* that he walked imaginatively on the outside of, perhaps feeding his imagination by eavesdropping, which provided the material for the exercise. 'These are the gloomy companions of a disturbed imagination', he typed at the top of his draft — probably, we may say on his own authority, before the work itself was actually begun — 'the melancholy madness of poetry, without the inspiration'. The quotation is from Junius, but it perhaps reflects a trace of the 'ill-health, debility or anaemia' one associates with the composition of *The Waste Land*. Those who saw Peter Wood's production of *Sweeney Agonistes*[1] will realize what a dramatist was lost when Eliot found himself, in his later plays, unable to follow the line here so promisingly begun. The characters are genuinely exteriorized, there is no suspicion that we can identify a *persona* of the author in any one of them. On the other hand, the poem as a whole is a reflection of the poet's mind as we feel we have a reflection of Shakespeare's mind in the later tragedies and tragicomedies. There is about the verse a gaiety which was certainly an element of Eliot's mind but rarely enough got through to his writing. It is not unrelated, perhaps, to the distance he felt between himself and his characters and to

[1] At the Stage Sixty Theatre Club, in June 1965.

what might well have seemed the hopelessness of the dramatic experiment. To the extent that Eliot found himself not only incapable of following up his success, but of completing *Sweeney Agonistes* itself, the attempt was in fact hopeless. The value of this work is, however, not only in the dramatic attempt, but in what strikes one as the extraordinarily veridical projection of the confusion of the poet's mind. The instinctive forces acquire a bleak objectivity in the persons of ladies who were not quite Mr Eliot's type. The male characters are Eliot's nearest approach to the man 'with talk clichéd for chat' of Wyndham Lewis or what one imagines is the Middle Western turn of Uncle Ez. It represents a facility of movement in this hard world which is far from Eliot's usual precise suavity. The very rhythms show an openness to the draughts of the great world which is attained nowhere else in the work of this poet.

> *Under the bamboo*
> *Bamboo bamboo*
> *Under the bamboo tree*

is not a 'crude' rhythm; it is one that drums into the mind and answers to profound movements of the near-consciousness more effectively than anything except the most telling parts of *The Waste Land*. The poem is concerned not with trivialities but with unusually unguarded moments of expression:

> I knew a man once did a girl in
> Any man might do a girl in
> Any man has to, needs to, wants to
> Once in a lifetime, do a girl in.

Let nobody say that there is anything in the creeping verse of the later *Quartets* which is more 'sincere' than that. And to what conclusion could Eliot bring his theme? A mystery which he could only express as a riddle. The last scene, in the *Final Version* published in the programme of the Stage Sixty Theatre Club's Homage to T. S. Eliot on 13 June 1965, ends with this:

> SWEENEY: When will the barnfowl fly before morning?
> When will the owl be operated on for cataracts?
> When will the eagle get out of his barrel-roll?

OLD GENTLEMAN:	When the camel is too tired to walk farther
	Then shall the pigeon-pie blossom in the desert
	At the wedding-breakfast of life and death.
SWEENEY:	Thank you.
OLD GENTLEMAN:	Good night.

There is at any rate a case for saying that *Sweeney Agonistes* is Eliot's best poem.

Sweeney Agonistes was not published in book form until 1932, when no doubt Eliot had given up hope of completing it. His subsequent attempts at drama were of an entirely different character. The thoughts which had accompanied the gestation of *Sweeney* have their bearing on this development, but what had been a groping became a deliberate effort. *The Rock* (1934) is not a play; it is a pageant. We look for — and find — something of the artificiality which appears in the seventeenth-century masque. But there is less sense of *rapport* with the audience than, say in Ben Jonson's masques. Jonson was doing something expected of him; Eliot was springing a poetic surprise. The prose Eliot wrote or permitted to be written to fill the interstices is appalling, and exhibits a lack of tact which, for such a man as Eliot, represents a degrading retreat into the superficialities of nice people. The verse of the choruses is excellent for declamation, and no doubt Eliot felt that he was making a useful step in the direction of a language which would be tolerated by the public. In *Poetry and Drama* (1951) he says some revealing things about the effect on his verse of his essays in dramatic speech. He found that 'a different frame of mind' was required for dramatic verse. In other verse one was writing 'so to speak, in terms of one's own voice'. The test is whether the verse is right to the poet; if it is, it may be hoped that other people will come to accept it in time. 'But in the theatre,' Eliot goes on, 'the problem of communication presents itself immediately ... You are aiming to write lines which will have an immediate effect upon an unknown and unprepared audience, to be interpreted to that audience by unknown actors rehearsed by an unknown producer.' These considerations had been absent in the composition of *Sweeney Agonistes*, which Eliot almost certainly regarded as a 'closet drama'. They offer an ingenious and incomplete apology for the change which was coming over the author. Shakespeare wrote for an ordinary stupid audience; Eliot would do the same. But the situation, at the end of a long

147

decadence of the theatre, differs entirely from the situation in Shakespeare's time. And Shakespeare, skilled man of the theatre as he was, managed his plays with a panache which gave the groundlings the impression that they were hearing something of interest without, one imagines, thinking that he had better put the thoughts of Lear in a language which would ensure that there was no misunderstanding and that immediate communication was achieved. In his later plays, Eliot's effort was to make the verse unnoticeable, while he affected a certain abstruseness of subject. Shakespeare was more given to taking a common subject and making of the verse what he liked.

There is, indeed, an ugly deliberation about Eliot's approach to the theatre. He was, after all, fifty when *Murder in the Cathedral* was published (1935). It was his first full play and it is late in the day for such an adaptation. No doubt the technical problems of the theatre — very special ones, however, until *The Family Reunion* (1939) when Eliot first entered upon the common stage — were a stimulus and an amusement; they certainly occupied him in a different way from the way in which they occupied the Elizabethan and Jacobean dramatists for whom they were part of the ordinary surroundings of their life, indeed of their profession. The choruses of *Murder in the Cathedral* are really words that a chorus can speak, and one should not under-rate the skill needed for that. But the dramatic verse is generally lifeless. The character of Becket is thought out in advance, like that of a character in an ordinary historical novel. The struggles of conscience are appallingly unreal, inexcusably so for a man who must have known what they could be. Eliot achieved a big social surprise — how astonishing that the Church could attract a poet, let us make the most of it — but no one who is moved by his earlier verse can doubt that the play represents a grotesque falling away.

Eliot himself quickly realized that *Murder in the Cathedral* did not solve 'any general problem' and that it was a dead end. He therefore turned, for his next play, resolutely in the direction of contemporary life. Why this conscious effort should have been needed, in the author of *The Waste Land*, is matter for speculation. One must suppose that the social tone of the Anglicanism of the time had been too much for him. There are those who have thought it too much for the Church. In *The Family Reunion* Eliot's first concern was the versification. He sought, as if it was a new problem — the matter is set out at length in *Poetry and*

Drama—'a rhythm close to contemporary speech'. He was, indeed, on a new and shallower level, going over the problem he must have faced at the outset of his poetic career. The excuse is the novelty to him of the drama, but one cannot but suspect that a profounder reason was that he had, somehow, turned his back on his earlier development. He found a verse 'in which the stresses could be made to come wherever we should naturally put them, in uttering the particular phrase on the particular occasion'. It is not unrelated to the verse of the later of the *Four Quartets*, which could hardly have been written as they are without it. The form continued to be used without essential modification in the verse of the later plays. The last play that could be thought to come in our period is *The Cocktail Party* (1950), which is surely already the verse of a dead man.

6

Eliot's final, and some would say crowning, performance as a poet was in the *Four Quartets*. In a sense, the title is a sleight-of-hand, for the sequence as now printed consists of an original poem, published in 1936, and a group of three developments of the theme which appeared in *The New English Weekly* in 1940–42. The first of the *Quartets* is decidedly best. The verse on the whole is tauter. The lassitude of the dramatic utterances has not yet overwhelmed it. Indeed it may be that, in *Burnt Norton*, the poet was trying to pull himself together. He must have been aware that *The Rock* and *Murder in the Cathedral* represented a slackening. Now he would get back to something which kept him ahead of the vulgar reader, as the earlier poems had done. He does achieve a certain novelty, but it is a novelty into which deliberation enters rather palpably.

> Time present and time past
> Are both perhaps present in time future,
> And time future contained in time past.

It is, at a lower intensity, the ratiocination for which, in the fifth poem of *Ash Wednesday*, he had turned to Lancelot Andrewes. As he develops the argument, another parallel comes to mind.

> If all time is eternally present
> All time is unredeemable.

What might have been is an abstraction
Remaining a perpetual possibility
Only in a world of speculation.

The ghost behind this is the young Eliot labouring at his thesis on
F. H. Bradley. Philosophy which, early, was a refuge against the
seductions of the muse, is clutched at as a raft to save the poet who
is swirling along in the wide Missouri. 'As to the problem of
knowledge, we have found that it does not exist,' he said in a
triumphal moment in *Knowledge and Experience*. But other
problems remained, the practical world, 'this real world, which is
not metaphysically the real world'. The self which was the
product of metaphysics had become, by 1929, the 'simple soul'
issuing from the hand of God. But the nakedness and simplicity of
the

　　　animula, vagula, blandula

are difficult to accept for the sophisticated mind, and the 'world
of speculation' retained its attraction for Eliot even though he
did not believe in it and he knew it was one he could not move in
with any great expertise. In *Burnt Norton* it quickly falls away
from him and he is left with the ordinary nagging memories,

　　　　　the passage which we did not take
　　Towards the door we never opened
　　Into the rose-garden.

It is a familiar theme in Eliot's poetry, but seen now from the
perspective of age —

　　　　　to what purpose
　　Disturbing the dust on a bowl of rose-leaves
　　I do not know ...

There is a congeries of recollections. The roses which

　　Had the look of flowers that are looked at

perhaps touch, in the bottom of his memory, the

> thousand
> Roses that grew in an enchanted garden

of Edgar Allen Poe, who must have been one of the poets of Eliot's youth.

> Clad all in white, upon a violet bank

— from the same poem, *To Helen* — must already have been not far below the surface when he wrote certain lines of *Ash Wednesday*.

> The surface glittered out of heart of light

recalls the much more impassioned moment of *The Waste Land* —

> Looking into the heart of light, the silence.

There follows, at the opening of the second section of *Burnt Norton*, what is, for a poet of Eliot's accomplishment, just a piece of poetry.

> Garlic and sapphires in the mud
> Clot the bedded axle-tree

— and so to 'the boarhound and the boar', regurgitated detritus like the nightingales singing near the Convent of the Sacred Heart. Then we move into a style of discourse of which the later *Quartets* are full. It does not convince us as poetic apprehension of something hitherto undiscovered. It is *not* a 'raid on the inarticulate' but the articulation of an idea already consciously accepted.

> I can only say, *there* we have been: but I cannot say where.

It is worthy of the doctoral thesis. As the exposition develops it is difficult not to grow impatient with it. Of course it is the writing of a man of immense accomplishment, but it is not the writing of a man impelled. The words come from a level where half-forgotten reasonings settle, not from profounder depths.

Nothing new has happened to the poet, and he is perhaps determined that nothing shall. Where we return to a visible world—

> Driven on the wind that sweeps the gloomy hills of London,
> Hampstead and Clerkenwell, Campden and Putney

—it is the world of *The Waste Land*, but again with the tem-
perature lowered and the concentration reduced. One cannot
withhold an inclination before the figure of this man, haunted by
his former achievements, wanting death but not finding it available.

> Words strain,
> Crack and sometimes break, under the burden,
> Under the tension, slip, slide, perish,
> Decay with imprecision,

—precisely—

> will not stay in place,
> Will not stay still.

Of course not. There is much to be said for silence, at the end of a
long life, but if one speaks, one must accept the movement of life
and language. And Eliot had, when he wrote *Burnt Norton*, still
thirty years to live—the years of his fame, indeed.

When he took up the themes of *Burnt Norton* again the marks
of decay were not less. *East Coker* begins with a tired rhythm:

> In my beginning is my end. In succession
> Houses rise and fall, crumble, are extended,
> Are removed, destroyed, restored, or in their place
> Is an open field, or a factory, or a by-pass.

The first words are striking enough; the rest is weak, nondescript
verse which, from an anonymous pen, would excite no interest.
One gets the impression, however, that Eliot is anxiously trying
for a new beginning. This was perhaps his mood at the time of the
last three *Quartets*; only the impulse is lacking. He goes forward
a few paces then changes his subject, or his image, not with the
152   force of dramatic contrast, as in the edited *Waste Land*, but

because it will not take him any further. There are passages which would not be negligible from a lesser hand, but which, from Eliot, horrify us with the superficiality of the impression. There are the figures in the deep Somerset lane

> Where you lean against a bank while a van passes.

Should he not have been content to give us these impressions of old age, without the portentous frame-work of time and eternity which is not a poetic apprehension, like Vaughan's

> I saw Eternity the other night,

but the worrying of an abstract bone which he has seen before. There are more pieces of poetry —

> Comets weep and Leonids fly
> Hunt the heavens and the plains

— as if the poet wants to reassure himself that his hand has not lost its cunning. But it has, as he lamely admits:

> That was a way of putting it — not very satisfactorily:
> A periphrastic study in a worn-out poetical fashion.

Alas, the 'wrestle' with words and meanings is no longer 'intolerable', though he pretends it is, though no doubt in his own mind he is thwarted and sick that he cannot do what he would. The 'autumnal serenity' and 'the wisdom of age' are a washout, but it is of no use to keep on saying so. *The Dry Salvages* and *Little Gidding* offer no novelties. It would have been harder, perhaps, for Eliot to have written what he had to say in prose, but he should have done, for he knew already what he meant, as far as he was going to know. Perhaps indeed he should have done a full-length study of Nicholas Ferrar, for he still had a better mind than anyone else who was likely to apply himself to the work.

The conditions in which poetry can be written are not usually, perhaps not ever, within the poet's control. It is useless — or almost useless — to speculate whether Eliot's immense literary skill could have been more fruitfully deployed in the latter part of

153

his life. But the identification of the point of his failure, and its nature, are of public importance because it is not for the health of the literature of the English-speaking countries that attention should be deflected from *The Waste Land*, *Sweeney Agonistes*, and *Prufrock*.

Chapter Eight

W. B. Yeats

I

When William Butler Yeats died, at the beginning of 1939, he
had had all the honours. The Nobel Prize for Literature had
come his way sixteen years before, just as he had completed a year
as a senator of the newly-established Free State. The French
government offered to bring home his remains in a destroyer, but
they had no luck that year and it was not until 1949 that the bones
were put in the shadow of Ben Bulben. The stone, by Yeats's
direction, says:

> *Cast a cold eye*
> *On life, on death.*
> *Horseman, pass by!*

Yeats was a great egotist, and frivolous enough to think it worth
while cutting a figure even after his death.

The career which brought him to this final gesture started in a
genteel, semi-detached house in Sandymount, near Dublin, in
1865. Three years later the family moved to London, where
Willie attended a 'rough' and 'cheap' school — the Godolphin,
Hammersmith. His father, who had started life reading for the
Irish bar, was an artist, and he had relatives in Sligo with whom he
spent holidays. With these advantages, he 'did not think English
people intelligent unless they were artists'. He was thus provided,
from an early age, with a situation which could give colour to the
sense of apartness so exceptional a boy might naturally feel. The
Irish must have suffered from a sense of inferiority in those days,
for there was an Irish master at school who made him stand up
and told him 'it was a scandal' he was so idle 'when all the world
knew that any Irish boy was cleverer than a whole class-room of
English boys'. When Yeats was fifteen the family returned to
Ireland, and he completed his education at the Dublin High

155

School, where he had to find other excuses for his dream of superiority, and at an art school, for his father, who was a man of great intelligence as his published letters show, thought that every boy, no matter what he was going to do, should have a training in art. Willie was already writing verses, and already 'composing in a loud voice', and was to be a poet. In 1887 the family was back in London, and Willie was cultivating publishers. *The Wanderings of Oisin* appeared in 1889. It was, as Louis MacNeice says, full of 'the languor of late Victorian old age', but John O'Leary collected subscriptions for it, presumably seeing the Irish bard under all this old stuff.

The curious mixture of aestheticism and dreamy nationalism from which Yeats started has a parallel, it is not often noticed, in the French nationalist movement at the end of the nineteenth century, but while Maurras and his friends could find an aesthetic in Racine and André Chénier the Irish had only a load of old fairy-stories and some improbable heroisms.

A tall lanky boy with deep-set eyes behind glasses, over which a lock of dark hair was constantly falling, to be pushed back impatiently by sensitive fingers ... a tall girl with masses of gold-brown hair and a beauty which made her Paris clothes ... unnoticeable, sat figuratively and sometimes literally, at the feet of a thin elderly man, with eagle eyes, whose unbroken will had turned the outrage of long convict imprisonment into immense dignity.

Thus Maud Gonne, for whom Yeats broke his heart, describes 'John O'Leary, the master, and his two favourite disciples'.[1] The auspices were perhaps too poetic for a serious writer. O'Leary himself must have been an impressive figure. He held, as he says in his *Recollections of Fenians and Fenianism*, 'that all agitating movements, however inevitable and necessary they may be, are at best but a necessary evil, involving all forms of self-seeking and insincerity, accompanied with outrage and violence, and opening up the widest field for the exercise of that treachery and cruelty which lies latent in human nature'. He preferred the older methods of Wolfe Tone, an engaging character who, as he said at his court-martial, 'designed by fair and open war, to procure the separation' of Ireland from England, and to this end arrived off the entry to Loch Swilly, in 1798, with a French fleet, ending his life shortly afterwards in the manner which might be expected.

[1] In *Scattering Branches*, 1940.

Yeats, of course, was of Anglo-Irish stock—not of the Scottish Protestants of the north but Church of Ireland people like Swift and Berkeley and the builders of eighteenth-century Dublin. To the distractions of aestheticism and romantic nationalism Yeats added that of magic. In 1885 he chaired the first meeting of the Dublin Hermetic Society and he dabbled in such rubbish on and off throughout his life.

The volume of *Last Poems* (1940) shows what was the terminus of Yeats's journey.

> You think it horrible that lust and rage
> Should dance attendance upon my old age;
> They were not such a plague when I was young;
> What else have I to spur me into song? [1]

Yeats is of course here cutting a figure, as in his epitaph (1938), which is also in this volume. The lines are not merely a statement of what he thinks. His mind is also on the spectator whose eye is supposed to be on him, but he is speaking out. Only the last line, perhaps, betrays the romantic figure who had become half an encumbrance to him. The 'spur me into song' is draped language, it is not how people speak, and even if Yeats himself had spoken in those terms—as well he might—one would have felt he was overdoing it a bit, providing something for his lovely voice to say, something he could flash his eyes over and shake his hair about. The line, does, of course, betray the enduring obsession about being a poet—as if this somehow took precedence over merely being a man, which is the subject of the most serious poetry. There is no doubt, however, that in these final poems Yeats is trying desperately to cast aside pretences and to get to the root of his mind. In a way the most impressive attempt—the most successful perhaps—is the brief *Chambermaid's Second Song*:

> From pleasure of the bed,
> Dull as a worm,
> His rod and its butting head
> Limp as a worm,
> His spirit that has fled
> Blind as a worm.

[1] *The Spur.*

It is the chambermaid who speaks, but it is the old man she sees, and he is no longer in a position to give himself airs. In *The Statesman's Holiday*, where the speaker is obviously a *persona* of the poet's, he is strutting, but there is a desperate throwaway air, as if he wished to make nothing of himself. The tone is not far from that which is found in certain of the songs in the song-books of the Restoration period — *Westminster Drolleries* and the like.

> With boys and girls about him,
> With any sort of clothes,
> With a hat out of fashion,
> With old patched shoes,
> With a ragged bandit cloak,
> With an eye like a hawk

—and so on. He writes ballads with what appears to be a deliberate recklessness:

> 'Because I am mad about women
> I am mad about the hills,'
> Said that wild old wicked man
> Who travels where God wills.[1]

But there is a pretentiousness about this which shows up at once beside this from the seventeenth century:

> My Cozen Moll's an arrant whore,
> And so is her sister Kate,
> They kicked their mother out o'dore,
> And broke their Fathers pate.[2]

Yeats is not merely singing a tune, and not merely uttering the lusts of an old man; he is also protesting, in a sort of last will and testament, that the world of the senses is more real than those abstractions which the world of the thirties was always trying to ram down people's throats, as the world of the seventies does too, though with a change of tone. 'In our time the destiny of man presents its meaning in political terms', he quotes Thomas Mann as saying, and his commentary is:

[1] *The Wild Old Wicked Man.*
[2] *Westminster Drollery* (1672).

How can I, that girl standing there,
My attention fix
On Roman or on Russian
Or on Spanish politics?...

But O that I were young again
And held her in my arms.[1]

It is understandable, but it is too preconceived to impress us as poetry.

Yeats's politics, which were really a department of his obsession with the dramatic, were with him to the end. We get recollections of the more colourful bits of the history which produced, in the end, the rather drab Republic:

Come gather round me, players all:
Come praise Nineteen-Sixteen,
Those from the pit and gallery
Or from the painted scene
That fought in the Post Office
Or round the City Hall.[2]

Parnell and Roger Casement have their poems, and from the contemporary scene there are O'Duffy's Blue Shirts, who had attracted Yeats for a time. *The Three Marching Songs* is better in the earlier version, published in *A Full Moon in March* (1935) as *Three Songs to the Same Tune* — and Yeats often in fact composed and chanted to a tune:

Grandfather sang it under the gallows:
'Hear, gentlemen, ladies, and all mankind:
Money is good and a girl might be better,
But good strong blows are delights to the mind.'
There, standing on the cart,
He sang it from his heart.

There is a sort of 'dare' about this, among the humanitarian liberalism of the thirties, and although one could not deny the lines a certain dramatic success, they are not the work of a man

[1] *Politics.*
[2] *Three Songs to the One Burden.*

who has faced reality very soberly. They strike a posture. Yeats was, in fact, defying the mob of inferior beings he was always apt to imagine around him, and he looked to O'Duffy's Blue Shirts to make good, in some way, the destruction of the great houses of his youth which of course, in Ireland, had been done physically by his friends the Irish revolutionaries though it would have happened, no doubt less dramatically, in any case.

> Down the fanatic, down the clown;
> Down, down, hammer them down,
> Down to the tune of O'Donnel Abu.

It is a sort of nihilism. Kipling is rather milk-and-water stuff beside this.

> When nations are empty up there at the top,
> When order has weakened or faction is strong...

Yeats's weakness, as when he sat at the feet of O'Leary, was for a little movement and colour in politics, without caring too precisely where it was likely to lead. But once again, it was an aspect of his distrust of abstraction:

> God guard me from those thoughts men think
> In the mind alone;
> He that sings a lasting song
> Thinks in a marrow-bone.[1]

This is one of Yeats's most successful statements of his final position, though the two remaining stanzas of *A Prayer for Old Age* (also in *A Full Moon in March*) slip back into the inferior dramatics of 'a wise old man', 'a foolish, passionate man' — figures of fun, equally.

Although the *Last Poems* and *A Full Moon in March* have so much interest as showing, with some bleakness, the point at which Yeats finally arrived, the essentials of this last philosophy are exhibited much more fully, and with more variety, in *The Winding Stair and Other Poems* (1933). Here the tensions are far better

[1] *A Prayer for Old Age.*

sustained. Old age still has for him something of the quality of a discovery. He is no longer the 'sixty-year-old smiling public man' of *The Tower*. Nor, on the other hand, has he yet been driven to the desperate gesticulations of the *Last Poems*, in which the voice is often more emphatic than the passion. The period in which most of these poems were composed began with Yeats being 'staggered', as he wrote in a letter to Olivia Shakespeare, by his 'first nervous illness'. There was an illness in 1927 from which he 'hardly expected to recover' but then he did expect it and started to write, his sense of life much sharpened by the nostalgia for it which can come to sick people. The volume starts with what, when one comes to think of it, was an astounding piece of insolence, a poem *In memory of Eva Gore-Booth and Con Markiewicz*, written while the sisters were still alive. These two friends of his youth had become old women; how could it be otherwise? It was long enough ago that they had played their part in his youthful frequentation of great houses. The poem has great charm but, viewed in this light, also a good deal of superficiality and some coarseness. It is a symptom of a general weakness in Yeats that, just as he himself struts and poses, except in his moments of greatest absorption, so he tends to see other people as archetypal figures, or masks, through his own preconceptions rather than for what they are. It is true that in this poem he gives colour to his attitude by asserting that it is their abstract, Utopian politics which has changed the girls to something 'withered old and skeleton-gaunt' but when one thinks of Yeats's own final fling, in *Last Poems*, in favour of politics of a different kind, one is less impressed. One might almost say that, in this dedicatory poem, Yeats is abusing his literary ability to strike an attitude of ego-tistical contempt. Were they more 'shadows' than he was? *He preferred them young*, of course.

The second poem in the volume, *Death*, starts as Yeats not infrequently does from a natural and truthful expression, only to find that the simple truth is not enough and take refuge in rhetoric.

> Nor dread nor hope attend
> A dying animal;
> A man awaits his end
> Dreading and hoping all;

—but he cannot stand at this point. He fumbles for his hero's mask and becomes

> A great man in his pride
> Confronting murderous men.

Should he not have known that, facing death, there are no great men, except for the spectator? Yeats has changed his ground and we feel we are being cheated. He was, after all, talking only to impress us. The *Dialogue of Self and Soul*, which follows, is hardly successful as a dialogue, because the characters are not sufficiently differentiated, but it contains lines which show Yeats painfully trying to look at the truth about his life, and to see clearly

> The ignominy of boyhood; the distress
> Of boyhood changing into man;
> The unfinished man and his pain
> Brought face to face with his own clumsiness;

but he steps aside for the attraction of

> The finished man among his enemies,

which is comforting stuff, for it is the 'malicious eyes' of others that have got it all wrong and he is, as he sees himself, a hero. There are, as so often, magnificent gestures as he struggles,

> A blind man battering blind men

till, with a final dramatic assertion, he claims to 'cast out remorse':

> When such as I cast out remorse.

The 'such as I' betrays him. There is more truth in the lines of *Vacillation* which Eliot pointed to as showing how Yeats 'achieved greatness against the greatest odds':

> Things said or done long years ago,
> Or things I did not do or say
> But thought that I might say or do,

Weigh me down, and not a day
But something is recalled,
My conscience or my vanity appalled.

In *Vacillation*, which is a series of eight short poems, Yeats is held
in the tension of conflicting impulses and it is this situation which
gives the poetry of this volume its strength. The figures he
conjures with here are not Casement or the men of 1916; they
are Berkeley, Swift and Burke — the great intellectual figures of
what, after all, still remains Ireland's most productive period.
He is still struggling, for some sort of intellectual solution which
will hold the opposing forces in balance.

Between extremities
Man runs his course;

between day and night, or some other set of antinomies. The
fumbling for a solution is understandably confused, and Yeats, as
ever feeling the need to speak out and to speak impressively, flings
himself into a sort of moral discourse:

Get all the gold and silver that you can,
Satisfy ambition, or animate
The trivial days and ram them with the sun,
And yet upon these maxims meditate:
All women dote upon an idle man...

There is a curious passion for generality in Yeats which contra-
dicts his declared hatred of abstraction. The types and mask with
which his work is littered are really a form of imperfect abstraction. He is not content to rest on his own experience, as a poet
more wholly of the century would be likely to do. No doubt the
moralism he favours is one which has come to him through a long
course of aestheticism, but it is a moralism all the same and in
this respect his attitudes are more akin than seems at first sight to
be the case to those of the Great Victorian poets. He is cut off
from any fruitful tradition — from Swift, Berkeley and Burke,
of whom in some ways he made so much — by the frivolous
attitude to Christianity exhibited in *The Mother of God* and in the
references to von Hügel. At moments he seems to approximate
rather to the Marquis de Sade, whose not very profound, and

163

perhaps insane, view was that the first duty of women was to lay themselves open to whatever lusts he chose to exercise upon them. There are moments when Yeats drops his moralism, and all his airs. The fourth poem of *Vacillation* shows him a London tea-shop — Lyons, probably. For a moment one sees the poet without affectation:

> My fiftieth year had come and gone,
> I sat, a solitary man,
> In a crowded London shop,
> An open book and empty cup
> On the marble table-top.

But even this attractive small poem ends with an assertion in which Yeats's egotism finds an outlet. He is 'blessed and could bless'; he sees himself as a source of power and puts the surrounding humanity in a different category. If we can provisionally accept Yeats's 'look at me' act, lyrics such as

> Acquaintance; companion;[1]

and

> I ranted to the knave and fool[2]

are impressive. They have great concentration and a spareness of diction which puts them, by any standards, high among the productions of the century. But when it comes, as he said in an earlier poem, to dining with Landor or John Donne, one can only conclude that though he may dine with Landor — no mean company — he will never dine with Donne, whose poetry is immeasurably nearer the bone.

The series of twenty-five short poems under the general title of *Words for Music Perhaps* are among the most remarkable productions of Yeats's deliberate art. The themes of lust and youth and age are presented in a sort of Punch and Judy show. Crazy Jane and the Bishop are both puppets, attempts no doubt to externalize the argument of life and death going on under the skin

[1] *The Results of Thought.*

[2] *Remorse for Intemperate Speech.*

of the ageing poet. While the impulse for the poems unquestionably comes from deep sources, there is a strong element of preconception in the subject-matter as, no doubt, in the form. It is in this paring down of language, in the later poems, that one suspects the influence of Pound, though F. R. Higgins, whether through observation or national loyalty, attributed the development rather to the influence of native Irish poetry. As to the subject-matter, the theme is set in the first encounter of Crazy Jane and the Bishop — Yeats's senile passion, perhaps, and the puritanism of De Valera's Free State. The mask Yeats wears is certainly that of the old woman recalling the lover of her youth, not that of the Bishop whose skin was

> Wrinkled like the foot of a goose.

It is as if, by choosing the more complete disguise of the female part, he could the more easily hide from himself the fact that his own skin is wrinkled and that he resembles the bishop more than the young lover Jack. The theme is developed with many variations and complexities in the best of the poems with a new tone in which realism is caught up in the lyric impulse. But the realism is elusive, and is perhaps less realism than a mask of harshness and ugliness which gives astringency to the beauty of the whole. Indeed, the exaggerated expressions of lust pass quickly into dream, to which world they belong:

> I had wild Jack for a lover;
> Though like a road
> The men pass over
> My body makes no moan
> But sings on:
> *All things remain in God.*

Those who think that realism should look up their Villon. The most successful parts of the series are perhaps those where meaning almost disappears in a cry of exultation or anguish, and the argument between Crazy Jane and the Bishop is lost sight of in a general cry of old age.

> Those dancing days are gone,
> All that silk and satin gear;

> Crouch upon a stone,
> Wrapping that foul body up
> In as foul a rag.

The lyric pitch is maintained to no small extent by the masterly use of refrain:

> *I carry the sun in a golden cup,*
> *The moon in a silver bag*

—in which Yeats owned he had a debt to Pound; or

> '*I am of Ireland,*
> *And the Holy Land of Ireland,*
> *And time runs on,*' *cried she.*
> '*Come out of charity,*
> *Come dance with me in Ireland.*'

The series ends, rather weakly, with some stuff about Plotinus.

There is, in the *Winding Stair* volume, a second, shorter series of lyrics, *A Woman Young and Old*, matching *A Man Young and Old* in *The Tower*, less desperate in tone than *Words for Music Perhaps* but with something of the same skill in handling short-lined stanza forms. The girl speaks, but it is the girl of a male observer.

> I admit that the briar
> Entangled in my hair
> Did not injure me;

still more in

> What lively lad most pleasured me
> Of all that with me lay?

There is nothing psychologically revealing about either series of poems; indeed the psychology may be said to be strictly preconceived. What is attempted rather is a sort of dogmatics of lust, not an easy subject, nor perhaps one which is capable of sustaining itself without support from elsewhere. Perhaps the chorus from the *Antigone* with which *A Woman Young and Old* concludes is intended, like the reference to Plotinus at the conclusion of *Words for Music Perhaps*, to indicate some support from a world of pagan theology, but it is not very convincing.

2

Although the development of Yeats's verse is from a Victorian tapestry, with plenty of adjectives and a romantic subject, to a spare line drawing, he never entirely moves into a world which is continuous with the world of prose. It is not merely that, to the end, he regards himself as entitled to use inversions—such as 'all that with me lay'. It is not, certainly, that his language always bears evidence of being the product of the release known as inspiration. No important writer of the century has more of an air of deliberation than Yeats has, and it is well known that a number of his poems were written out first in prose, and then converted. It is rather that one feels that Yeats is claiming for his work a certain sort of protection. He is the man in the poet's mask. His prose is 'the prose of a poet', exhibiting in turn great intellectual force and silliness, both in the same portentous language, and intended to be taken with equal seriousness because the poet has so delivered himself. At the outset of his career, Yeats made a pronouncement about his intentions, in *The Celtic Twilight* (1893), which he lived up to until the end. 'I have desired,' he says, 'like every artist, to create a little world out of the beautiful, pleasant and significant things of this marred and clumsy world.' Yeats's conception of the beautiful and the significant changed with fashion. In place of romantic love we have, in the late poems, the exertions of copulation. The world he made was still collected in order to impress. Yeats always seems to demand to be listened to on his own terms. The test of a poet, in the end, is, however, the extent to which he can be taken on other people's terms. With regard to his native country, Yeats's intention was 'to show in a vision something of the face of Ireland to any of my own people who would look where I bid them'. He would point to what was 'beautiful, pleasant and significant' to himself, rather than elucidate what was there. The contrast with Swift, whose companion he liked to think himself, could not have been more absolute.

A more illuminating comparison may be made with the great theorist of the theatre, Edward Gordon Craig. Craig was a man of great intelligence and invention who devoted himself, largely in vain one might think, to the revivification of the theatre by the application to it of the lessons of tradition, eclectically gathered in a manner which is reminiscent at times of Ezra Pound searching the classics of many countries for a modern idiom. He wanted an unnatural mode of speech, an unnatural mode of delivery, actors like marionettes, disguised beyond recognition, conventionalized movements and expressions dependent on masks and formal movement. You might say that this programme, which Craig intended for the theatre, was adopted by Yeats for himself. One has only to put Yeats's work beside that of Hardy to be aware of the stiffness of his clothes. There is no psychology in Yeats, only magic. There are no people, only dolls — of elegant and dramatic appearance, very often. Craig went so far as to say (in *The Theatre Advancing*) that 'no matter what the work is to be, if it is to be called an art work it must be made solely from *inorganic* material'. It needs the satiric genius of a Lewis to apply this principle, even partially and intermittently, to the art of literature. Yeats was not the man for such ruthlessness. His portrayals are of conventionalized types — the beauty, the aged lecher, the hero and, of course, The Poet. We do not learn anything from them, but they amuse us.

Yeats was, of course, far too intelligent not to understand the danger of his preoccupation with types and images, and with himself as a formal actor. The realization came most fully at the end of his career, when it was too late to un-pretend. The character of his work was fixed. The *Long-Legged Fly* and *The Circus Animals' Desertion*, both in *Last Poems*, are the clearest statements of his repentance. The *Long-Legged Fly* presents the characteristic dolls — 'our master Caesar', 'that face' at the 'topless towers' — but Yeats would like to identify himself with the man who becomes nothing, to lose himself in his work. Even to make this point he chooses, from force of habit, the archetypal artist, the *famous* artist, though the point could be made without fame.

> There on the scaffolding reclines
> Michael Angelo.
> With no more sound than the mice make
> His hand moves to and fro.

The 'long-legged fly upon the stream' whose 'mind moves upon silence' is, however, itself a symbol or at any rate an object and Yeats, for all his aspiration, hardly succeeds in becoming the mere fly skating on the water.

168

It is in *The Circus Animals' Desertion* that he is most explicit about the confusion wrought by his preoccupation with images. He recognizes that the main course of his life has been among them:

> Winter and summer till old age began
> My circus animals were all on show

and he finds it difficult to do anything but 'enumerate old themes'. Once, however, one is on the track of Yeats's weakness, one is not easily convinced even of the truth of his confession.

> Players and painted stage took all my love,
> And not those things that they were emblems of.

But the question is, whether images and emblems can take all of anyone's love. If not, is Yeats not still pretending to have had a special kind of heart, a poet's heart no doubt, quite different from a man's? Is not all this tied up with the phoney Platonism represented by the 'pure mind' of the last stanza?

3

The Tower (1928) is usually thought the high point of Yeats's art, when *The Winding Stair* is not. It starts with an artifact of singular power and elaboration, *Sailing to Byzantium*. It is the poet's most consistent attempt to give himself over to the intellect, as *Words for Music Perhaps* is his most consistent attempt to give himself over to the body. Both are reactions to old age. Both represent a clinging to life, a determination not to give up in the face of failing powers, and have the panache of spirited old people who show a defiant energy. For the Yeats of *Sailing to Byzantium*,

> An aged man is but a paltry thing,
> A tattered coat upon a stick, unless
> Soul clap its hands and sing, and louder sing
> For every tatter in its mortal dress.

The 'soul' of this poem is an entity which can make itself more athletic by intellectual studies, which, as the title poem of *The Tower* puts it, can

Choose Plato and Plotinus for a friend.

Byzantium with its elaborate toys

Of hammered gold and gold enamelling[1]

is the destination of this non-natural, aspiring intellect. It is a vanity if ever there was one, a conception which comes in direct line from the Art for Art's Sake of the nineties. The artifice breaks into what is certainly among Yeats's most telling poetry with

> Sick with desire
> And fastened to a dying animal
> It knows not what it is.[2]

But the 'artifice of eternity' into which Yeats asks to be gathered has no existence beyond the poem. It is part of a gesture, impressive in the poet, but meaningless for common life when one closes the book.

The Tower, the second poem in the volume of that name, is an example of Yeats's best rhetoric. The first section is a mask of old age.

> Never had I more
> Excited, passionate, fantastical
> Imagination, nor an ear and eye
> That more expected the impossible —

This lively old gentleman — can it really be good for him to be so excited and passionate? — supposes that he must abandon 'the Muse' and give himself over to abstractions. One knows perfectly well that he intends nothing of the kind, but the threat arouses our sympathy. In the second part of the poem Yeats brings out all his dolls. The great houses are evoked, with Mrs French and her 'serving-man'; 'a peasant-girl commended by a song'; 'the man who made the song', blind, of course, like Homer who, although

[1] *Sailing to Byzantium.*
170 [2] *The Tower.*

Yeats did not read Greek, is readily brought out to mime the part of The Poet; and so on. In the third and final part of the poem,

It is time that I wrote my will,

the poet works himself up into a final resolution which is essentially that of *Sailing to Byzantium*:

Now shall I make my soul,
Compelling it to study
In a learned school
Till the wreck of body,
Slow decay of blood,
Testy delirium,
Or what worse evil come —[1]

—until the death of his friends, even of his girl friends, seems nothing. All this is bravado. We learn nothing of the real old man, who took to reading detective stories and, if he ignored the death of his friends, did so not because he had a full-fashioned soul but out of selfishness, like the rest of us, and particularly the old.

In the *Meditations in Time of Civil War* is, similarly, a parade of conventional conceptions. Yeats broods on the great houses which fascinated him when he was a young man, and helped him to build up his grandiose conception of himself, or rather perhaps to provide a symbol for the isolation from inferior persons which he felt already. In prose terms it is rather absurd. There is a great circumlocution to come to the conclusion that merely to dawdle around the achievements of another age gets you nowhere. In the second part of the poem he describes his house—the tower of Ballylee he acquired shortly before his marriage, and which he had managed to buy for what must have been the very satisfactory price of thirty-five pounds. When Yeats had first known this establishment, years before, it had found a sensible contemporary use as a farm with a mill attached. Yeats turned it into a poetic house. In his poem the farmer and the miller, and the other intervening nondescript persons, have disappeared. He thinks of the 'man-at-arms' who first lived there, a Norman no doubt, then presents himself as the second 'founder', though what he is

[1] *The Tower*.

founding is, of course, nothing so useful as a strong place to a Norman invader; it is somewhere where his heirs might find — as presumably they did not — somewhere

> To exalt a lonely mind,
> Befitting emblems of adversity.

But of course in the twentieth century a re-furnished Norman tower, so far from being an 'emblem of adversity', could only be a luxurious cottage for some well-to-do person to fill with antiques, something which Harrods, or some agent in New York, would sell at a better price than thirty-five pounds. As for the poet's work-room

> *Il Penseroso's* Platonist toiled on
> In some like chamber

— Yeats was, unquestionably, not a man for Making It New but for making it old. The scene he sets is a preconceived one. A sword given him by a visiting Japanese completes the décor. He might well be pleased with it, but there is more than a touch about him of the collector who wishes to impress you with a personal distinction which has rubbed off from his collection. The most convincing part of the poem is that in which Yeats describes a brief encounter with a Republican soldier,

> An affable Irregular
> A heavily-built Falstaffian man

— for he too is described in conventional, literally *stage* terms rather than seen with the naked eye —

> Comes cracking jokes of civil war
> As though to die by gunshot were
> The finest play under the sun.

He is jealous at even this clouded encounter with reality.

> I count those feathered balls of soot
> The moor-hen guides upon the stream,

To silence the envy of my thought;
And turn towards my chamber.

Those lines sound authentic.

The impact of public affairs did, undoubtedly, have its effect on the development of Yeats's poetry. His romantic imagination was with the ghost of O'Leary, but he was himself a man of the English ascendancy. It is only when caught off his guard that he speaks in this character, as he does in *Sixteen Dead Men* (from *Michael Robartes and the Dancer*, 1921).

O but we talked at large before
The sixteen men were shot,
But who can talk of give and take,
What should be and what not
While those dead men are loitering there...

It is borne in upon him that the Anglo-Saxon game of compromise is finished. He is appalled, and as a man with a foot in both camps explains the position. The shooting of the rebels of 1916 was a tactical mistake, one of those fatal martyrdoms of which more is apt to be heard. The whole poem has a clarity and directness which Yeats rarely achieves for long without a touch of marmoreal elaboration.

The Wild Swans at Coole (1919) contains some of the best poems in the plain deliberate manner of the second part of Yeats's career. With this plainness and deliberation comes a certain hardening of the perceptions, not unconnected, perhaps, with whatever desire to elude reality it was which drove him to compress into a logically coherent system the odds and ends of visions and magic that he had always played with. There is also the influence of the theatrical doctrine of masks, unhappily translated to a place where it does not belong. Although one may come to feel forcibly these limitations, this decline in poetic candour at a time when Yeats's technical capacity was increasing, there is no denying the strength of the writing, in its kind. There is a sense in which the later Yeats is more rhetorician than poet, and a poem like *In Memory of Major Robert Gregory* marks this development powerfully. Before he calls up Robert Gregory himself — the son of his friend and collaborator Lady Gregory, and killed in the war — he evokes other friends of his youth:

> Lionel Johnson comes the first to mind,
> That loved his learning better than mankind,
> Though courteous to the worst

—these are nice things to say about a man, but they do not get very near their subject, nor probably were they meant to. Yeats is as it were creating a figure which will serve instead of Lionel Johnson in the eyes of posterity. He is making a historical mask behind which his friend can shelter. Lionel Johnson would probably have appreciated the kindness, but in the long run it must show up that it is not the truth that Yeats was concerned to tell. One could not be further from the *Nihil excipio, sed in omnibus te nudatum inveniri, volo* of the author of the *Imitation*. Yeats is peopling a story-book, and among these fustian characters he was, in the end, to be not the least. The method is a first, immensely talented sketch of the method of creating bogus personalities which has become one of the diseases of the age, with every scruffy talker seeking to pass himself off—on the television screen if nowhere else—as a fascinating personality. The stanza rises in a sort of *crescendo* of impressiveness, of a kind which is a characteristic weakness of Yeats's later work, to the vacuity of

> A long blast upon the horn that brought
> A little nearer to his thought
> A measureless consummation that he dreamed.

Then John Synge is called up

> That dying chose the living world for text

and succeeded in hiding himself behind a stylized picture of the people of Arran, a race, Yeats says, in his best fustian vein,

> Passionate and simple like his heart.

George Pollexfen comes next, and then he turns to Robert Gregory himself, to dress him up as

> Our Sidney and our perfect man,

and to account for his absence there is that precious phrase about 'the discourtesy of death'. These are things which, if said in conversation among friends, could only seem embarrassing and pretentious. Yeats gives a not dissimilar treatment to himself in a poem in the same volume on the doubtful theme of *Men Improve with the Years*, where he asks us to regard him as

> worn out with dreams;
> A weather-worn, marble triton
> Among the streams.

If anyone thinks that serious he should refresh himself with a course of Sir Thomas Wyatt. Yeats is better, at this stage in his career, when he is frankly playing, as in *Solomon to Sheba*. He makes a pretty thing with his two dolls:

> Sang Solomon to Sheba,
> And kissed her dusky face,
> 'All day long from mid-day
> We have talked in the one place,
> All day long from shadowless noon
> We have gone round and round
> In the narrow theme of love
> Like an old horse in a pound.'

Here there is no pretence; the puppets are puppets. The result is that the poet, moving with a skill which comes of much training, manages to convey, indirectly, a genuine, fleeting impression from his own experience. There are a number of short poems in this volume in which Yeats uses his immense competence unpretentiously and with great effect. The accent of truth is in *A Song*:

> I thought no more was needed
> Youth to prolong
> Than dumb-bell and foil
> To keep the body young.
> *O who could have foretold*
> *That the heart grows old?*

The life of the sentiments transmits itself to the verse. There is the short poem *To a Young Girl*—presumably to the now nubile daughter of Maud Gonne, who was the romantic passion of his youth.

> My dear, my dear, I know
> More than another
> What makes your heart beat so;
> Not even your own mother
> Can know it as I know,
> Who broke my heart for her
> When that wild thought,
> That she denies
> And has forgot,
> Set all her blood astir
> And glittered in her eyes.

The best example of Yeats's more deliberately stylized presentations at this period is the poem *Upon a Dying Lady*. The subject was a perfect one for his method, and the scene and the properties introduced are closely modelled on reality. The poem describes how Aubrey Beardsley's sister Mabel entertained her friends, and they her, when she was dying of cancer.

> With the old kindness, the old distinguished grace,
> She lies, her lovely piteous head amid dull red hair,
> Propped upon pillows, rouge on the pallor of her face.

She conducted herself with great courage, torn between amusing herself with improper stories and the rather pathetic 'O yes I shall go to heaven. Papists do'—which Yeats characteristically elaborates into

> Thinking of saints and of Petronius Arbiter.

There are dolls about her, which her friends have made for her, and these toys help to give the scene the exterior qualities his dramatization requires. He picks up the theme in

> She is playing like a child
> And penance is the play,
> Fantastical and wild
> Because the end of day

Shows her that someone soon
Will come from the house, and say—
Though the play is but half done—
'Come in and leave the play.'

For a moment Yeats's desire to make a pretty, formalized scene
and his feelings of pity in the presence of the dying woman
become congruent. It is not grief that the poem conveys; it is
hardly concern for the chief character; it is a sense of the propriety
of her having been so perfect a piece of furniture in the poet's
ambiance.

Responsibilities (1914) contains some short poems in the plain,
emphatic manner which Yeats had not yet made enough his own
to write at length in. We get

Toil and grow rich,
What's that but to lie
With a foul witch[1]

—and there are poems which reflect Yeats's implication with the
affairs in Dublin, the affairs of the Abbey Theatre and of the
Municipal Art Gallery. He is showing already the scorn of what
he regarded as the mob which become so prominent in his later
work. There are also more wavering lines not half-way from an
earlier manner, such as

Poets with whom I learned my trade,
Companions of the Cheshire Cheese[2]

—a reminiscence, of course, of the Rhymers' Club. But the
emergence of the later from the earlier Yeats is seen more clearly
in the preceding volume, *The Green Helmet* (1910). There are
the lines, to which he had to give the rather grandiose title of
The Coming of Wisdom with Time:

Though leaves are many, the root is one;
Through all the lying days of my youth
I swayed my leaves and flowers in the sun;
Now I may wither into truth.

[1] *The Witch.*
[2] *The Grey Rock.*

Yeats was conscious of the change, which in *Responsibilities* had become explicit as

> there's more enterprise
> In walking naked,[1]

though the later work hardly lived up to this resolution. *The Fascination of What's Difficult* reflects the tension between the artist of the nineties, with his Pateresque sense of the status of the beautiful and the privileges of the man who invents a work of art, and the man bedevilled by the cares of a less insulated life — in Yeats's case the work of the Abbey Theatre:

> My curse on plays
> That have to be set up in fifty ways,
> On the day's war with every knave and dolt.

No doubt the dragging of his art into the public world made his tongue rougher, and gave him a certain sort of maturity. At the same time something was submerged — what, can be guessed at from *His Dream*, a curious romantic ballad which probably comes nearer to expressing his profound concerns than the more patently outspoken poems:

> I swayed upon the gaudy stern
> The butt-end of a steering-oar,
> And saw wherever I could turn
> A crowd upon a shore.

> And though I would have hushed the crowd,
> There was no mother's son but said,
> 'What is the figure in a shroud
> Upon a gaudy bed?'

Here the poet is one of the ghosts; he is in a situation in which he cannot resist his dream. The crowd on the shore watched him, but he had to take up their song:

> And running crowd and gaudy ship
> Cried out the whole night long.

178   [1] *The Fascination of What's Difficult.*

The poem was the transcription of a dream, and the wilful attitudes which dominate the later poems were exluded.

Backwards from *The Green Helmet*, through *In The Seven Woods* (1904) and *The Wind among the Reeds* (1899) to *The Rose* (1893) and the beginnings, one comes upon the post-Pre-Raphaelite who is a poet of the end of the nineteenth century rather than a beginner of the twentieth. There is much to be found in these volumes of a languid charm which has by no means entirely faded. Yeats began, so to speak, from a dead end, and the history of his development is the history of his struggles to get out of it. How far he climbed out into the daylight of natural speech is a matter about which there can be more than one opinion. Time will make the matter plainer, but it is possible that, in the long run, the best of the earlier poems, precious though they are, will seem a more direct expression of the poet's mind than what came later. At any rate, *The Happy Townland*, *The Folly of Being Comforted*,

Who will go drive with Fergus now?[1]

—*Innisfree* itself, are keys with which to unlock the later poems and are not more likely than they to be forgotten.

[1] *Who Goes With Fergus?*

Chapter Nine

Herbert Read ; Robert Graves ; Edgell Rickword ;

---

the influence of the prose of James Joyce and
D. H. Lawrence

I

If Yeats was a Victorian Great Man, extending himself by force
of will right up to the outbreak of the Second World War, and
adapting for his own use certain technical lessons of the twentieth
century, Herbert Read was, at any rate in certain aspects, a man
blown by every modern wind that passed his way. Indeed, before
he died he had written a mountain of books explaining everything
that anyone with pretensions to be an intellectual in his time
wanted to know. Amidst the literary left-wingism of the thirties
he was always active, but heading for an anarchism which was
proclaimed as being necessarily implicated with peace, freedom,
and art, things so patently good that one wondered why so much
explanation was necessary to recommend them, and so elusive
that one might think that no amount of shouting could ensure
one's achieving them. For many years no creative enterprise could
hope to start without the recommendation of this friend of culture. It was a dangerous role, which could hardly be played for a
long series of years without the performer looking a little ridiculous. But the causes were by definition noble and Herbert Read
certainly the most intelligent and attractive figure who ever lent
himself to so much nonsense.

   In the history of poetry Read's place is a much more modest
one. It would be a pity, however, if, as the great abstract scaffold-
ings he loved to build fall down one by one and reveal that there
was no building inside them, his genuine performance as a writer
should be lost sight of in the more spectacular discredit. Read was,
at bottom, diffident and serious-minded to the point of boredom. It
was his facility in exposition which from time to time concealed
these qualities from view. His origins were not of a kind which
generally gives rise to intellectual frivolity. He was born, in 1893,
on a farm in a remote Yorkshire vale. He has described his early
surroundings vividly in *The Innocent Eye*. The vale was 'a basin,

wide and shallow like the milk-pans in the dairy; but the even bed
of it was checkered with pastures and cornfields, and the rims
were the soft blues and purples of the moorlands'. Here he spent
the first ten years of his life amidst all the business of corn and
cattle. There was the blacksmith's shop, the church with its service 'of extreme simplicity and despatch' and its sundial with the
inscription, 'This is daeges sol merca aet ilcumtide.' When
Read's father died there were candles burning 'on a table laden
with cold meat and cakes'. Everything in the farm was sold up
and although the boy's life thereafter followed a different course,
he had acquired the indelible knowledge of a world dominated by
the changes of nature, not by those of technology. 'As this body
of mine passes through the rays of experience,' he says at the conclusion of *The Innocent Eye*, 'it meets bright points of ecstasy which
come from the heart of this lost realm. But the realm is never
wholly lost: it is reconstructed stage by stage whenever the
sensibility recovers its first innocence, whenever eye and ear and
touch and tongue and quivering nostril revive sensation in all its
child-godly passivity.' This early experience, and this attitude
towards it, are crucial elements in Read's poetry, in which the
sophistication is all of the surface.

Read spent the five years following his father's death at an
orphanage school where the regimen was, by any standard now
recognized, spartan. He then took a job as a clerk in Leeds and
finally found his way to the university there. The decisive event
of his early manhood, however, as was inevitable to one of his age,
was the outbreak of war in 1914. He was commissioned in the
Green Howards, and served with distinction on the Western
Front. But before this happened he had already enrolled himself
with Elkin Matthews as a poet, with verses of which he quotes a
specimen in *Annals of Innocence and Experience* — not without a
qualm, he understandably says:

> I pluck a daisy here and there —
>   O many a daisy do I take!
> And I string them together in a ring,
>   But it's seldom the ring doesn't break.
>
> O daisies rosy, daisies white!
>   If I could string them in a ring

> They'd make a bonny daisy chain —
> O why is a daisy a delicate thing?[1]

This is not the surface of the verse which appears in the *Collected Poems* from 1914 onwards. Read early became acquainted with the more enterprising of the literary work that was going on in London, and in the latter part of the war he met Ford, Flint, Aldington, Pound, Eliot, Wyndham Lewis and Orage. Many of the poems in *Eclogues* (1914–18) recall the farm in Yorkshire, but the technique is now modern.

> The farm is distant from the high-road
> half a mile;
>
> The child of the farm
> does not realise it for several years;
> He wanders through the orchard,
> finds mushrooms in the paddock,
> or beetles in the pond.

The rhythm is secondary to the effect of the poem, and unpromising. This idiosyncrasy recurred in most of Read's work throughout his career. For those who regard rhythm as of the essence of poetry, this marks a limitation which leaves him with a very modest place as a poet. For Read himself, whether the theory preceded the practice or — as is much more probable — the practice the theory 'the distinction between Poetry and Prose is not and never can be a formal one'. 'No classification of metre,' he says in the introduction to his *English Prose Style* (1928), 'no theory of cadence or quantity, has ever resolved the multiple rhythms of Poetry and the multiple rhythms of Prose into two distinct and separable camps.' So far so good, but there is, as Read himself allowed, 'a surface distinction' between prose and poetry, and the general truth of the theory is a poor reason for ignoring this difference in practice. Read was the exponent of another theory, which cut across the differences of prose and verse. He saw poetry as a special form of mental activity, one in which 'there is no time interval between the words and the thought'. That is exact. He is on less sure ground when he goes on to say that poetry may inhere in a single word or phrase — as of course it may — while

[1] *A Little Girl.*

prose is dead words given life by rhythm. As in all such para-
doxes from a man who has thought about and practised the art of
writing, this presentation of the problem has its share of truth in
it. On the other hand, the implied playing down of the role of
rhythm in verse is a weakness to which his own practice as a poet
does not reconcile us.

Read turned from the bucolic scenes of his childhood to the
scenes of the Western Front. The earlier war poems are laconic.
Imagism has done its work on the young infantry officer, and it
enables him to speak quietly of the corpses, the mud, the refugees,
the fear and the heroism. One imagines that this manner of
speech suited the undemonstrative Yorkshireman, with a mind
which absorbed all the horrors imaginatively but, as it were, stood
quietly back from them. Once again, it is rarely that the rhythm
compels attention, which is held rather by the interest of the
subject-matter. *Kneeshaw* recounts, with deliberate flatness, the
military career of a dazed recruit who was the antithesis of
the poet in courage and detachment and who 'delivered
his body to fear'. Most of the poems tell merely of scenes and
occasions.

> A man of mine
> lies on the wire[1]

—it is the rhythm of

> Meine Ruh' ist hin
> Mein Herz ist schwer.[2]

He describes his oscillation between

> A giant attitude and godlike mood [3]

in which he discovered in himself hitherto undetected qualities of
traditional valour and a contrasting patience. 'Then again,' he
says

[1] *My Company.*
[2] Goethe: *Faust.*
[3] *My Company.*

I assume
My human docility,
Bow my head
And share their doom.[1]

If there is in all this only a flickering and intermittent poetry there is a delineation, more or less faint, more or less clear, of a mind which no danger or exhaustion could deprive of its charm or dignity.

Read's most satisfactory record of his experience at the front is to be found not in his verse but in the prose narrative, *In Retreat*, which he published in 1925. It is his journal of the withdrawal of the Fifth Army from St Quentin in March 1918. It is not written to bring tears to the eyes, to express a futile protest against superior commanders, or for any other irrelevant purpose. It is the cool, imaginative account of an officer finding his way through a series of tactical situations of great difficulty, doing his duty to the utmost with a constant care for the men under his command. There can be few finer narratives of its kind in the language.

I lay on my belly in the grass and watched through my field-glasses every minute trickling of the enemy's progress. Gradually they made their way round the rim of the redoubt, bombing along the traverses. And now we only held it as lips might touch the rim of a saucer.

Miles further back:

I took off my clothes to dry them, and sat on a bench in my shirt. If I had been asked then what I most desired, besides sleep, I think I would have said: French bread, butter, honey, and hot milky coffee. The forager soon turned up. God knows where he got that food from: we did not ask him. But it was French bread, butter, honey, and hot milky coffee in a champagne bottle! We cried out with wonder: we almost wept. We shared the precious stuff out, eating and drinking with inexpressible zest.

And at the end: 'In this manner we marched by easy stages down the valley of the Somme, halting finally at Salenelle, a village near Valery, and there rested four days.' It is a narrative to set beside Raleigh's of the last fight of the *Revenge*. Nothing Read ever wrote in verse equals it.

Read returned to the subject of the war in a long poem pub-

[1] *My Company.*

lished in 1932, *The End of a War*. It is in three parts. The first is the *Meditation of the Dying German Officer* who was killed by an English corporal after he had betrayed them into an ambush by giving false information. It attempts to re-create the mind of the highly disciplined Prussian officer of the First World War, the creature of a military civilization. It is written in an unaffected irregular blank verse which manages to follow a living rhythm for much longer bursts than Read managed elsewhere in his poetic work.

> God dies in this dying light. The mists receive
> my spent spirit: there is no one to hear
> my last wish. Already my thoughts
> rebound in a tenement whose doors
> are shut: strange muscles clench my jaws
> these limbs are numb.

There is no doubt that Read is echoing profound thoughts of his own, wrung from the experience of the battlefield. The second part of the poem is a *Dialogue between the Body and the Soul* of a young girl left naked and dismembered by the retreating Germans. The soul says:

> War has victims beyond the bands
> bonded to slaughter. War moves with armoured wheels
> across the quivering flesh and patient limbs
> of all life's labile fronds.

The interchange between the two partners is of touching simplicity.

> BODY: Mary Aegyptiaca
>   is the pattern of my greatest loss.
> SOUL: To whom in nakedness and want
>   God sent a holy man.
>   Who clothed her, shrived her, gave her peace
>   before her spirit left the earth.

The incident of the ambush, and the murder of the girl, were matters of fact, taken by Read 'as a focus for feeling and sentiments otherwise diffuse'. Read does not regard it as his 'business as a poet to condemn war'; he only wishes 'to present the universal aspects of a particular event'. It is a moral many writers of verse could with profit attend to that 'judgment may follow, but should never precede or become embroiled with the act of poetry'. The third and last section of the poem is the *Meditation of the Waking English Officer*, with whom his identification is obviously complete.

> I felt no hate
> only the anguish of an unknown fate
> a shot, a cry: then armies on the move.

He hesitates between belief and disbelief, or rather trust and distrust, in God. Read did not call himself a Christian after his fifteenth or sixteenth year. He ends this meditation with

> God is love:
> in his will the meek heart rejoices
> doubting till the final grace a dove
> from Heaven descends and wakes the mind
> in light above the light of human kind
> in light celestial
> infinite and still
> eternal
> bright.

A comparison with the *Four Quartets* is instructive. Read speaks as a Christian *malgré lui*.

The End of a War is certainly Read's best poem — some might say his only poem. The status of most of his writing in verse is uncertain. It is plainly the work of an intelligent man; but that is not enough. It presents us intermittently with glimpses of this wavering, unpretentious mind, the best part of the man who became so chronic an expositor of 'the modern'. But that is hardly enough either. It is as if the facility of Read's discursive mind was such that the barriers to expression, the sense of which is often a preliminary to poetry, did not exist. The spring was drained off before it was operating at any pressure. One can almost see the process at work at the conclusion of the title poem of *A World within a War* (1944):

His nature is God's nature: but torn
How torn and fretted by vain energies
The darting images of eye and ear
Veiled in the web of memory
Drifts of words that deaden
The subtle manuals of sense.

But the pattern once perceived and held
Is then viable: in good gait and going
In fine song and singular sign: in all
God's festival of perfect form.

The poet's mind has gone, as it were almost in one leap, to theory.

2

Born two years after Read, in 1895, Robert Graves likewise encountered the full rigours of life as an infantry officer on the Western Front. The two years made a difference. Herbert Read was already an undergraduate at Leeds when the war broke out; he had begun to look at the world with the eyes of a young man. Graves was still a schoolboy, and went straight from Charterhouse to the army. Read had been born lucky, far from literary influences and had had to make his own difficult way to poetry. Graves was born in Wimbledon, the son of an inspector of schools who had pretensions as a poet and indeed was one of a literary family. He had to take care that the verse he contributed to *The Carthusian* 'was not the easy showing-off witty stuff that all the Graves write and have written for the last couple of centuries'. When he went to the Welch Regiment he was impressed by their etiquette and one might almost say that he saw the officers' mess as a kind of more rigorous prefects' common-room. The temperamental differences between the two men were, however, more profound than any differences of age or social background. Graves was turbulent and perhaps cantankerous. He was a boxer, with a sense of his own presence, while Read was a natural intellectual who took to action only because the situation demanded it.

Graves has written the history of his early years, and more particularly of his years in the army, in *Goodbye to All That*. The book had a rapid success when it appeared in 1929 — the same year as Richard Aldington's *Death of a Hero*. It should be read by anyone who wants to understand Graves's poetry. How much 187 one finds in it is perhaps a matter of temperament. No doubt on its appearance it found an audience largely on account of its subject-matter. There was ready a corps of readers who had gone through more or less of the fighting in France and were anxious to check their memories against what was so vividly set down by Graves. Others who had missed the fighting had begun by 1929 to want to find out what they had missed. Some of both groups had also their public schools to look back on, and there was in the inter-war years also a — not very notable — literature of the public school. In some ways the book is a curious production for so intelligent a man as Graves. Where the interest of the subject-matter flags — as for many readers it will when he is not discussing the operations in which he took part — one is struck by what looks like a deliberate superficiality, a mere chattiness which seems designed to appeal to the Wimbledon milieu, shocking them and rubbing them up the wrong way, of course, as is expected of the *enfant terrible* of a solid family, but definitely directed to that milieu rather than concerned with the elucidation of truth. There is a certain pawkiness about the style which gives the impression of a determination not to hug reality too closely, not to submit to it, above all, and admittedly in those early years Graves had plenty not to submit to. There is a certain defect of sensibility, which is by no means wholly a negative quality. Ben Jonson carries certain defects to the point of a new cardboard creation. In Graves, one simply misses a certain depth and humanity, the kind of deficiency which led him to say, in *A Survey of Modernist Poetry* (with Laura Riding, published in 1927), that there are 'very few real poems and very few real children', although in fact all children are real and no cleverness will tip the scale even a fraction in the other direction.

The Graves family claimed that they went back to the Conquest, and Robert says that the pedigree 'is good as far as the reign of Henry VII' — far enough for ordinary purposes; an element of fantasy enters into most pedigrees before that date, if not indeed later. The point is that Graves started as a self-conscious gentleman, a situation in which personal prowess is often confused with hereditary distinction; that after all is what hereditary distinction is for. A disposition which one might conclude to be naturally unsympathetic built on this foundation to produce a kind of arrogance which may be all right to see one through this world but does not wear too well in a book. There is also the odd fact—or perhaps it is not so odd—that it was only after his enterprises on the Western Front that Graves first fell in love 'with a woman'; earlier there had been the ordinary public-school affections. The places where, in *Goodbye to All That*, Graves speaks out most clearly are not those where he speaks most loudly. Often it is on the subject of literature that he writes most revealingly. He commits himself in passing to the judgment that Galsworthy is a better writer than Wells, which shows a certain cult of deadness. He gives a most interesting account of a visit he and his first wife paid to Thomas Hardy at Max Gate and his account gives the impression that he was hardly aware what a touchstone he had touched. Hardy seems to have been—for his years—at his best at the time of the visit. He countered the information that Mrs Graves—Nancy Nicholson, daughter and sister of the painters—did not use her married name, with a story of an old couple in Dorchester who had done the same sixty years before. So much for modernity. When it was explained to Hardy that the Graves had not had their children baptized he remarked that 'his old mother had always said...that at any rate there was no harm in it'. When they came to the subject of poetry, Hardy asked whether Graves wrote easily and on being told that a current poem was already in its sixth draft and 'would probably be finished in two more', said: 'I have never in my life taken more than three, or perhaps four, drafts for a poem.' Poetry was 'always accidental'.

When Graves was still suffering from the shock of the war, it seemed to him 'less important to be well than to be a good poet'. This might be heroism but it could be folly. It is true, as Eliot remarked, that poetry might come more easily in a period of poor health. Wilfully to keep oneself in such a condition in order to produce verses is another matter. It displays an indifference to Hardy's principle that the tensions which produce poetry must be accidental. It may also denote a certain vanity and a certain frivolity in the poet's attitude to life, which is sure to show up in the quality of the poetry. Art readily finds out the weak places of the inventor. Graves himself has said, in *A Survey of Modernist Poetry*, that 'genius in the poet is a sympathy between different parts of his own mind'. A certain integrity—in the radical sense of wholeness—is of the essence of the art. Graves at times exhibits an acute understanding of what is required. He says, for example, that 'all dead movements are focused on the problem of style' and that 'the reader should enter the life of the poem and submit himself to its conditions to know it as it really is'. There is on the other hand a certain impatience about his mind, or you might call it wilfulness, which makes it difficult for him to stay long in a world of 'negative capability'. He had like Yeats a passion for revision. In the foreword to the 1959 edition of his *Collected Poems* he comments on his habit of throwing out, in each successive edition, 'poems that no longer pass muster'—a laudable practice enough, but when 'the survival rate' is said to have 'kept fairly even…at five poems a year', one may suspect the imposition of criteria which bear little relation to the original inspiration.

In fact the quality of Graves's production has varied considerably over the years. Perhaps his inherited facility at first betrayed him. At any rate the early verses are those of a pretty versifier rather than of an urgent poet. This is not to deny them their charm :

> Love without hope, as when the young bird-catcher
> Swept off his tall hat to the Squire's own daughter,
> So let the imprisoned larks escape and fly
> Singing about her head, as she rode by.[1]

That could not be written without a genuine talent and some serious training. But the theme, of course, is mere pastoral fantasy, a memory of fairy-stories and picture-books. The war, in which Graves performed so notably and from which he suffered prolonged nervous consequences, did not concentrate his mind. He took less to the war than Rosenberg or even Owen, and his war verses are not impressive. There are rather crude applications of the theme of David and Goliath, a rather superficial comparison with the life of the Roman legionaries, some more direct impressions of the Western Front, but, on the whole, nothing that amounts to much after fifty years. It was afterwards, when the war haunted him from a distance, that we get the more authentic comment :

> Asleep, amazed, with lolling head,
> Arms in supplication spread,
> Body shudders, dumb with fear;

[1] *Love Without Hope.*

There lifts the Moon, but who am I,
Cloaked in shadow wavering by,
Stooping, muttering at his ear?[1]

A poem which presents this haunting more indirectly is *The Pier-Glass*. It is of this poem that he speaks, in *Goodbye to All That*, when he tells how he feared to be cured lest the 'haunting would end' and he should become 'merely a dull, easy writer'. The ghost here is female:

Lost manor where I walk continually
A ghost, while yet in woman's flesh and blood.
Up your broad stairs mounting with outspread fingers ...

This poem is one of those which Graves truncated, out of a sense of tidiness, in the 1959 *Collected Poems*. It is a pity, for it is the more original and more intimate part of the poem which is lost.

A rumour, scarcely yet to be reckoned sound,
But a pulse quicker or slower, then I know
My plea is granted; death prevails not yet.
For bees have swarmed ...

They are sinister bees:

Bee-serjeants posted at the entrance chink
Are sampling aech returning honey-cargo
With scrutinizing mouth and commentary,
Slow approbation, quick dissatisfaction.

The lines are among the most telling in Graves's *oeuvre*, and they end with a complicated, unexplained memory in which the war was certainly for something:

Kill or forgive? Still does the bed ooze blood?
Let it drip down till every floor-plank rot!
Yet shall I answer, challenging the judgment: —
'Kill, strike the blow again, spite what shall come.'
'Kill, strike again, again,' the bees in chorus hum.

[1] *The Incubus.*

That is poetry which cannot be made up by any skill or ingenuity; it is a reluctant deposit on the floor of the mind. There are several poems of this period which have this involuntary quality — for example, *Down*:

> Mouth open, he was lying, this sick man,
> And sinking all the while; how had he come
> To sink?

It is himself that he is presenting, with great clarity of mind, in a period of comparative ill-health. No man in his senses wishes to live permanently in such a world, and Graves in fact climbed out of it, aided, it seems, by some study of psychoanalysis.

By the time we get to *Poems 1926–1930* the mood and tone are entirely different. To some extent Graves is drawing on his old facility in versification, but he has by now invented intellectual difficulties enough to set him problems and tauten up the writing. This is the period when Graves worked in association with Laura Riding, whose ingenuity clearly stimulated his own. There are still poems which, like the Blatant Beast in *Saint*, feed on the ancient residues, but the characteristic of the period is a return to a more superficial operation of the mind. The new superficiality is, however, different from the old. It is that of a man who knows something of the darker places of the mind, but is witty and sociable enough not to dwell on them. Graves had by now observed a good deal of the world; there is experience behind his wit, as in *Brother*.

> It's odd enough to be alive with others,
> But odder yet to have sisters and brothers
> To make one with a characteristic litter —
> The sisters doubtful and vexed, the brothers vexed and bitter
> That this one wears, through praise and through abuse
> His family nose for individual use.

The poem underwent some changes in the later edition, one of which is worth noting — *puzzled* for doubtful — an improvement certainly. *Brother* is not the sort of poem young men write when they first issue from the protection of their families. *In Broken Images* is likewise the product of some weighing against other men. It cannot be said, however, that Graves really lives up to these promises of development. As one turns over his volume of *Collected Poems*, one can find many ingenious poems which entertain for a moment, few that leave any impression that is not a commonplace or a quirk. Somehow the life that is undoubtedly in him does not flower, and he remains a very marginal poet. For the most part there is little of technical interest, and although technique is nothing in itself it is one of the manifestations of the poet. The quality of Graves's mind is in such verses as

> The Philatelist Royal
> Was always too loyal
> To say what he honestly
> Thought of Philately.

It is neatness itself, and neatness is one of the elements of literature.

3

Another poet who had a significant part of his education on the Western Front is Edgell Rickword. His poetry was written almost entirely between 1918 and 1930, most of it in the middle twenties. Unlike Read and Graves, he has produced no narrative of the war years. He did, however, produce a few necrophilous poems, which are like nobody else's and which combine recollections of the trenches with a rather sinister eroticism. One might do worse than look at Aldous Huxley's novel *Point Counter-Point* for an impression of the socio-literary atmosphere of the twenties. Edgell Rickword might have been a character in it. He is, however, no mere emanation of a milieu but a person in his own right, self-contained and indeed surrounding himself with defences of one sort and another.

Rickword was one of the joint editors of *The Calendar of Modern Letters*, which started in the spring of 1925. It is astonishing now to reflect that England could then support a periodical of this quality at the same time as *The Criterion*, then in its third year. The contributors included Robert Graves, D. H. Lawrence, Wyndham Lewis, Edwin Muir, Liam O'Flaherty and E. M. Forster. The editors of *The Calendar* did not lay down any programme, except so far as their programme was not to have one. 'A conviction of the value of spontaneous

¹ *Philatelist Royal.*

growth,' they said '(or growth which seems spontaneous to the watching mind) and of unpoliced expression, is as near as we come to any public challenge or editorial doctrine.'[1] They were, however, committed to a sort of individualism—a pessimistic sort, as far as the editors were concerned. E. M. Forster might evoke an aroma of Cambridge and Abinger with the assertion that in the universe, or in Europe, 'nothing, nothing matters… except distinction of spirit',[2] but the editors saw the other side of this model of the world and thought that 'perhaps the streams of people in the street are not so dissimilar as autumn leaves, manure for next summer's generations'[3]. There was, anyway, an openness to winds blowing from several quarters which Edgell Rickword hardly maintained in his later years, when he was associated with the *Left Review*. The number published in February 1926 even contained an article by Wyndham Lewis proposing that 'an Italian Proconsul could be established in Downing Street or elsewhere and a Fascist nobility supply a long-felt British need'[4]—a form of humour not likely to have been appreciated by the politicians of the thirties.

Edgell Rickword seems to have been the first to use the term 'scrutiny' in the literary-critical sense in which it has been made current by F. R. Leavis; a series of assessments was published in *The Calendar* under the general title of *Scrutinies*. Rickword was concerned with what he called *The Re-Creation of Poetry* through the use of 'negative' emotions. He attempted to revive the somewhat creaking ghost of Charles Churchill and, more hopefully, drew attention to the merits of Swift's verse, then certainly not much read. He noted that 'an effect of the triumph of the romantic movement in the last century' had been 'to separate the poet from the subjects which abound in ordinary social life, and particularly from those emotions engendered by the clash of personality and the hostility of circumstances'. He made the excellent point that the exclusion of these emotions had had the same effect on poetic language as the distinction the French classicists made between 'noble and vulgar emotions'—'the erection of a literary language'. Rickword was, therefore, mid-way through the half-century, defining a new point of attack against the literary code from which the main figures of this

[1] and [3] 'Comments and Reviewers' in Vol. 1, No. 1.

[2] 'Edward VII'.

[4] 'The New Roman Empire'.

history had been seeking emancipation in one form or another. It cannot be said that he made much contribution to the technical development of literature. His contribution was through a sensibility which extended the subject-matter of verse. The area of his conquest was that explored by the Marquis de Sade, an author who is worth looking at in passing but should not be made too much of. Rickword contributed to *The Calendar* a study of de Sade which also draws in Schopenhauer and Baudelaire and takes the argument into the realm of politics.

For society must have a positive sadistic tendency if it is to exist in a healthy state, or the surrounding egos, races, or 'lower' forms of life will absorb it for their own purposes. The policy of statecraft, probably most effective when least cognisant of the ends in view, is to sift the natural givers and the natural takers, those who suffer and bestow, and those who exert and assert, into positions where they can satisfy these tendencies, and to provide a system of easy compensations for the dualistic majority.[1]

The passage will bear reflection by the reader who turns to the satire on non-intervention in the Spanish civil war which Rickword contributed to the *Left Review* in March 1938.

It was probably to Baudelaire that Rickword looked in the first place for the liberation of his sensibility. The war, however, had taken him into fields that Baudelaire did not know. The negative emotions appear with some force in *Trench Poets*, which is not merely silly:

> I knew a man, he was my chum,
> but he grew blacker every day,
> and would not brush the flies away.

Rickword goes on to tell how he used to read

> to rouse him, random things from Donne —
> like 'Get with child a mandrake-root.'
> But you can tell he was far gone,
> for he lay gaping, mackerel-eyed
> and stiff and senseless as a post.

When the poet got as far in his reading as the bit in the *Elegies* about a woman not needing more covering than a man, the corpse

---

[1] 'Notes for a Study of Sade'.

grinned nastily, and so I knew
the worms had got his brains at last.

In a vein which owes more to his French predecessors, he writes in
another poem of the moon rising over the battle-field 'with the
grand air of a punk':

Then I thought, standing in the ruined trench,
(all round, dead Boche white-shirted lay like sheep),
'Why does this damned entrancing bitch
seek lovers only among them that sleep?'[1]

It was natural after this for Rickword to pursue a course as the
baudelairean poet of cities:

The long, sleek cars rasp softly on the curb
and twittering women rise from cushioned nests[2]

—a period touch that, for women do not twitter any more or

the loutish mass with lingering moonish smiles
on vast cod-faces swimming crowded lanes

from the more ambitious *Prelude, Dream and Divagation.*
Rickword produced a number of poems which present with
actuality the crowded, lust-ridden streets of London, in a manner
different from Eliot's; he is nearer than Eliot to the squalor he
describes; the orgasm and the pain are never far from his mind.
There is an inevitable subjectivity in all observation, but what
Rickword sees is there all right. It is what he excludes which
gives his impression its peculiar shape.

Rickword's peculiar preoccupations were so intense that he
cannot be said to have made much progress in 'the subjects which
abound in ordinary social life', as his critical writing suggests he
may have wished to do. Or when he did, he abandoned poetry.
There are, however, elements of genuine social satire in *The*

[1] *Moonrise over the Battlefield.*
[2] *Luxury.*

Encounter, in which he describes a meeting in Regent Street with an intellectual pathic, charmingly named Twittingpan:

> being two days nimbler than the smartest clique
> he gave the cachet to the safest chic.

The eighteenth century — so difficult to avoid in the satiric heroic couplet — was too strong for him and he did not succeed in inventing a modern social genre. In his own, idiosyncratic vein, however, Edgell Rickword is an original figure.

4

The scene can hardly be set for the poetry of the thirties and forties without some mention of two prose writers whose influence on the second quarter of the century is comparable to that of Ford Madox Ford in the first quarter. These are James Joyce and D. H. Lawrence, without some knowledge of whom neither the technique nor the ethos of the poetry in the latter part of our period can be understood. Something has already been said about Joyce's verse, charming and limited and uninfluential. His prose is another story.

James Augustine Joyce was born in Dublin in 1882, not of Anglo-Irish stock, like Yeats, but of the Papist strata. His father came from Cork. When James, the eldest son, was born, and for some years afterwards, he was employed in the office of the Collector-General of Rates in Dublin — to which he had apparently been appointed as a reward for services to the Liberal party. The post seems to have been one of the older type of official appointment, well-paid and not onerous. The career of John Stanislaus Joyce is described in Herbert Gorman's biography as 'a blithe and unfaltering march downhill from modest affluence to actual cramping poverty'. Joyce's mother was the classic subdued and devoted wife required for the full flowering of such a character. Both parents were musical. James's education was at the hands of Jesuits — Clongowes Wood College, Belvedere College, and University College, Dublin. By heredity and training Joyce was as deep in the Irish socio-political thing as Hardy was in the English. His reaction was to be bored with the Gaelic revival and to look to Henrik Ibsen as a liberator.

Joyce spent some months in Paris when he was twenty, living on so little that he may be said to have starved his way through the winter. It is curious that one of his major pieces of reading, at this time, was the works of Ben Jonson. Or perhaps not so curious, for Jonson is a great master of the deliberate surface. The young Joyce was dogmatically for the intellect and deliberation. In an interesting passage in *Stephen Hero* he says:

He persuaded himself that it is necessary for an artist to labour incessantly at his art if he wishes to express completely even the simplest conception and he believed that every moment of inspiration must be paid for in advance. He was not convinced of the truth of the saying 'The poet is born, not made' but he was quite sure of the truth of this at least: 'The poem is made not born.' The burgher notion of the poet Byron in undress pouring out verses just as a city fountain pours out water seemed to him characteristic of most popular judgements on aesthetic matters…

There is a perceptible air of the nineties about the deliberation and cadence of this prose. It carries the weight of a powerful intellect, but it is part of the movement of refinement which, from Pater to Ford, brought back to English prose a touch of Gallic clarity, superficial or not. Joyce went straight from Dublin to Paris, hardly stopping in London, and jumped from the slightly delayed aestheticism of his province into the world in which he was the contemporary of Pound and Eliot. His Jesuit training and the liberation of Ibsen, between them, would in any case have made most of the intellectual excitement of pre-First World War London seem rather beside the point. The stories of *Dubliners* must have owed a good deal to the sort of French influences which moulded the work of George Moore. But Joyce's work exhibits a personal temper rather than a fashion. The grave, analytical young man is — whether he charms or irritates — the vehicle of a peculiar artistic mission of which the rendering of thought in a simple, lucid prose is only the first task. It is significant that this work of the surface was the first work, because it is not in that direction that the influence of Joyce has been most telling. *A Portrait of the Artist as a Young Man* was published by the Egoist Press in 1916, and from that moment Joyce may be reckoned to have been a prominent figure of the vanguard. It was, however, with the technical innovations of *Ulysses* (1922) that he shook the world — or as much of it as is shaken by such things. If the opening pages have the gravity and lucidity of *A Portrait* the end falls into that internal and almost interminable monologue in which syntax and punctuation are dissolved. It was this novelty, of course, which delighted the men of literary fashion. A little of what then passed for obscenity also helped. Because the monologue was incoherent, by the standards then accepted, Molly Bloom's reflections were supposed to represent the depths of the mind, although in fact, as in the earlier prose, it was a surface which was exposed. The puns, parodies and other verbal antics of the intermediate parts of the book exhibited an ingenuity which has few equals. Only the subject-matter of the book flagged. It was, as in *Stephen Hero* and *A Portrait*, the inhibited, prurient world of Joyce's adolescent mind. 'Isolation is the first principle of artistic economy,' he had said in *Stephen Hero*, and the sentence has a special sense in relation to Joyce's own work. The comedy saves *Ulysses*; the emotional atmosphere is unilluminated.

The verbal acrobatics in which Joyce excelled became an obsession for him. He might move continuously in the prison of his particular Dublin, but in a certain logomachy he had no equal. These tricks, continued page after page in *Finnegans Wake*, passed into popular mythology, like Molly Bloom's mutterings, as a revelation of the contents of the mind — all mind, so great was Joyce's linguistic prowess and so many more the languages laid under contribution. No doubt the perfection of this literary exercise enabled Joyce in the end to tap recesses of his own thought. That was his trick, however, the result of deliberate training and much erudition. The influence of his work has been quite different. The mere superficialities of a disintegrated syntax came to be regarded as a way of revelation, so that incoherence came to be thought of as a mark of profundity. In the eyes of fashion, there seemed to be a connection between this idiosyncratic way of writing and the emptying of the inner chambers of the mind represented by psychoanalysis. The language of the deep, so to speak, became the recognized intellectual medium of the twentieth century. The way to all kinds of poetic pseudo-profundity was opened up, to the great confusion of shallow minds.

The other great prose influence on the poetics of the second quarter of the century was of a different kind. D. H. Lawrence, a Nottingham miner's son, started his literary career with what any reader of H. G. Wells or Arnold Bennett would recognize without difficulty as being novels. He was born in 1885; *Sons and Lovers* was published in 1913. Lawrence offered no technical innovations which could be put beside those of Joyce. The novelty he contributed was temperamental. This is no place to

199

explore his peculiarities, or to discuss how far they amounted to a philosophy. There is no question of his extreme sensitivity, or that he effected a temperamental revolution, less drastic no doubt than Rousseau's but not altogether dissimilar in kind. Lawrence's sense of physical reality is tender to the point of a shudder, not merely in the matter of sex—though it is that which has got most prominently caught up in the scandal and commerce of the century—but in relationships with animals and with natural objects. Lawrence was a prophet warning the world of what technology was costing it. When he wrote well it was by genius; his conscious efforts, and his ratiocinations, are generally deplorable. Lawrence was not, of course, without the capacity to argue about technical matters in literature. He was able to give lessons to Edward Marsh, the editor of the Georgian anthology.

I think I read my poetry more by length than by stress [he wrote in a letter in 1913]—as a matter of movements in space than footsteps hitting the earth...It all depends on the *pause*—the natural pause, the natural *lingering* of the voice according to feeling—it is the hidden *emotional* pattern that makes poetry, not the obvious form.[1]

It is typical of Lawrence. He starts by being instructive, but is soon down to the emotions. Whatever is the distinguishing mark of poetry, it is not they. 'It is the lapse of feeling, something as indefinite as expression in the voice carrying emotion.'[2] Lawrence could not keep off the subject. Of course emotion may be expressed in poetry. So it may by a cry of pain or flood of tears. The *mode* of expression constitutes the art. Lawrence was apt to believe that whatever he poured out, so long as he felt strongly about it, was important. But nothing is more trivial, to those not immediately concerned, than the belly-aching of a man of feeling. As a writer of verse, Lawrence was temperamentally well suited to breaking away the shackles of post-Victorian poetics, but he lacked the reticence, and the ear, for achieving a satisfactory new form. There is little doubt that the subject-matter of much of his verse is, in any case, too little matured to be a fit subject for art. At times he writes what he calls verse because he is too lazy to turn out a decent piece of prose, or because what he has to say is nothing but petulance. A good example of this superficial

[1] and [2] Letter to Edward March, 19 November 1913.

recording is *Last Lesson in the Afternoon*, an account of his school-mastering, which sinks to:

> What does it matter to me, if they can write
> A description of a dog, or if they can't?
> What is the point? To us both, it is all my aunt!
> And yet I'm supposed to care, with all my might.

A poem like *Last Words to Miriam* again is merely a trivial statement about personal emotions, indeed a rather tedious bit of waspish self-justification.

It is by these two things—a writing without ear or sense of balance, and the setting down of direct, untransmuted feelings—that the influence of Lawrence on subsequent verse has mainly been felt. If Lawrence may be said to have cast an influence over the thirties, Joyce, in the manner indicated, did so over the forties; they imagined themselves drunk with words which came, in fact, from a rather deliberate and sober mind.

Chapter Ten

The thirties: W. H. Auden; Stephen Spender;
Clere Parsons; William Empson

I

W. H. Auden was born in York in 1907. His father was a doctor,
and shortly after the birth of Wystan — the third son — the family
moved to Birmingham where Dr Auden became Professor of
Public Health. Wystan went to a preparatory school at the age of
eight, to a public school at the age of thirteen, and to Christ
Church, Oxford, when he was eighteen. At his preparatory
school he met Christopher Isherwood. At Oxford he met Cecil
Day Lewis, with whom he edited *Oxford Poetry, 1927* and
Stephen Spender, who printed his poems on a hand press. Stephen
Spender was to become co-editor in turn of *Horizon* and *Encounter*.
Cecil Day Lewis was to do well at the Arts Council and become
Poet Laureate. Isherwood was to be a successful novelist and
subsequently a guru. Auden himself had, by the age of thirty,
had a double number of *New Verse* devoted to him, with tributes
from twenty writers including Graham Greene, and had been
awarded the King's Gold Medal for Poetry.

The explosion — it was no less — of W. H. Auden was, it will
be seen, not unassisted by fortunate circumstances. It was,
however, not merely that he early acquired friends whose considerable talents included a gift for public relations. He was also
carried forward on the waves of liberal-communist sentiment
which, before the Second World War, were supposed to signify
understanding of the issues at stake in the advent of Hitler and in
the Spanish civil war. It is unthinkable that he should have been
awarded the King's Gold Medal in 1937 if his politics had been
those of Wyndham Lewis. The explosion of Auden was, however,
also a genuine literary phenomenon. Bearing in mind that Yeats
was an Irishman and Eliot and Pound Americans, it might
reasonably have been said of him — as it was more questionably
said of Stephen Spender on the appearance of the latter's *Poems*
in 1933 — that the quality of his verse had not been surpassed 'by

any other English poet since the war'. Mere quality of writing never produced such adulation in England, or perhaps anywhere else, and certainly not such almost instantaneous success. But Auden's *Poems* (1930), contained, from the first page to the last, unmistakable proof of force and originality.

The book opens with *Paid on Both Sides*, a short play which Auden called 'a charade'. He probably felt the need to give some indication that this was not a straight play, as understood by the tedious theatre of the day. It is in fact a poetic drama not strictly comparable to any that had come before. The subject-matter has been variously accounted for. It certainly owes something to Icelandic sagas, as the verse owes something to Anglo-Saxon, in which J. R. R. Tolkien had been his guide at Oxford. But the scene is a version of the contemporary English north. The world of the sagas is no longer seen through a mist of romantic time, but with a direct, contemporary eye. The dominating influence, however, is an overpowering adolescent, if not boyish, fantasy. There is fighting and killings between the rival gangs — a violence one might sense in the air of the thirties but which was not yet actual. The result is a play which, for all the improbability of its theme, carries conviction as psychological and social truth. No poet since Isaac Rosenberg — who was not much in anybody's mind at the time — had conveyed such a sense of having urgent imaginative secrets to convey .The urgency is there in the first words of the opening prose dialogue. The speakers are Trudy and Walter, who are on the Nower side of the argument between that family and the Shaws:

T: You've only just heard?
W: Yes. A breakdown at the Mill needed attention, kept me all morning. I guessed no harm. But lately, riding at leisure, Dick met me, panted disaster. I came here at once. How did they get him?

It is masterly. The breathless, clipt sentences, with their fusion of modernity and archaism, take one at once into the heart of the feud. The 'breakdown at the Mill' gave the struggle an industrial reference which had some desperation at a time when the quarrel was not about wage increases but about poverty and hunger. Trudy goes on, in language which goes back to Auden's Oxford studies and to the roots of English:

In Kettledale above Colefangs road passes where high banks overhang dangerous from ambush. To Colefangs had to go...

There had been an ambush; Red Shaw with ten men, and one of the Nowers had been shot. At this news Joan delivers her baby prematurely, and comes in with the child and a corpse, saying forebodingly — in the first verse lines of the play —

> Not from this life, not from this life is any
> To keep.

It is heavily loaded speech, in convincing rhythms. There could be no doubt that here was a poet who was starting out for himself. Joan looks forward to the time when the baby will take up the quarrel, and the chorus — this was four years before *The Rock* — comes in with its reflections, in an original, urgent verse which carries a reminiscence of Old English without a trace of pedantry:

> Can speak of trouble, pressure on men
> Born all the time, brought forward into light
> For warm dark moan.

There is observation as well as prophecy in the verse:

> We pass our days
> Speak, man to men, easy, learning to point,
> To jump before ladies, to show our scars.

The poet can convey a shudder of feeling:

> O watcher in the dark, you wake
> Our dream of waking, we feel
> Your finger on the flesh that has been skinned.

To a generation which had been taught by Eliot the lesson — which it badly needed — of sparse utterance, and which had in a manner frozen under the instruction, this easy, powerful speech was a liberation. It seemed as if poets might again speak familiarly, without the restraint of more than their personal mannerisms. The dialogue that follows the chorus is again in prose, till Walter and Trudy start to brood on the killings while they wait for news of the revenge planned against Red Shaw. Their language is full of poetic surprises:

His mother squealed like a pig when he came crouching out.

Or this:

> I will not say this falsely; I have seen
> The just and the unjust die in the day,
> All, willing or not, and some were willing.

The Nowers and some others come in, and in heavily-stressed verses on the Anglo-Saxon pattern tell how Red Shaw was found asleep with a woman

> Upstairs together Tired after love

and there is fighting in which Shaw is shot as he tries to escape across a ford. Soon afterwards the chorus, switching to a more plausible modern scene, introduces matters of commerce and industry:

> The Spring unsettles sleeping partnerships,
> Foundries improve their casting process, shops
> Open a further wing on credit till
> The winter.

This is no longer commerce introduced for a shocking contrast with the 'poetic', as in *The Waste Land*. Auden's verse can include such matters in its normal discourse. There is an interlude with Father Christmas and some farcical matter, for Auden is attempting a synthesis across the whole range of feeling, an enterprise of extraordinary scope. He was twenty-two at the time. There is a marriage between John Nower and Anne Shaw, as if the feud were to be patched up. But there is an ambush at the wedding party and John Nower is killed. So to the final magnificent chorus:

> Though he believe it, no man is strong.
> He thinks to be called the fortunate,
> To bring home a wife, to live long.

> But he is defeated; let the son
> Sell the farm lest the mountain fall;
> His mother and her mother won.

Besides *Paid on Both Sides*, the 1930 volume contained thirty poems, nine of which had appeared in the collection printed by Stephen Spender on his hand press. Although Christopher Isherwood says, in his notes on the early poetry in the *New Verse* Auden Double Number (November 1937), that Auden would sometimes compose poems regardless of grammar or sense out of odd lines from poems which were not otherwise allowed to survive, and that 'this is the simple explanation of much of Auden's celebrated obscurity', it would be surprising if any of the best poems in this volume were composed in that way. If they were, it must have been done in response to some other compulsion than Isherwood's taste for some miscellaneous odd lines. The poems which make most impact certainly give the impression of having been composed in a single spurt or in one or two spurts. On the other hand there is a remarkable unity about Auden's work at this early period, so that in a sense all his compositions were one. Several of the poems in *Paid on Both Sides* were written before the play as such was conceived although, Auden has said, 'they seemed to be part of something.' It is the sense of being 'part of something' larger and more significant which gives Auden's early work its freedom of movement and its sense of import. The details do not matter; the poet is hurrying on to explain further the great matter he has in hand. This gets us past the untrimmed obscurities. But he is capable of great lucidity, without loss of power:

> The crowing of the cock
> Though it may scare the dead,
> Call on the fire to strike,
> Sever the yawning cloud,
> Shall also summon up
> The pointed crocus top,
> Which smelling of the mould,
> Breathes of the underworld.[1]

There is also the less interesting lucidity of Auden's Kiplingesque vein, as in the poem beginning

Get there if you can and see the land you once were proud to own[2]

[1] IX.

[2] XXII.

The verse is certainly no better than Kipling's — it is not as good —
but the subject-matter was naturally more topical for the youthful
audience of the thirties:

> Lawrence was brought down by smut-hounds, Blake went dotty as he
> sang,
> Homer Lane was killed in action by the Twickenham Baptist gang.[1]

The best poems, however, are those in which Auden himself is
still puzzled, or where he is making a discovery as he writes:

> Nor was that final, for about that time
> Gannets blown over northward, going home,
> Surprised the secrecy beneath the skin.[2]

Or:

> Sir, no man's enemy, forgiving all
> But will his negative inversion, be prodigal.[3]

Auden has never surpassed these original accesses of discovery.

Auden's second volume, published in 1932, was *The Orators*,
which he was later to call 'a case of the fair notion fatally injured'.
It is a medley of prose and verse, full of hints and puzzles like
Paid on Both Sides, but Auden was already beginning to feel his
way more surely towards explanations. The nature of the explanations that appealed to him is indicated by the first words of
the prologue:

> By landscape reminded once of his mother's figure.

Auden had read a good deal of psychology — of the psychoanalytical
variety — and put his faith in that. There is something in the
discordant note introduced into the Auden double number of
New Verse by Edgell Rickword, who says: 'his failure to analyse
the social movement which so profoundly affects his work often
leads him into emotionally irresponsible statements.' This was of

[1] XXII.
[2] XXIII.
[3] XXX.

course said from an orthodox Marxist point of view, Edgell Rickword having by this time thoroughly bound himself in those boring chains. There is, however, undogmatic good sense in the suggestion that Auden (and his collaborator Isherwood) were evading the social issue 'by tackling the problem in psychological terms'. There is much hinting, in *The Orators*, of a marvellous cure just round the corner for sick minds. There are threats of the imminent downfall of the world of

Majors, Vicars, Lawyers, Doctors, Advertisers, Maiden Aunts

but it is evidently to this sort of world that the author himself belongs and indeed he and his friends exude sharply the odour of spoilt children from protected homes. It was perhaps unfortunate that, on leaving Oxford, Auden went after a year in Germany to teach in such an establishment as The Downs School, near Malvern. The protective covering must have been pretty thick there. It is not very brave to shout boo to your maiden aunt from such a hideout, and to associate yourself vaguely with the threats of death and revolution, and of the irruption of a rough proletariat turning nasty on the dole, which was so much in the air of the thirties. The whole tone of *The Orators* is vitiated, even more than that of the earlier volume, by the cosiness of the hero's situation. The combination of revolution and privileged self-interest—the old Whig formula—was the whole tone of that Oxford Communism of the thirties which has been so successful in its social adaptations in the following years. In Auden the aroma of the prep school is also strong. There really is no imaginative leap into a wider world. There is something hopelessly juvenile about the little group of Wystan, Stephen, Christopher and Cecil at this epoch. For intellectuals in the van of politico-literary movement they are boobies. There is, however, in Auden, great psychological acuity, swift observation and a powerful neurotic imagination. There is also a literary inventiveness unequalled by any near contemporary. *The Orators* opens with an *Address for a Prize Day* in absorbing, rapid prose. In a parody of the language used on such occasions Auden gives a popular analysis of the various mis-directions of love, 'those who have been guilty in their life of excessive love towards themselves or their neighbours, those guilty of defective love towards God and those guilty of perverted love. Have a good look at the people you know; at the boy sitting next to you at this moment, at that chum of yours in the Lower School. Think of the holidays, your father, the girl you met at that dance. Is he one? Was she one?' And so on. The analysis is pursued in various forms, in the sections that follow. Auden goes round removing the comfortable chairs from under everybody else. He probes his own wounds—at least one supposes that is what he is doing. 'Eighteen months ago, if anyone had foretold this to me I should have asked him to leave the house.' 'Auden expresses'— to quote Edgell Rickword's note again—'more poetically than any of his contemporaries, the feeling of insecurity that afflicts a section of the middle classes as the ceaseless concentration of capital into fewer hands undermines their comparatively privileged position. His early verse prophesies and threatens the imminent downfall of a system which has become inimical to good living. Ruined boys, handsome and diseased youngsters, stupid valitu-dinarians, implacable gangsters in a meaningless feud, these are some of the symbols which haunt his first volume of poems.' This is the world which comes further to light in *The Orators*. The verse sections of the book show a notable development in the direction of a forthright, popular satire. In the poem to John Warner he comes as near to a devastating verse-oratory as was possible from the milieu Auden inhabited. For a moment it seemed possible that poetry might again burst on to the popular world. At its simplest we get to

Their day is over, they shall decorate the Zoo
With Professor Jeans and Bishop Barnes at 2d a view,
Or be ducked in a gletcher, as they ought to be,
With the Simonites, the Mosleyites and the I.L.P.

The poem ends with an *Envoi*:

Go south, lovey, south by the Royal Scot.

This is, distinctly, a new verse *con gusto*. As an editorial note of Geoffrey Grigson's put it, Auden exhibited a 'broad power of raising ordinary speech into strong and strange incantation'.

Incantations are dangerous, however. Auden had developed his natural gift of impressive speech to the point at which he could hardly avoid wizardry. It was genuinely of a novel kind. The 'magic' is no longer a 'magic' left over from the nineteenth century; it belongs to this one, indeed to Auden personally. It is in evidence again in *Look, Stranger!* In this volume Auden's later manner came clearly to light and his poetic was in some sense fixed. While a reader who finds interest in Auden's subject-matter and manner of discourse will wish to follow him in the later volumes, those interested simply in his contribution to literary invention may stop here. They will find an accomplished reversion to established verse forms and the grave, somewhat formal unrhymed speeches he has used from time to time since. Auden shows all the marks of facility in versification; it is doubt-ful whether anyone since the death of Swinburne has exercised a similar mastery. The second of the *Two Songs for Benjamin Britten* — a significant beginning for Auden's interest in the opera — shows signs of a reading of Dryden:

> Underneath the abject willow,
>   Lover, sulk no more;
> Act from thought should quickly follow:
>   What is thinking for?[1]

It is an admirable tone of public discourse, clearer than any that had sounded in English verse since Kipling. But Auden never really succeeds in being a poet of the great world. His bent is towards the psychological and his milieu is a personal one:

> Lucky, this point in time and space
> Is chosen as my working-place;
>   Where the sexy airs of summer,
> The bathing hours and the bare arms,
> The leisured drives through a land of farms,
>   Are good to the newcomer.[2]

His eye like the moon's is on

> The healers and the brilliant talkers,
> The eccentrics and the silent walkers.[2]

The atmosphere is one of frankness among friends, with a certain holding back on all outsiders, including the reader. There is also a

[1] XXII.
[2] II.

complacent sense of decay, justified still by a belief in a proletarian revolution which will shortly put all to rights. All this is as dated as *Little Arthur's History of England*, but of course it meant that the *Zeitgeist* was waiting to cheer Auden on and has since kept his memory green among old-fashioned literary journalists.

> For what by nature and by training
> We loved, has little strength remaining:
>   Though we would gladly give
> The Oxford colleges, Big Ben,
> And all the birds in Wicken Fen,
>   It has no wish to live.[1]

The imaginative ambition of Auden and his friends at that time was

> To hunger, work illegally,
>   And be anonymous[2]

but in real life none of these things was much in their line.

The trouble about Auden's verse in discursive vein is that he is not, as he writes, in the process of discovering something for himself; he is the pedagogue or doctor advising others what truth is. The result is a certain superior languor. The lines are filled out with easy words:

> Nor was every author both a comforter and a liar;
> Lawrence revealed the sensations hidden by shame,
>   The sense of guilt was recorded by Kafka,
>   There was Proust on the self-regard.[3]

This facility vitiates most of Auden's later work. It is as if the tensions necessary for the production of poetry had departed — as they often do — leaving a notable literary talent playing with some ideas. It is not a common talent which can produce such verses as the *Letter to Lord Byron* (1937). But the letter is a form of journalism, dependent on a technique already well known and making entertaining play with received ideas. In *New Year*

[1] II.
[2] III.
[3] XXXI.

Letter Auden turned to the octosyllabic couplet. It needs some pressure greater than a desire to explain things to make anything new of that. In fact, Auden is drawing largely on the tricks of the author of *Hudibras*,

> The Devil, as is not surprising —
> His business is self-advertising —
> Is a first-rate psychologist
> Who keeps a conscientious list,
> To help him in his ticklish deals,
> On what each client thinks and feels,
> His school, religion, birth and breeding,
> Where he dined and what he's reading...[1]

But Samuel Butler has never been beaten on his own ground.

2

Another, beside the Devil, who has had an interest in advertising is Stephen Spender, though perhaps he was so infected by the *Zeitgeist* that no great effort was needed. He was born in 1909 — two years after Auden — in a well-known Liberal family. The atmosphere was politico-professional. When Spender says, in his autobiography, *World within World*, that 'the war had knocked the ball-room floor from under middle-class English life' it is — of the many groups this phrase can be taken to indicate — of the well-to-do upper middle classes that he is speaking. 'People resembled dancers suspended in mid-air yet miraculously able to pretend that they were still dancing.' The explanation is that, relatively speaking, they still were. After mentioning some of the ordinary social phenomena of the twenties which his father deplored., Spender says: 'We knew vaguely but surely that our generation would inevitably have less than his.' He was, to all intents and purposes, one of a race of Whig seigneurs who could pretend to descend the social staircase a little and still remain very well-placed as compared with those who were coming up. And as in fact the whole social-intellectual movement of the inter-war years was — as Wyndham Lewis grew unpopular in pointing out — pseudo-revolutionary, such people were in fact exactly at the point from which it was easy to move into positions of advantage in the changed world. It is amusing to find Stephen still saying, in

[1] *New Year Letter.*

the middle of the century, that his father 'supported Liberal causes of which there seemed little left but the idealism', as if that differentiated him in some way from his son. And if the older Spender was brought up 'in a style of austere comfort against a background of calamity', that, *mutatis mutandis*, is precisely the sort of atmosphere in which Stephen achieved and even held on to some kind of fame. The role his father played in his imagination was determined by the fact that he died when Stephen was seventeen, the age, as he says, 'when sons react most strongly against their parents' and, it might be added, pretend they are most different from them. His mother, said by her son to have been 'hysterical, and given to showing violent loves and hates, enthusiasms and disappointments', had already died. Under her reign, 'cooks, governesses, relations, friends, were for ever entering our lives, sunning themselves in radiant favours, only to commit some act which caused them never to be mentioned again, unless with an air of tragic disapproval.' Her 'painting, embroidery and poetry had a sacred, unchallenged reputation' in the family.

At the age of fifteen, Spender came under the influence of his maternal grandmother. She was a Schuster, a member therefore of another seigneurial Whig family. She was not politically inclined. She loved the children and wanted them to be happy. 'Thus she was ready,' Stephen say, 'to sympathise with our every wish.' She saw at once that Stephen's father 'could not understand' his son's taste for 'modern painting, theatre, literature'. She supported the boy in every way and piloted him according to his true nature. With this favoured background, it is rather astonishing to learn that, when he got to Oxford, he attributed the differences between himself and his fellows to the fact that he was 'a new boy among public schoolboys, who thought that not to come from a public school was as ridiculous as to be a foreigner'. In this distressing position he had to consort with 'Prince Radziwill from Poland, Count Czernin from Austria' and an American Rhodes scholar.

A certain painful and priggish sincerity disengages itself from the pages of Spender's autobiography. 'Most of my weaknesses,' he says, 'even if I have learned something from them, are' — and why should it be supposed that we should think otherwise? — 'still with me.' It is the tone of a man who attaches an infinite importance to his own emotions, and to himself as a 'personality'. Not for nothing did he dream as a child of being Prime Minister, 'acclaimed by crowds who whispered' as he passed 'It's He', making decisions on which the world waited, and always astonishing everyone by the simplicity and naturalness with which he spoke 'to quite unknown people whose names never appeared in the newspapers'. Stephen early contrived to know an unusual number of prominent writers. It was not merely towards Bloomsbury that he was drawn — or towards which he drew. At the age of twenty, four years before the publication of the first volume of his'poems, he was already lunching with T. S. Eliot. Few poets can have expended so much care in establishing professional connections; certainly few can have been so successful in the matter. When his *Poems* were published in 1933, Allen Tate was recruited to review them for *New Verse*. After benefiting from all the revolutionary passions of the thirties, Spender moved into position for the fifties. In October 1939 he was planning the review *Horizon* with Cyril Connolly, and in the summer of the next year they 'received letters from pilots fighting in the Battle of Britain, often saying that they felt that so long as *Horizon* continued they had a cause to fight for'. *Horizon* represented a consolidation of literary power for the figures of the thirties. The Comment in the first number said that 'a magazine should be a reflection of its time' and *Horizon* certainly succeeded in being that. There is a good deal of comedy about Connolly's moralizings. The war was being 'fought for culture'; that would no doubt explain the attitude of the grateful pilots. When Goronwy Rees, with 'a mind numbed by soldiery', made some tactless remarks, the Comment explained that 'the whole distinction which Rees makes between soldiers and artists is one which will disappear, for eventually we shall all be fighting'. It did not quite come to that, nor were 'the conscript fathers of *Horizon*' ever 'drafted into the dashing Rees's awkward squad'. Indeed the institution persisted until after 1945, to ensure, as far as might be, that those who had provided the 'culture' of the thirties should continue their government in the post-war years.

Spender's poetic *oeuvre* is slight but genuine. At his best he succeeds in being the disarming and disarmed character he pretends to be. He cannot be said to have made any contribution to the technique of verse though he has, at times, a personal limpness. He has, however, at times also a clarity which might have been the vehicle for imparting more interesting truths, if the mind behind this style had been more interesting. Allen Tate's review of the first volume of *Poems* was entitled *A New Artist*, but with Spender, as with the immeasurably more powerful Lawrence, being an artist is not a primary vocation. What he is about is well defined by Allen Tate: 'Within the general terms of the intellectual crisis of the age, Spender has defined a personal crisis of his own.' Stephen looms comically large in this picture, and he sees the 'crisis of the age' very much in undergraduate or journalistic terms; but it was this, of course, which gave his poems their impact when they were first published. He says in the introduction to his *Collected Poems* (1953): 'Poetry is a game played with the reader according to rules, but it is also a truth game in which the truth is outside the rules.' He accepts the existence of a truth beyond the limits of his art, and it is this which gives his work a certain puzzled seriousness. But of course a man is an artist only so far as he restricts his writing to the area within which, for him, the rules and the truth coalesce. This involves a standard of discipline which Spender rarely manages to maintain throughout a complete poem.

While Eliot and Pound had gone farther afield for influences which could help them to an individual expression, Spender slumped back on more proximate sources. Tate noted the traces of the later Yeats in

> Now I suppose that the once envious dead
> Have learned the strict philosophy of clay[1]

and there are echoes of Wilfred Owen:

> Time merely drives these lives which do not live.[2]

One of the most complete poems in the first volume, *The Prisoners*, is unthinkable without the man who thought the poetry was in the pity:

> They raise no hands which rest upon their knees,
> But lean their solid eyes against the night,
> Dimly they feel
> Only the furniture they use in cells.

[1] *In 1929.*
[2] Untitled poem.

Their Time is almost Death. The silted flow
Of years on years
Is marked by dawns
As faint as cracks on mud-flats of despair.

Spender is rather a social than a literary phenomenon, and the most interesting verses, after all, are those in which, without pretension, he 'defines his personal crisis' in terms which go beyond his own tears. There is the plain autobiography of

My parents kept me from children who were rough
Who threw words like stones and who wore torn clothes.
Their thighs showed through rags. They ran in the street
And climbed the cliffs and stripped by the country streams.

I feared more than tigers their muscles like iron
Their jerking hands and their knees tight on my arms.
I feared the salt coarse pointing of those boys
Who copied my lisp behind me on the road.[1]

Or these lines which are the classic delineation of the less cynical part of public-school/Oxford communism of the thirties:

Oh young men oh young comrades
it is too late now to stay in those houses
your fathers built where they built you to breed
money on money it is too late
to make or even to count what has been made
Count rather those fabulous possessions
which begin with your body and your fiery soul:
the hairs on your head the muscles extending...[2]

A good deal has happened since then. The tone of Spender's later verse is, naturally, less juvenile, but he might have done better not to have gone beyond his charming first volume. His work as a whole is diffuse and talkative, and it is for those who are fascinated by his personal crisis to follow its autobiographical course to the end.

3

Clere Parsons was a near contemporary of Auden and Spender. Born in 1908, he died in 1931, and his *Poems* were published in

[1] and [2] Untitled poems.

the following year. They are no more than the thumb-nail sketch of a possible *oeuvre*, but they have a clarity and elegance which is not exactly like anyone else's work and that, for a young man of twenty-two or three, is notable. The introductory poem says:

> Mallarmé for a favour
> teach me to achieve
> the rigid gesture won only with labour
> and comparable to the ease
> balance and strength with which the ballet-dancer
> sustains her still mercurial pose in air.[1]

That is the work — and not merely the sentiment — of a poet who is setting out to learn his trade as Pound and Eliot set out. In spite of occasional archaism, as unfashionable when the verses were written as it is now, the tone of the volume is not merely contemporary but new:

> April who dost abet me with shy smiles
> If I made bold by amorous fancy touch
> Suddenly with my lips thy shining lips which
> Are the smooth tulip and chaste crocus bulb
> Lady be swift to pardon me thus much
>
> This day cannot long delay his choice between
> Whether to be spring or remain winter still
> — Behold the impetuous sun flings light like scarves
> On petalled lace to dazzle the ocean and
> With silver lance our wintry moods to kill
>
> Sweet month thou dost incite me to review
> My fearful ship that hath all hopes in hold
> O august bark of destiny bear me on
> Safely those difficult and deep tides to where
> No bird of fire shall steal my apples of gold.[2]

The lines sing and there is about them a quality at once airy and metallic. There is no doubt that they emanate from a literary talent of distinction. *Garden Goddess* perhaps indicates the quality of his work.

[1] *Introduction.*
[2] *Suburban Nature Piece.*

Cool is this wind which laps the leaves
And fans me to sleep. The drowsy hours
Curl round my head like heavyscented flowers
Whose rare perfume with every breath I breathe

The lake by lazy swans patrolled
Fluidifies her lovely line;
Fingers disturbed in that blue calm, divine
How cold in champfered folds the marble flows

Now joy's cartographer I trace
My acres of gay and wellbeing's land
O my summer be music be Proust and Sisley and
With me in the dead season, pastoral days.

4

Undoubtedly one of the most respectable names to emerge in the
thirties was that of William Empson. Empson was born in 1906
and his first book — appropriately, perhaps, a book of criticism —
appeared in 1930. This was *Seven Types of Ambiguity*, which has
certainly had a profound influence on the literary sensibility of the
age, so that it has been possible for a man well versed in poetry and
poetics, who happened not to read the book until a relatively late
date in his career, to say that it contained nothing he had not
already absorbed through other channels, though at the time of its
publication the work was certainly one of great originality. The
book may be regarded as a consequence of I. A. Richards's prolonged insistence that there was no harm in attaching meaning to
poetry. Whereas, however, *Principles of Literary Criticism* and
Practical Criticism, so influential in their day in Cambridge and
beyond, were the work of a man who himself had no great gift for
literature, *Seven Types of Ambiguity* bears on every page, in the
texture of its prose style, the evidence of a subtle literary talent.
Empson's thesis is that 'the machinations of ambiguity are among
the very roots of poetry', and he defends it against 'the objection
that meaning does not matter, because it is apprehended as Pure
Sound, and the objection that what really matters about poetry is
the Atmosphere'. He pursues this idea through seven types of
ambiguity and innumerable examples, taking 'almost always'
poems that he admires for, he says acutely, you must 'rely on each
particular poem to show you the way in which it is trying to be
good; if it fails you cannot know its object'. There is no suggestion

in his method of tearing up flowers or butterflies because the pleasure of doing that is greater than the pleasure of looking at them. Empson's attitude is that of Rémy de Gourmont's naturalist who starts from the contemplation of a skeleton leaf. The merit of the book is exactly what, in the last paragraph, he claims it to be: 'that for those who find this book contains novelties, it will make poetry more beautiful, without their ever having to remember the novelties, or endeavour to apply them. It seems,' as he fairly says, 'a sufficient apology for many niggling pages.' The book is as necessary to the contemporary understanding of literature as *The Sacred Wood* or *How to Read*. If none of Empson's later critical work is of comparable value, that is only because the standard he set is so high—and because his subject in this book so entirely suited his caste of mind.

The type of mind operating in Empson's poems is evidently, sometimes irritatingly, the same. The extreme acuteness and the erudite pursuit of detail give the verse a peculiar character. Empson's mind is scientific and positivist; within this reference, he exercises with an ingenuity which it is hard to find a parallel for without going back to the Metaphysicals of the seventeenth century. Empson is well aware that the repeated introduction of abstruse references and odd facts may be tiresome, and he is far from wishing to mystify. 'It is impertinent,' he says in a note originally appended to his *Poems* (1935),

to expect hard work from the reader mèrely because you have failed to show what you were comparing to what, and though to write notes on such a point is a confession of failure it seems an inoffensive one. A claim is implied that the poem is worth publishing though the author knows that it is imperfect, but this has a chance of being true. Also there is no longer a reasonably small field which may be taken as general knowledge. It is impertinent to suggest that the reader ought to possess already any odd bit of information one may have picked up in a field where one is oneself ignorant; such a point may be explained in a note without trouble to anybody; and it does not require much fortitude to endure seeing what you already know in a note.

Empson is simply accepting a principle which is an everyday matter in the worlds of science or affairs, but which is a late-comer to the world of polite letters. There is good reason for the reluctance of poets to accept the specialists' disintegration of knowledge. On the other hand, Empson's workmanlike acceptance of the situation and its consequences are admirable, for they make the general problem clearer. The situation is new only in degree, not in kind, and Wordsworth had already noted that the obscure discoveries of scientists might become matter for poetry when they had become assimilated in the common stock of experience. In so far as Empson's practice of obscurity, helped out by notes, implies an abandonment of the notion of a common mind within which interchanges can be made, it may be contended that his tolerance has gone too far. But there has, in fact, always been the field of all knowledge, larger than the individual poet could manage, and the test of the poet is his ability to give importance to what he selects from it. A merely specialist importance will not do, and a mind so tenacious of miscellaneous fact that it is apt to produce the irrelevant detail may well be impeded in its communication with the ordinary run even of intelligent men, whether in verse or in common conversation.

While it cannot be said that Empson wholly escapes from the inconveniences to which his abnormally ingenious mind exposes him, his poetry — precisely because he is, in fact, a considerable poet — is marked by an appeal to a wider, imaginative apprehension. He can and often does write so that pleasure precedes the reader's understanding of the sequence of ideas in a poem. There is a quality of incantation about:

Not but they die, the teasers and the dreams.
Not but they die,
                         and tell the careful flood
To give them what they clamour for and why.[1]

As a good specimen of Empson's contorted early style one may take the *Invitation to Juno*:

Lucretius could not credit centaurs;
Such bicycle he deemed asynchronous.
'Man supperannuates the horse;
Horse pulses will not gear with ours.'

Johnson could see no bicycle would go;
'You bear yourself and the machine as well.'
Gennets for germans sprang not from Othello.
And Ixion rides upon a single wheel.

[1] *The Teasers.*

Courage. Weren't strips of heart culture seen
Of late mating two periodicities?
Could not Professor Charles Darwin
Graft annual upon perennial trees?

Yet Empson's range extends to the lucid verses of *The Birth of Steel*, a masque he wrote for the Queen's visit to Sheffield, and it is a mark of his skill that he always manages to keep the verse taut, whether the subject is complicated or straightforward. *Aubade*, which gives an account of an earthquake in Japan — for Empson has been an academic visitor to the Far East — shows how his sinewy verse can be managed for simple description:

Hours before dawn we were woken by the quake.
My house was on a cliff. The thing could take
Bookloads off shelves, break the bottles in a row.
Then the long pause and then the bigger shake.
It seemed the best thing to be up and go.

Useless to complain that, with so much talent, Empson is a poet who illuminates the interesting detail rather than effects any larger re-orientation in the reader. He has nothing to impart at large other than the common enlightenment of the age, but it is a merit that he does not pretend to have more than that.

Chapter Eleven

Wyndham Lewis; Roy Campbell; Hugh MacDiarmid

I

It is difficult to know how one should treat, in a history of poetry, the work of a writer of the stature of Wyndham Lewis whose predominant work was in other fields. Lewis is, by any standards, one of the major figures in the literature of the twentieth century, as well as a major figure in English painting and draughtsmanship. No one should approach his relatively restricted work in verse without some awareness that it is merely a facet of a much larger and more complex structure, nor be content with his reading of *One-Way Song* until he has acquainted himself at least with *Time and Western Man*, *The Wild Body* and *The Human Age*. Lewis has featured little in the vast corpus of critical commentary on the poetry of the twentieth century, and the multitudinous anthologizings of the same. Yet his work in verse is important and his work as a whole is of such a character as to modify judgment of the whole poetic production of the age. No one who does not give it a proper place is in a position to arrive at a sober judgment of the poetry of Pound, Eliot or Yeats, to say nothing of lesser figures. One might as well try to weigh up the poetry of 1700–1750 without setting a value on the prose work of Jonathan Swift.

The peculiar importance of Lewis in this context is in his appreciation of the role of the human mind, of the traditional instrument of *homo sapiens* as exemplified in great creative figures such as Shakespeare or Leonardo, in the shoddy, erupting world of the twentieth century. Born in 1882, Lewis was of an age to be dewy-eyed at the beginning of the century. His father was an American, his mother an Englishwoman of Scottish-Irish extraction, and he was brought up and schooled in England, ending his rather diversified formal education at the Slade. After that he spent several years abroad, in Germany and above all in Paris, and came back to London in 1909 well equipped to take an external view of the follies of Anglo-Saxondom. The pre-First World War years were a time of great literary and artistic inventiveness, in which Ford Madox Hueffer, Pound and Hulme were in their various ways sapping under the surface of received ideas. In this world Lewis was a powerful, and certainly the most versatile, figure. He was, of course, much concerned with visual art, but by 1914 he had produced most of the stories now collected in *The Wild Body* as well as an extraordinary play, *Enemy of the Stars*, characterized by a fusion of the manners of casual chat with a stand-offish highbrowism of content—a fusion which is a recurrent feature of Lewis's writing and one which has perhaps done something to impede its recognition by the professorially-minded as well as by the even larger public. The mood and attitudes of *Enemy of the Stars*, as well as its technique—at once visual and didactic—are prophetic of much in Lewis's later work: to describe them as anti-romantic suggests their invective force too feebly:

Loud feeble sunset—blaring like lumpish, savage clown, alive with rigid tinsel, tricked out in louse-infected pantaloons, before a misty entrance, upon the trestled balcony of a marquee, announcing events in a stale programme of a thousand break-neck sports—of poodles that sit up to tea, and of handcuffed men who eat their food or paint a landscape with the sole assistance of their feet—promising laughter and death mixed—of fat-bottomed pantomimes and mortal accidents from trapezes in the roof—the pink-tighted flesh of the female and the frisking beneath it of a milk-white horse-flesh to delight the horsy, punctuated throughout with the chatter of skilled Fools: a showman who bellows down to penniless herds, their eyes red with stupidity, crowding beneath him clutching their six-pences.

From this satirical vision we are invited 'to take a header into the boiling starry cold'. This is, briefly, Lewis's position as a satirist. *Enemy of the Stars*, first published in *Blast* in 1914, was accompanied when it was reprinted in book form by 'a metaphysical commentary', the *Physics of the Not-Self*, which explains that the intention was 'to show the human mind in its traditional role of the enemy of life, as an oddity outside the machine'. The machine itself was the object of the satire.

Lewis's characteristic literary art developed outside the bounds of metre, but he started, like so many others, with verse. He recalls in *Rude Assignment* how, about the time he went to the Slade, he 'began to write Petrarchan sonnets, but soon changed to

Shakespearian. They were easier to do'. Lewis claims that 'some were so like Shakespeare's' that as he remembered lines in them he was never quite certain whether they were Shakespeare's or his own. Then he wrote that the sonnets had been lost from view for some time; they had been lent to a friend who had cut his throat and whose corpse was gnawed by rats. The sonnets turned up after Lewis's death, in the Cornell collection, and it can now be said that the confusion with the work of Shakespeare is unlikely to persist. One can see that Lewis had been reading Shakespeare. These exercises in verse show markedly that adolescent receptivity to others' words which is a symptom of the incipient writer. There is also extant, of Lewis's early work in verse, a poem of some fifty lines written while he was visiting Normandy and Brittany with his mother. This is *Grignolles*, which was published in 1910 in *The Tramp*, 'an Open Air Magazine' edited by Douglas Goldring, who was an associate of Ford Madox Hueffer:

> Grignolles is a town grown bald
>   With age; its blue naked crown
> Of houses is barer than any hill,
>   On its small hill; it is a grey town.
>
> It is like a cathedral, crowding and still,
>   All of a piece, like one sheer house;
> Like a town built for worship, and called
>   Grignolles, from the land thereabout.
>
> But it is like a cathedral from which have decayed
>   All afterthoughts and generous things
> Added — the warm gradual weft —
>   All down-coverings from its naked wings.
>
> It seems only first buildings are left,
>   The virgin soul of first architects;
> Only the first dream of a town as it leapt
>   In the brains of the lonely peasants — projects
>
> Which the dim granges shaped from their sides,
>   And a wilderness of gaunt fields that
> Needed a house as each holding does —
>   But a great, warm house more human than that.

Now something of that first savageness,
    And the keen sadness of first plains
(Although the country's grown *bourgeois* and green)
    To the town has come as its soul wanes.

The poem bears unobtrusive marks of unassailable originality.
No one, in 1910, could have taught Lewis to write like that. Of
contemporary influences on the style of the verse, only Hardy
seems a possibility, and that only because of Hardy's plainness and
awareness of fact, and his disregard of the conventions of pretti-
ness in setting down what he has to say. But a different and more
powerful mind is in play in *Grignolles*. With hindsight, we can say
that it is the work of a man who knew the contemporary influences
and chose to ignore them, deliberately and even a little woodenly
going his own way. The movement of the verse is uneasy; it is
plain that — despite the sonnets — this is an unaccustomed medium.
An incautious reader of *The Tramp* might have thought the poem
the work of a *naïf* of some sort. The rhymes are properly matched
only when it suits the direct sequence of what the author has to
say, as if he could not manage any better or even had not noticed
his lapses. There is none of the wilfully experimental air of, say,
F. S. Flint, who was in essence much more conventional. New
wine is deliberately being put in old bottles.

Within, Grignolles is listless and sweet;
    Its veiled life is not conscious how
Its wandering cairn of walls can suggest
    In one wild whole things dead now:

Just as man forgets Time's waste,
    And his soul's crumbling, and is blind
To a grandeur a little distance gives it —
    Lives a life veiled, moody, and kind.

The final stanza reverts to a bleak rendering of the surface:

As over the porch hangs mistletoe.
    Its houses are bleak, windy fronts
With stormy windows; or cabins low;
    And wandering convents, and sheds chapels once.

A quarter of a century of work — several men's work, it might   225 be said—as painter, novelist, and author of such critical and theoretical work as *The Lion and the Fox* and *The Art of Being Ruled*, not to mention service in the artillery in the First World War, lies between *Grignolles* and *One-Way Song*, which was published in 1933, the year in which Hitler came to power. Since the end of the First World War, Lewis's eye had become increasingly fixed on what he called—long before politicians began to present their shallow and opportunist version of the same charge—'this vast fossilized colony of twentieth-century Britons'. In 1930 he had paraded, in *The Apes of God*, a circus of personalities who had dominated the socio-cultural stage of London before the rise of a new brand of pseudo-revolutionaries in the thirties. The year of the publication of *One-Way Song* saw also the publication of a short tract called *The Old Gang and the New Gang*. In this Lewis gives an account, at once simple and elusive, of the political mechanisms involved in 'the deliberate "Youth-hysterics" of now ageing men' and the illusions of Mr and Mrs Everyman who—and is it different now?—'were in the habit hazily of considering themselves as the representatives of "the New"'. This lesson has never gone home to the people, and did not go home to the intellectuals who, at the time, were in the process of succumbing to a new wave of bogus political novelty and youthfulness at the hands of Spender and Auden. *One-Way Song* is not the book one should go to for a fundamental understanding of what Lewis is saying about the intellectual situation of his time. It is a vigorous supplementary attack, important in this history because it brought back to English verse a kind of boniness and prickliness, and a verve which is of rare occurrence and had long been absent, though Auden, as we have seen, had in his more acceptable way already enlivened the field. And in the matter of verve one should perhaps spare a thought for Roy Campbell.

The media Lewis used for his only volume of verse were, as in *Grignolles*, adaptations of standard forms. He could not make his form as Eliot and Pound had done, but uses fourteeners and heroic couplets in the knowledge that his energy, and the pressure of what he has to say, will disrupt them into a certain novelty. The book opens with *Engine Fight-Talk*—the deliberate ungainliness of the title sets the tone. In this poem Lewis assumes the role of a teacher before an improbable class of boys whom he lectures, somewhat allusively, on the concept of time and its relationship with literary romanticism. The result is a comic poem of considerable strength and great liveliness. Bouts of argumentation are interspersed with vignettes of the classroom :

> Tapping my mouth, in the same unbending tone,
> I said (my voice is never raised the jot of a note above
> The merest conversational half-drone),

or

> They hurled their class-books at each other's heads, there were roars
> upon earsplitting roars.

The class entertains the prejudices that might be supposed. When the teacher says rude things about 'the marxist mahomet' he has to use all the best pedagogic tactics to bring them round again :

> They found this a little difficult. 'False colossus' was very bad.
> I could see them biting their fingernails behind the breastworks of
> their cribs.
> I did not speak for a minute. I knew they must take for a cad
> A man who was brutal to Marx, or at best to be regarded as mad.
> So I had to win back their confidence. I did it with sundry fibs,
> And looks of bursting conceit. At his ease at once each small lad
> Rewreathed his smiles, asked to leave the room, or went back to his
> fish and chips.

The next poem is *The Song of the Militant Romance*, in which Lewis announces his intention of putting a squib under the Scots, a bit of starch into the Irish, and generally improving 'all that is slender' in Anglo-cum-Oxfordshire-Saxony'. While this ambitious programme may not be completed in the poem, Lewis utters in it a miscellany of diatribes to some effect. As to the manner :

> As to the trick of prosody, the method of conveying the matter,
> Frankly I shall provoke the maximum of saxophone clatter...
> I shall drive my coach and four through the strictest of hippical
> treatises
> I do not want to know too closely the number of beats it is.

Alan Bold fairly points to these lines as illustrating the point that 'Lewis's rhymes equal Byron's in their deliberate corniness'—but whether this is a merit in either poet is another matter. The poem is aggressive about literary sentimentalities. Byron and Keats are given a blow in passing for their real or alleged sensitivities:

> A couple of rubber teats
> Should have been supplied beyond any question to these over-touchy pets —
> For me, you are free to spit your hardest and explode your bloody spleen
> Regarding my bold compact Fourteener, or my four less than fourteen.

The rest of the volume is divided between two long poems, *If So the Man You Are* and the *One-Way Song* itself. It is in the former that Lewis comes nearest to a twentieth-century version of the classic satire of the Juvenal–Dryden–Pope kind. There are typically Lewisian shifts of position as he hunts down his prey. In spite of all the noise and bustle Lewis is always the man of peace and quiet, whose object is to get on with his work as an artist — or would be, if the conditions of the age allowed it. At the centre of all Lewis's satire is the principle, stated in Manifesto II of the first issue of *Blast*: 'We fight first on one side, then on the other, but always for the SAME cause, which is neither or both sides and ours.' It is a confusing but vivid method.

> Ours *is* a clownish age. If so the man
> You be to understand it then you can
> Scarcely be other than a Man in an Iron Mask
> Or choose but choose a most invidious task.

There are various characterizations before Lewis's most customary mask, that of the Enemy, is put on. Contemporary *mores* are reflected

> I'm no He-man you know, I'm not a He.
> I'm not a chesty fellow that says *Gee*!
> I'm not you know a guy that lives on pep.
> I'm not a red-blood person who snaps *Yep*!

—and so on. The elements to which Lewis is friendly or unfriendly are closely mixed up, so that the satire is partly against himself, as good satire should partly be. Possibly the figure of

228

T. S. Eliot was in his mind, though it was certainly not all that was there, when he wrote the third section:

> The man I am to live and to let live.
> The man I am to forget and forgive.
> The man I am to turn upon my heel
> If neighbours crude hostility reveal...
> To tread too softly, maybe, if I see
> A dream upon my neighbour's harsh tapis.
> The man I am to exact what is due to men,
> The man to exact it only with the pen.

In the interlude which follows the stage direction 'ENTER THE ENEMY (cloaked, masked, booted and with gauntlets of astrakan)' we move on to clearer ground and come nearest to a personal statement. In the opening canto of this part (Number 13) Lewis unleashes a direct indignation at the neglect of his work.

> Must I be given *nothing*, lest I take
> Too much from the world's *trop-plein*? Fake after fake,
> Encouraged, must usurp the place is mine?
> And yet had I demanded a gold-mine,
> Or aimed to be dictator of the West,
> I could not be regarded as a pest
> More than I am by asphalt-inkslinger
> Alike, and in-the-manger monied cur.

The reason for his untouchability comes near to being that of the classical moralist:

> What is it that men fear beyond everything?
> Obviously an open person. Bring
> One of us 'truthful ones' too near, their nests
> Would be unfeathered. Experience invests
> Us with such terrors, us whose tongues are clean...

It is dangerous ground, and uncharacteristic. Typically, as Roger Sharrock has pointed out, Lewis 'is not interested in ethics, but in metaphysical experiment; he is not going to be driven out of his mind by the human assault on reason, since it is part of his premises'.[1] But Lewis had certainly received treatment which

[1] Reviews of *Self-Condemned*, by Wyndham Lewis, and *Wyndham Lewis*, by Hugh Kenner, in *Essays in Criticism*, Vol. V.

it would have been inhuman not to resent. To the critic who asks why, if he is as good as he thinks, he is not all the rage, he replies

> Because you are so the man to boost the flea!

which of course is done daily and weekly. There is a satisfactory panache about Lewis's gestures in the accusatory parts of his poem. A good example is Section 17 which derides the common Everyman in satire that is simple and straightforward:

> If so the man you are commissionaire,
> If so the man *marchand de mégots* there,
> If so the man you are, *oh merde alors*!

A series of uniform denunciations follows, ending with the throw-away:

> If so the man that's Everyman, these words,
> If so the man, we throw to the dicky-birds!

—a realization that satire cannot attain its objective because its most suitable objects are impervious to it.

The *One-Way Song* — the title poem of the book — is the most subtle piece of argumentation put into English verse in the twentieth century — and one could go back further. It is the peculiarity of Lewis's theoretical writing that he advances repeatedly on his game, with what looks like menaces, without actually killing it. One might say that his books are haunted by the unkilled spectres of his chase. This is partly because, as he approaches nearer, he sees more intensely the complexity of his subject. He is striving for clarity, and a firm line; reality remains in its bewildering complexity. When he returns to a theme, there-fore, it is not merely to reiterate some concluded theory, it is to continue his examination — and his worrying — of the prey. Although in *One-Way Song* Lewis takes up his old wrestling-match with the conception of Time, one does not feel that he is telling you what he has told already in *Time and Western Man* and elsewhere. There is, in almost every line of the verses, a tension which arises from the fact that the argument is not yet complete, and one has the general drift but it is not yet explained precisely what he is driving at. For Lewis himself, no doubt, the act of intellectual apprehension is still going on as he writes. He writes from a great fullness, but he is driving all the time into emptiness, or into 'the boiling starry cold'. No doubt the lack of final explicitness is in part due to the medium, as he says in canto xxiv, but in fact Lewis's method in his prose is less fundamentally different than he would have us believe. He is always an artist, accepting the complexity of the world, rather than a professional person explaining it, however much he may affect the *persona* of the pedagogue.

> I can only release, as elegant as deer,
> A herd of wandering shapes, which *may* go straight,
> But are just as likely to have grandly strayed,
> Before we write finis out of sight and reach.
> I cannot help this. It is noblesse oblige.

It is in fact the habit of telling the truth as he sees it. The inspirational thing, in literature, is not to be deflected by the pressures and temporizings which do in fact deflect us in our ordinary talk and affairs.

> I demand no absolute, except only God

he says, and this line the later parts of *The Human Age* illustrate profoundly. Lewis is in deadly earnest in his time themes. It is, as he says, 'a man singing and not a bird'. His probing, now this way, now that, of what seemed to him the morbid relationships of his contemporaries with past and future — the *evocations* of what is not there and the *being carried forward* to what is not there either, is his central contribution to cleaning up the Augean human image.

That *One-Way Song* occupies a place of relatively small dignity on the official contemporary Parnassus shows only the immense and sinister frivolity of that institution, in its various forms. It cannot be said that Lewis is completely master of his medium, but while most versifiers fail from sheer lack of anything to say, his verse bursts with a plethora of material.

2

Roy Campbell had the distinction of writing a review of *The Apes of God* which the *New Statesman* declined to publish on the grounds that he took 'a far more serious view' of the merits of the book than the acting editor thought justifiable and indeed took 'Mr Lewis altogether' too seriously. In favour of Ellis Roberts's letter on this subject one can say only that it was better than the more deadly weapon of silence, in such a case. But when one thinks of the books which are praised as a matter of course, in the journal in question as elsewhere, this makes pretty good reading:

My serious complaint against the notice, in so far as it concerns Wyndham Lewis, is that you ignore what seems to me an obvious lack of composition — he can only *write* in sentences, or occasionally in paragraphs.

The offer, which Campbell rejected with scorn, was to publish the review, unsigned, 'with such modifications' as this super-critic thought fit.

Campbell followed this up by publishing his review — which was a sober affair giving an excellent account of the nature of Lewis's satire — with other material about the book, in a pamphlet which contained also Lewis's essay on *Satire and Fiction*. It was the sort of trouble he liked. His militancy was very different from that of the Enemy. Lewis had an uncommon intellectual apparatus, with an industrious grounding in more than one art and in several related studies. He was well equipped, by his early training, to arrive at an understanding of the currents of fashion and ideology which swept over Europe in his life-time. Roy Campbell had neither a comparable intellectual equipment nor so instructive a background. He was born in Natal in 1901, and the country in which he grew up 'bore little resemblance' — as a later and better poet from South Africa, David Wright, says — to the one which now exists in its room. The family were among the first settlers in Natal, and Roy's father was an eminent and energetic doctor — a brilliant scholar who 'read Latin authors easily, especially Lucretius'. Roy was able to wallow in the natural plenty which was already being fast destroyed by European weapons, and grew up to ride and hunt where the game still came readily into the sights. For a man of boisterous temperament this made the discipline of the narrower spaces and the modern world not only unacceptable but to some extent unintelligible. Campbell himself recognized that he had not been through the right mills, and was suspiciously boastful about the matter. He left South Africa in 1918, and stayed around Oxford for about a year, no doubt because
232 he had hoped this might be the fountain-head of a sophistication

which he lacked. In fact the interlude served some purpose, for he met William Walton, Wyndham Lewis, T. S. Eliot and the Sitwells and so in a few years was not badly placed either for orientation or for circulation. He had a considerable, disorderly talent for language, and an immense energy of the kind called explosive, and all this he put into *The Flaming Terrapin* (1924), a poem which he called a 'symbolic vision of the salvation of civilization', though he was hardly qualified to have a vision of this particular object. His models were Shelley, Keats and Byron, and he added the modification of a sub-tropical imagery. He was, however, already a reader also of Dryden and Pope, and it was to a version of their couplet he turned for his most militant excursions. He did not succeed as Lewis did with the adaptation of this medium because he was more imitative and, for all his exuberance, had not really enough to say that was new. Instead, he was tempted to a prolixity which was natural enough to him anyway. This is not to say that there are not couplets, and longer passages, in *The Wayzgoose* or *The Georgiad*, which manage to encase some of his ebullient life, but for the reader who knows his Dryden there is no great *literary* point in reading these verses. *The Georgiad* is of interest as an essay in literary politics. It can raise a smile with contemporaries, and is perhaps otherwise not unuseful, to poke fun at a clever and shoddy journalist-versifier like Humbert Wolfe, but the victims of the *Dunciad* are of interest now only because of the precision of the blows with which they are struck down. The then recent affray over *The Apes of God* is naturally not forgotten:

> How Ellis Roberts, stuttering, explains
> His bright blue funk of honesty and brains,
> And trapped, repents the evil of his ways
> Stampeding headlong into frantic praise.

Other notable reviewers are thrown with equal energy:

> How Nicolson who in his weekly crack
> Will slap the meanest scribbler on the back,
> Who praises every Gertie, Bess or Nelly,
> That ever farrowed novels from her belly,
> At the mere thought of Lewis goes quite blue
> And to a cackle turns his weekly coo...

But in the face of genius Campbell was modest. He was once taken to Max Gate to meet Hardy but was too awed to enter the house, and stayed in the car, drinking whisky from a hip flask, while his friends went in.

When he was not engaged in satirical assaults Campbell wrote romantic verse which is remarkable mainly for the energy it manages to enclose at that late date in the movement. *Adamastor* (1930) is the crucial volume for this aspect of Campbell's work. Such discipline as the poems possess probably came from a reading of Rimbaud and Baudelaire. It is arguable that Campbell is at his best when establishing contact with a poet in a language other than English. There is the tribute to Camoes in *Talking Bronco* (1946), which has genuine vigour and at least the historical interest of conveying a mood of the Second World War soldier overseas—

> Camoes, alone, of all the lyric race,
> Born in the black aurora of disaster,
> Can look a common soldier in the face:
> I find a comrade where I sought a master;
> For daily, while the stinking crocodiles
> Glide from the mangroves on the swampy shore,
> He shares my awning on the dhow, he smiles,
> And tells me that he lived it all before.
> Through fire and shipwreck, pestilence and loss,
> Led by the ignis fatuus of duty...[1]

After the end of the period with which this history is concerned Campbell produced translations of St John of the Cross (1951) and of Baudelaire (1952) and perhaps this is where he should have started.

3

A different—harder and more serious—turbulence prevails in the work of Christopher Murray Grieve, who for the most part has written under the name of Hugh MacDiarmid, to ensure, no doubt, that he is not taken for an Englishman, as to which race he has the strongest preconceptions, or has drawn from his experience the most rigorous conclusions. So powerful are the anathematizations which stream from him across the border that there is a sort

[1] *Luis de Camoes.*

of moral impropriety about including him in a history of *English* poetry. His works are public, however; a good proportion of them are written in the *lingua franca* and will inevitably make their impact on all who write in it. Being a part of English literature is something the Scottish poet, however umbrageous, cannot avoid — any more than the American can — whatever place he may hold in the sub-category to which he belongs by place and history. *English* in the term *English literature* refers to the language and is without prejudice to any independences, rebellions, hostilities or national distinctions whatsoever. The dialect of Burns, or the synthetic Lowlands — they call it Lallans — of MacDiarmid and his collaborators, does not take the authors concerned out of English literature any more than William Barnes is outside because he wrote in the language of Dorset, but it can be admitted that these departures from the general idiom narrow the impact and it would perhaps be tactful to admit that Lallans is not exactly English.

Grieve was born in the tiny town of Langholm in Dumfriesshire in 1892, and for most of his life his eye has been passionately on that border, much as that of Barrès was on the line of the Vosges. At moments Grieve has felt that most of the northern territories of England should come under his sway, as differentiated from the decadent south, but for the most part he has stuck firm to his line, insisting on the other hand on an identity of race and interest with the Celtic fringe, though to the foreigner the Highlands and Islands might seem not self-evidently more akin to the Lowlands than, say, Carlisle is. All that matters here is that the humours of nationalism have bitten deep into Grieve/MacDiarmid, and his work is unintelligible without them. Grieve's home in Langholm was in the same building as the public library, a convenience of which he early made use. His father was a postman, active in Kirk, Cooperative and Trade Union, and Radicalism and Republicanism were something the poet had later to develop rather than invent for himself. He was in the family tradition, though no doubt the postman could hardly have imagined the varieties of nationalism and communism which his son has at various times conceived, or the lessons of gratitude to the Russians which he has found occasion to give to ungrateful Czechs and Hungarians. It must be admitted, however, that whatever the aberrations — as they must seem to all but the most sympathetic observers — of his politics from time to time, he has a long,

235

consistent record of hostility to England, more particularly since his stay in England in 1929–31. He has not been at peace even with Scottish Nationalists, among whom as in other parties there are legitimate factions, but he has consistently been a political force, of the kind which bureaucratic governments think nothing of and are completely defenceless against. By the very force of his disapproval MacDiarmid has had a considerable influence on the course of public affairs in Scotland, although — or because of the very fact that — he protests against the idea that 'any scheme to do anything at all, political economic, commercial, or industrial — except to rouse a distinctive and dynamic spirit in Scotland' — has 'anything whatever to do with Scottish nationalism'. To some extent the object of hostility may be less England than the great British shawl that anyone in these islands who wants to breathe has to get out from under — a task which the English themselves may be less well placed to perform than the Irish, Scotch or Welsh, so that they are likely to be the last of the nationalities to re-emerge, if anybody in the end really succeeds in doing so.

Grieve started to train as a teacher, rather half-heartedly, and instead became a journalist. He was at this time in contact with Keir Hardie. In 1915 he joined the R.A.M.C. Unlike those who fought on the Western Front, his war seems largely to have been 'comparative stagnation and monotony and gruesome dull routine of disease and misadventurous death, unaccompanied by the flame and guns and the glitter of steel'. But in Salonika as elsewhere, there was 'the sacrifice of youth, the long, hard separation of lovers, the rush of death, the insupportability of the apparent triumph of the powers of darkness, the deep thoughts in the sentinel night, the sharpened memories of home constantly coming with an unspeakable newness'. These impressions are set out in *Four Years' Harvest*, which is to be found in *Annals of the Five Senses* (1923), a book — published under the name of Grieve — which is full of lively indications of the uncertainties from which the author set out. Although 'the impression had obtained at home that but for the prevalence of certain diseases life in Salonika would have been little short of a picnic' it did not seem so to the exiles. The impressions were 'beyond the possibility of assimilation' and he wanted 'additional skull space' to cope with them. It was because Grieve's mind was open to so much that he felt he could make little of it. The effort to find an order in the objects of his vast receptivity has been a constant preoccupation of his struggle. 'He could not see any internal centre from which sprang anything he thought or did' but then came, following the pattern of the extreme Evangelical Christianity in which he was brought up, 'strong and swift with perfect purification…the full tide of a stirring lay sermon which a socialist comrade had delivered'.

After the war followed years in Montrose, where he was a Labour member of the town council and a J.P. In 1928 he became one of the founders of the National Party of Scotland. His activities, as well as his reading and his writing, have been multifarious. Scarcely any literary figure of the century has given proof of such abundant energies. In the tangle of Communism, Nationalism and Social Credit he has pushed here and there, to the dismay of moderate and reasonable men but with his sights always on the objectives to which Scotland, and Scottish literature, ought in his conceptions to move. His battles have often been waged in conditions of great hardship—in the Shetlands, as a manual worker on Clydeside, as a man merely ignored and without enough to live on. A certain arrogance is not out of place in one who has done so much, in the face of so many difficulties, but it cannot be said that his boring Scottish insistence on whatever he happens to be saying has done his work no harm. Add to that his formidable memory, and his grim determination to reproduce what he remembers, including dreary and trivial statements by third-rate minds as well as more significant extracts, and you have the clue to the more rebarbative aspects of his genius. His appetite is better than his digestion, and we are invited to watch the great gobbets floating around in his stomach. There is none of the natural selectivity and the urge to discard which makes the erudition of Pound or Eliot so profitable.

The prose sections of *Annals of the Five Senses* are interspersed with verse, the product of an epoch when he was denouncing the idea of preserving the Scottish language as a reactionary idea and urging that English was 'an immensely superior medium of expression'. This verse is on the whole less lively and prickly than the prose with which it is mixed. On the whole he goes for a poetic subject and writes prosily—or at least extensively—about it. *A Moment in Eternity* covers six and a half pages, a recollection of a Spanish girl with whom he apparently spent a night in Salonika nearly five. These are short-breathed stretches compared with

237

many of MacDiarmid's later performances, but they show that from the first his English verse did not tend towards concentration. It may well be that the move into a Scots which was at once a literary language, drawing on the older writers, and an excursion into homely speech, enabled him to hold more firmly to the permanent and essential and to discard some of the mere talk which is the recurrent weakness of his writing. *Sangschaw* (1925) flew in the face of his own recently emitted theories about the superiority of the English language, and no doubt no mere theory would hold MacDiarmid back when he had a poem to write. The artificiality of his Scots language did not, however, present more than a momentary impediment — if it did that — to his loquaciousness and facility and *A Drunk Man Looks at the Thistle* (1926) runs on to over two-and-a-half thousand lines. This, however, is nothing to the man whose English poems run into tens — perhaps hundreds — of thousand of lines. There has, in fact, for years been an immense work building up, in which the vast bulk of what MacDiarmid has written could find a place, if indeed there is a distinct *place* for anything in this great eruption of formless energy. It is as if the poet's skin had come off and he was walking around with his guts hanging out.

Yet MacDiarmid's achievement is, undoubtedly, one of the most important of the half-century. Leaving aside his work in Lallans, which one who is not familiar with the language can merely suspect of including his most refined performances, what he has done of great significance for the future is to achieve a plainness and obviousness in his handling of English verse which makes it a possible vehicle for any and every subject. It would be a pity if the bulk and content of the major poems — or poem — resulted in the shorter English poems passing from view. The volume entitled *Second Hymn to Lenin* (1935) contains a few which can stand beside the strongest of Kipling and any but the best of Pound. There is *Folly*, a sort of epitaph on one who threw away his energy 'on puss and on booze'.

> Yet there he was. The fool just chose to *live*,
> Gratifying follies and powers that would have sufficed
> To carry him high in commerce, church or state — giving
> Himself to high jinks instead — a barbarous choice that surprised
> All who spend their lives wasting the reasons for living.

The last line is a twist of

Propter vitam vivendi perdere causas.

There is also *Another Epitaph on an Army of Mercenaries*, in reply to A. E. Housman's.

It is a God-damned lie to say that these
Saved, or knew, anything worth any man's pride.
They were professional murderers and they took
Their blood money and impious risks and died.
In spite of all their kind some elements of worth
With difficulty persist here and there on earth.

At his most serious MacDiarmid is wrestling with the main poetic task of the century—the task he has in mind in *To Circumjack Cencrastus* (1930) when he says:

And men hate poems dry and hard and needs
Maun hae them fozy wi' infinity.

He is wrestling with it in these short poems, but his idiosyncratic achievement is to provide a language for the long poem. It is a weakness that his ultimate poem is not so much long as endless—for knowing when to shut up is also a merit—but who else could have been such a bore without being dead? The type of dead long poem in this century is Bridges's *Testament of Beauty*; only Pound, besides MacDiarmid, has produced a live one. It is in the nature of MacDiarmid's diffuse achievement that one cannot give an adequate idea of it in short quotations. There is in *Lucky Poet*— a prose self-study published in 1943—a 'comprehensive manifesto' on *The Kind of Poetry I Want*. This great slab of versification, which had been read by Eliot and others but which it had hitherto not been possible to publish, is of course a chunk of the major, endless MacDiarmid outpouring. The 'kind' wanted is stated in one way after another. This is merely one way:

A poetry the quality of which
Is a stand made against intellectual apathy,
Its material founded, like Gray's, on difficult knowledge,
And its metres those of a poet

Who has studied Pindar and Welsh poetry,
But, more than that, its words coming from a mind
Which has experienced the sifted layers on layers
Of human lives — aware of the innumerable dead
And the innumerable to-be-born,
The voice of centuries, of Shakespeare's history plays
Concentrated and deepened,
'The breath and finer spirit of all knowledge,
The impassioned expression
Which is in the countenance of all science.'

MacDiarmid had absorbed a large miscellaneous scientific reading as well as reading in the general literature of several languages. His verse holds all these references. So we are told — in *In Memoriam James Joyce*, which, though not published till 1955, was written soon after Joyce's death in 1941 —

We have of course studied thoroughly
Alspach, English, and the others who have written
On 'Psychological Response to Unknown Proper Names',
Downey on 'Individual Differences in Reaction to the Word-in-Itself'.
Bullough on 'The Perceptive Problem
In the Aesthetic Appreciation of Single Colours',

and so the catalogue goes on for nearly two pages. We then learn:

The following order represents the success with which
Images of a given kind were aroused
Through direct suggestion — auditory 46·8 per cent.,
Olfactory 39·3, cutaneous 35·5, organic and pain 30·7,
Gustatory 14·2.

There is nothing then that MacDiarmid cannot put into verse, muscled if not vivid and certainly alive. In a sense such verse represents the longest distance travelled, in the period covered by this history, from the romanticism of the last century, for it is verse used once again as a common medium of expression, fit for any matter. It is of interest to recall that MacDiarmid, looking back to a Scottish poet of the nineties, has said that 'what Davidson, alone of Scottish poets, did was to enlarge the subject-matter of poetry, assimilate and utilize a great deal of new scientific and other contemporary material'. MacDiarmid is a more than worthy successor in this line.

In hammering out his peculiar brand of hard, all-purpose verse MacDiarmid was without doubt much assisted by his studies of the great 'makers' of the fifteenth and sixteenth centuries, Henryson, Dunbar, Gavin Douglas and Sir David Lindsay. What he had first to overcome, as a Scottish poet, was the predominance of Burns, not that Burns is not a fine poet but that he had become a point of obsession and formed an opaque barrier between the present and the earlier Scottish tradition. The tradition was, of course, also an English one, for Henryson represents the influence of Chaucer a couple of generations after the English poet's death. But there is an astringency about the work of Dunbar, Douglas and Lindsay which differentiates them clearly from Chaucer's milkier verse. One cannot say that Gavin Douglas is *more* readable than Chaucer, but the *The Bukes of Eneados of the famose Poete Virgil* are extremely readable and so is the much slighter *Historie and Testament of Squyer William Meldrum* of David Lindsay; and the asperity of these Scots may offer a more direct clue to the needs of current verse than Chaucer himself does. It is certainly the case that if one compares the poems in *Annals of the Five Senses* with MacDiarmid's later English verse, one is aware of a peculiar hardness — different from Lewis's — which had been missing from the language for a long time. This hardness springs, in part at least, from his recognition of the 'makars'.

Chapter Twelve

The forties: George Barker; Dylan Thomas;
Patrick Kavanagh; David Gascoyne

I

The poetry of George Barker in a sense marks the beginning of a
retrogression. It began to appear in the early thirties but it was
clearly distinguished from most of the work appearing in *New
Verse*. There was of course no common style in that periodical,
but there was a fairly general aspiration after facts of a public
kind, and the language, in its several varieties, was composed of
words which had been purged of certain associations by the inter-
vention of Pound, Eliot and Joyce. The cord which tied English
poets to the nineteenth century had been cut. The language
Barker used had its novelties, but it was in the Keats–Tennyson
succession. Without allowing that the typical poets of the
thirties were anything that could be called classical, one might
say that with Barker romanticism had raised her pretty head
again. It was not of course that he was unaware of what had
intervened.

George Barker was born in Essex in 1913. His father, whom he
oddly refers to as a policeman, and

> a little low
> In the social register,[1]

was the son of a Lincolnshire farmer and became a colonel in the
Coldstream Guards. His mother was an Irish peasant from
Drogheda, the daughter of a marine pilot. She was clearly a
woman of genius, as he describes her:

> Under the window where I often found her
> Sitting as huge as Asia, seismic with laughter,
> Gin and chicken helpless in her Irish hand,

242 [1] *The True Confession of George Barker.*

Irresistible as Rabelais, but most tender for
The lame dogs and hurt birds that surround her.[1]

He was educated at elementary schools and the Regent Street
Polytechnic, and so avoided taking colour from the ordinary
undergraduate life of the day. He was, in any case, in several
senses probably too near the ground for politics of the Auden-
Spender variety. His apartness from that stampede is certainly
related to the idiosyncratic quality of his work. In his *Funeral
Eulogy* he does not speak of Garcia Lorca as a Republican hero,
but as one who 'died because he had no cause' and 'took a bullet
from the side that had most guns and most murderers'. Those who
remember the passions aroused by the Spanish civil war will
recognize that there is an element of dogged independence in
these words. Barker early made the acquaintance of T. S. Eliot,
to whom his poems contain more than one personal tribute.
One, written at the approach of war, sees Eliot

Expecting a bomb or angel through the roof,
Cold as a saint in Canterbury Cathedral,
This gentleman with Adam on his mind[2]

and concludes, not without affection,

And when the bomb or angel breaks the vaulting
Trust he remembers, among the others, my name.[3]

The other poem, written on the occasion of the sixtieth birthday,
sees Eliot less conventionally and less remotely. Barker himself is
nearly ten years older:

By that evening window where
His accurate eye keeps Woburn Square
Under perpetual judgment so
That only the happy can come and go
About the gardens and not be
Tested in that dark neutrality.[4]

[1] *To My Mother.*
[2] and [3] *To T. S. Eliot.*
[4] *Verses for the Sixtieth Birthday of T. S. Eliot.*

Eliot invited Barker to do some work, including some reviewing, for the somewhat austere *Criterion*, a fortunate circumstance for a young man still training himself to write.

Although he has from time to time held academic appointments, in Japan, the United States, and in this country, Barker could not be described as having any other profession than that of a poet. He has said that enough has not been made 'of the simple argument that writing serious English poetry is a full-time occupation. A certain amount of reading has to be done, a certain amount of writing has to be done, a certain amount of living has to be done.'[1] One of his early attempts to meet the problem was to withdraw to a cottage in Dorset, but since then economic pressures and the usual restlessnesses have taken him to many places, including the great cities of several countries, none of them no doubt providing continuously all that his programme requires. 'The poet needs three things to go on being a poet,' he says; 'a dictionary, alcohol and love.'[1] The dictionary seems to be all right, but he reports difficulties from time to time with the other ingredients. However, he has perhaps not been short of them, by ordinary standards.

From the first Barker exhibited a slightly excessive facility with evocative words. It was as if he could sit burping gently, whatever his thoughts, and enjoy the aroma of past feasts.

> Venerable all hills, all valleys
> Avalanched with immaculate quietude, air
> Falls through autumnal halls, in which infrequent airs
> Blown from the few instrumental leaves
> Fall again in infrequent falls, in rains.[2]

One cannot avoid the suspicion that he is less concerned to say something clearly than to say it in a way which will be recognized as being poetical. The big words — venerable, avalanched, immaculate, quietude — come rather thick and fast. The next stanza brings us more:

> Again formidable winter strikes the winds
> Crystalline immobile, all still,

[1] *Essays.*

[2] *Venerable All Hills, All Valleys.*

The third:

Against the interminable grieving of the sea.

There is great verbal talent in these verses; there is also an appearance of complacency in an easy magic. There may be some deliberate trying out of sounds in such verses; Barker was still learning his trade. There are internal rhymes, such as, in this poem

Incipient gaieties of the impending spring, sending
Messengers

—or, in *The Leaping Laughers*

Many men mean
Well: but tall walls
Impede, their hands bleed and
They fall, their seed the
Seed of the fallen.

It is impossible not to feel that the thought is being led by the words. It is this no doubt wilful reversal of the direction in which the language of poetry had been developing since the nineties which makes Barker seem to belong rather to the forties than to what has gone immediately before them. Of course in the composition of poetry words must take command but they can also be discarded and there are unquestionably, in different writers and in different epochs, differences in the principle on which they are discarded. Theory cannot do much for us in this field, but there is a relationship between theory and the unconscious which has a bearing on practice. But, as MacDiarmid says

Joyce in turn
Is richt, and the principal question
Aboot a work o' art is frae hoo deep
A life it springs.[1]

The danger of the poet yielding too readily to the seduction of

[1] *Second Hymn to Lenin.*

words is, precisely, that he may become content to draw from too shallow wells.

In *Calamiterror* (1936), Barker comes nearer to writing the sort of poetry which his more deliberate early work seems to be groping towards. The artificial use of big words has gone; the level of evocation is deeper. One may guess that the surface of the mind has been broken by profound and novel experience. At any rate we feel that Barker is trying to say something, only it is too difficult:

> What when born upward breaking from heaven downward
> Is my bare bloodred babe.

Or

> Who is the parent of the innumerable plant,
> The gladiola, the hidden violet, the sweet onion.

The best — on the whole the earlier — parts of *Calamiterror* have a novelty of subject-matter which could only have been reached by the track of verbal technique which Barker followed. The continuity of the world from the viscera to the tree-top in

> What is the green dream in the summer tree,
> Which like a vague womb rests on the dark boughs;

and

> The blood cataract leaping along the arm
> Boiling with foam of perspiration pearls

are new perceptions. Barker, as it were, speaks from inside the body or sees the body around him as he speaks.

These intuitions haunt all Barker's poetry. The question is how often he is willing to meet the ghosts, and how often he puts between him and them a smother of words or an evasive pose. He is not above toying with a ready-made poetic role. In *Vision of England '38* he evokes Chatterton, Wilde and Keats — not very bracing company.

O lamentable lips that ragged showed their burns,
As that beautiful youth with Saint Mary Redcliffe in hand
Stepped forward and fell at my side and murmured:
'I warn you, not poison.'

Who took my hand and left an orchid there,
With the mark of his lips that parted their shapes
To speak a word of hope: was it salacious Oscar
Or the lost Orphic who coughed blood at Naples?

Everywhere the truth flickers in the background, as in *Elegy No 1*, with

Look how Tottenham and the Cotswolds, with
More mass than a man, lie easy under the sky,
Also awaiting change they cannot understand.

But there is also

I sip at suicide in bedrooms or dare pessimistic stars

—which is sensationalism. It is as if Barker is tempted to snatch at any excitement which looks like offering material for verse, instead of going on living and allowing the poetry to make itself out of whatever residues are involuntarily left. He is most convincing when caught unawares, as perhaps in the second of the *Pacific Sonnets*, presumably written in connection with his war-time journey to Tokio:

Those whom I may not meet pester me now
Like dogs I lost seem leaping at my breast,
But lost, lost across space, found in a day-dream
Only, or foundered in the floundering west
Go under whispering messages that blow
Over the world and pester me with home.

The more pretentious poems are often the least satisfactory. The *Secular* and *Sacred Elegies*—insufficiently differentiated to bear these titles, one might think—seem to be elaborated in order to impress. There is a lack of intellectual discipline behind such work. In spite of his claim in his sonnet, Barker does not

serve
Much the same master[1]

as Baudelaire.

The resolution of these uncertainties comes in *Goodman Jacksin and the Angel* and above all in the First Part of *The True Confession* — the second part is outside the period of this history. *The True Confession* was omitted from the *Collected Poems, 1930–1955* at the request of the publisher, presumably on account of its occasional obscenity. In this poem Barker found the tone, and the technique, which perfectly suited his humorous but otherwise unrigorous mind. He treats extensively of his favourite subject of copulation, vacillating between worldliness and a spirit of sensual inquiry. The complete lack of pretension enables him to write with clarity, the stanza-form is one he handles with perfect ease and to which he imparts novelties of rhythm.

> Today, recovering from influenza,
>   I begin, having nothing worse to do,
> This autobiography that ends a
>   Half of my life I'm glad I'm through.
> O love, what a bloody hullaballoo
>   I look back at, shaken and sober,
> When that intemperate life I view
>   From this temperate October

—and so on through nearly a thousand lines. He pretends to no more seriousness than the years have left him with; and therefore cannot be faulted as far as he goes:

> What's the point of a confession
>   If you have nothing to confess?
> I follow the perjuring profession
>   —O poet, lying to impress! —
> But the beautiful lie in a beautiful dress
>   Is the least heinous of my transgressions:
> When a new one's added, 'O, who was it?'
>   Sigh the skeletons in my closet.

[1] *To Charles Baudelaire.*

The intuitions with which his poetry began are packed around with years which have not been lacking in observation :

> I looked into my heart to write.
>   In that red sepulchre of lies
> I saw that all man cherished
>   Goes proud, rots and perished
> Till through that red room pitiless night
>   Trails only knife-tongued memories
> To whose rags cling, shrieking, bright
>   Unborn and aborted glories.

It is difficult to understand why this has not become one of the best known poems of the century; the omission from the collected volume was unfortunate.

2

Dylan Thomas was the son of the senior English master at Swansea Grammar School. He was born in 1914 and educated first at a small private school in the town and then at the Grammar School, which he left before he was seventeen. He was not interested in academic studies and apparently did not consider going to a university. Instead, he became, for a year, a reporter on the *South Wales Daily Post*. After this he did a little acting. His main occupation, however, from the age of sixteen was the writing of poems. Indeed, his late teens were his most productive period. At the age of nineteen poems of his were published in, successively, *The New English Weekly*, the *Sunday Referee* and the *Listener*. He was quickly in touch with T. S. Eliot, Stephen Spender, and Geoffrey Grigson. His reading after this was not much; he relied on beer and genius. His social circulation has been extensively documented. He did some work on films during the war, and on the B.B.C., mostly afterwards. He died on his fourth trip to the United States, in 1953.

Thomas's first volume, *Eighteen Poems*, was published soon after he was twenty and the second, *Twenty-Five Poems*, a couple of years later. They both received enthusiastic reviews, Edith Sitwell taking up the trumpet in 1936. There was, certainly, something very noticeable about these volumes. Words were hurled around in a way which did not make much sense, and the confusion was attributed to poetic force. Amidst the general adulation Thomas could hardly be blamed for not insisting on his own diagnosis, which he gave in a letter to Pamela Hansford Johnson, a friend of his ingenuous youth, in 1934: 'I'm a freak user of words, not a poet. That's really the truth. No self-pity there. A freak *user* of words, not a poet. That's terribly true.'[1] And so it was. What was undoubtedly taken by many, on the first appearance of the poems, to be an outpouring from a deep uncon-sciousness — which would account for the obscurity — was largely the effect of deliberate working over. He told Pamela Hansford Johnson, in the letter already quoted: 'All day yesterday I was working, as hard as a navvy, on six lines of a poem. I finished them, but had, in the labour of them, picked and cleaned them so much that nothing but their barbaric sounds remained.' A factitious quality, evident if one compares Thomas's work with the best surrealist work, or indeed with any natural poetry, can be felt on every page.

> I, in my intricate image, stride on two levels,
> Forged in man's minerals, the brassy orator
> Laying my ghost in metal,
> The scales of this twin world tread on the double,
> My half ghost in armour hold hard in death's corridor,
> To my man-iron sidle.[2]

Or

> Then swift from a bursting sea with bottle-cork boats
> And out-of-perspective sailors,
> In common clay clothes disguised as scales,
> As he-God's paddling water skirts.[3]

These are, so to speak, deliberate wonders. Thomas claimed that much of his obscurity was 'due to rigorous compression', but the effect is rather of little being conveyed in many words than of the reverse. There is, indeed, a lack of emotional and intellectual development about Thomas which makes his work boring, once the first surprise has worn off. A poet has to have something to say and Thomas had, in fact, very little. A poet also has to take

[1] Letter of 9 May 1934.
[2] *I, in My Intricate Image.*
[3] *Once Below a Time.*

the words he is given, and not bully them. But Thomas is histori-
cally important as the prototype of much of the literary pretension
of the forties.

3

Patrick Kavanagh came from a world beside which the Swansea of
Dylan Thomas was metropolitan. He was born in Monaghan,
on the Eirean side of the Ulster border, in 1905. His father was
a small farmer and a shoemaker, and apparently acted as local
adviser on other matters as well. Kavanagh senior seems to have
been a man of parts who found multifarious uses for his talents,
in a way which has disappeared from more urbanized and mobile
communities. He was not well off. 'My childhood experience,'
Patrick Kavanagh says in his *Self-Portrait* (1964), 'was the usual
barbaric life of the Irish country poor.' He goes on to say that he
has 'never seen poverty properly analysed. Poverty is a mental
condition. You hear of men and women who have chosen poverty,
but you cannot choose poverty. Poverty has nothing to do with
eating your fill today; it is anxiety about what's going to happen
next week.' This in itself would explain a certain difference in
tone as compared with, say, Auden and Spender, whose contemporary Kavanagh more or less was. It also explains Kavanagh's
relatively slow emergence to notice. His first volume of verse,
The Ploughman and Other Poems, was published in 1936.
Kavanagh was still living on what in retrospect he called his
'comfortable little holding of watery hills beside the Border'. He
went to Dublin in 1939, and made his living writing columns for
the *Irish Press*, the *Standard* and the *Farmer's Journal*. It was
almost inevitable that, with the restlessness which came of his
abilities, he should want to leave his narrow circle in Monaghan.
He might afterwards regard the move to Dublin as 'the worst
mistake of his life', but that was in the wisdom which immersion
in a larger world had given him. 'It would not have been easy,'
he says, 'for a man of sensibility to survive in the society of my
birth, but it could have been done had I been trained in the technique of reserve and restraint.' It is a noble piece of retrospective
criticism, both of art and life. Kavanagh got to know the literary
world only to understand that in the confinement of his youth
there was something of infinitely greater value. The 'Irish
literary affair was still booming' when he arrived in Dublin.
'Ireland, as invented and patented by Yeats, Lady Gregory and

Synge' was still all the rage. Whatever charm it might have for urban and middle-class Dublin, it is easy to see why it should disgust the man who had spent thirty-five years in 'the watery hills' — 'And me with health and strength to dig ditches, or to leap them anyway with a sack of white flour on me back'. He had, when he wrote the poems in *The Ploughman*, his own vision of Ireland:

> We are a dark people,
> Our eyes are ever turned
> Inward
> Watching the liar who twists
> The hill-paths awry.[1]

The vision took more definite shape in *The Great Hunger* (1942), a long poem which brought him a considerable reputation, more on account of its Irishness than its literary qualities, as he must have reflected with some bitterness. It is a notable piece of work, if perhaps too directly autobiographical, under the chosen *persona* of Maguire, to equal the best of the short poems in which, earlier and later, he presented a distillation from his hard experience.

> O he loved his mother
> Above all others.
> O he loved his ploughs
> And he loved his cows
> And his happiest dream
> Was to clean his arse
> With perennial grass
> On the bank of some summer stream;
> To smoke his pipe
> In a sheltered gripe
> In the middle of July —
> His face in a mist
> And two stones in his fist
> And an impotent worm on his thigh.

The suppressed lust, the colour and light of his fields, the sense of companionship in a world where 'one talks to the horse as to a brother', which are themes of *The Great Hunger*, all re-appear in

[1] *Dark Ireland.*

Tarry Flynn (1948) a novel which perhaps contains the best of Kavanagh's work and, as Kavanagh himself claimed, 'not only the best but the only *authentic* account of life as it was lived in Ireland this century'. The book weakens only for a moment at the end, with the appearance of a rascally old uncle who for a moment is passed off as representing liberty. The rest is a steady reflection, many-coloured because veridical. It does not denounce, though there are some harsh things said in the book, for to denounce would be to write in accordance with a set of ideas about this rural community, and Kavanagh is presenting the facts. So if in this world 'decency' refers 'to the size of the property and not to the character of the individual' and the priest is more romano-gaelic than catholic, there is among all the avidity an intrusive natural beauty and the characters stand out raggedly, naked of the commercial pretension of more urbanized circles.

The most prominent *general* idea is a negative one, as perhaps must be the case of a man who is struggling to liberate himself and to allow reality to triumph in him over preconceptions. He discovered that 'the Ireland thing' got in the way, and he aspired to free himself from it. Because he was an Irish peasant he wanted to rid himself of the *notion* of the Irish peasant. 'A poet is an original who inspires millions of copies,' he said. In the end the original mind contributes to the preconceptions of those that follow, and Kavanagh has no doubt done his share of that. But his constant preoccupation is to see the world otherwise than through ideas, and so, at his best, he sees it.

> The only true teaching
> Subsists in watching
> Things moving or just colour
> Without comment from the scholar.[1]

His conclusion is:

> So be reposed and praise, praise praise
> The way it happened and the way it is.[2]

In what may have been his last poem, published in the Dublin

[1] *Is.*
[2] *Question to Life.*

periodical *Holy Door* in 1966, Kavanagh defined his position in
some lines addressed to Yeats:

> Yeats it was very easy for you to be frank
> With your sixty years and loves (like Robert Graves)
> It was thin and in fact you had never put the tank
> On a race. Ah cautious man whom no sin depraves
> And it won't add up at least in my mind
> To what it takes in the living poetry stakes
> I don't care what Chicago thinks, I am blind
> To college lecturers and the breed of fakes
> I mean to say I'm not blind really
> I have my eyes wide open as you may imagine
> And I am aware of our own boys such as Ben Kiely
> Buying and selling literature on the margin
> Yes Yeats it was damn easy for you protected
> By the middle classes and the Big Houses
> To talk about the sixty year old public protected
> Man sheltered by the dim Victorian Muses.[1]

The lines are among the best extant criticism of Yeats. They
exhibit Kavanagh as possessed of a fine critical intelligence and
with a profound understanding of his fellows — which is not a
very different thing.

4

David Gascoyne is a poet of quite a different order of seriousness.
Born in 1916, he was educated at Salisbury Choir School and for
six years sang daily at Mattins and Evensong in the cathedral.
He then found his way to Regent Street Polytechnic, and so like
both Barker and Thomas avoided the university influences of the
thirties. His first volume of poems, *Man's Life is This Meat*, was
published when he was twenty, and by this time he had already
produced *A Short Survey of Surrealism* (1935), which points to
his having acquired at a very early age an extensive knowledge
of contemporary French poetry. Gascoyne also made his way
into some of the more interesting recesses of German literature,
and in 1938 published *Hölderlin's Madness*, an introductory essay
followed by 'what may perhaps be regarded as a *persona*' consisting of adaptations of extracts from Hölderlin's poetry interspersed

[1] *Lines to Yeats.*

with entirely original poems. Further volumes of Gascoyne's poems were published in 1943 (*Poems 1937–1942*) and 1950 (*A Vagrant and Other Poems*). The whole *oeuvre* to date is slight in bulk. Gascoyne seems to possess in an abnormal degree the gift of writing only when he has something to say.

Gascoyne's early interest in surrealism had nothing in it of mere attachment to a passing fashion. The *Petite Anthologie poétique du Surréalisme*, with a long introduction by Georges Hughnet, had appeared in 1934 and in preparing his short book Gascoyne had been in touch with André Breton and Paul Eluard as well as with Hughnet. He studied the documents of the movement with care, and the English reader who wants to understand its origin and development can still not do better than turn to his work. Gascoyne's interest in the subject was far from being an academic one. It was the form taken, at the age of nineteen, by his involuntary inquiry into the nature of poetry and indeed of the human mind.

Confined from early childhood in a world that almost everything he ever hears or reads will tell him is the one and only *real* world and that, as almost no one, on the contrary, will point to him, is a prison, man — l'homme moyen sensuel — bound hand and foot not only by those economic chains of whose existence he is becoming ever more and more aware, but also by chains of second-hand and second-rate *ideas*, the preconceptions and prejudices that help to bind together the system known (ironically, as some think) by the name of 'civilisation', is for ever barred except in sleep from that other plane of existence where stones fall upwards and the sun shines by night, if it chooses, and where even the trees talk freely with the statues that have come down for ever from their pedestals.[1]

The world of dream was, he said, regarded much as, during the Victorian era, 'the erotic domain' had been regarded. 'That the dream is useless, an escape from reality, the dreamer a self-indulgent and lazy person, is the accepted view of an overwhelming majority.' For Gascoyne concern for poetry was, from the first, identified with concern for the truth. Although surrealism, as a movement, had the weakness of other organized movements that it dragged in the train of its theory many more than were able to comply with its spirit, it provided, for a young Englishman before the Second World War, a point of view which enabled him to stand back a long way from the Anglo-Saxon prejudices

[1] *A Short Survey of Surrealism.*

of the thirties, whether literary or political. As to the latter, while it cannot be maintained in retrospect that the French left showed any greater foresight or prudence than the left in this country, it was certainly nearer the heart of the struggle, as young men demonstrating and being beaten up in the *quartier latin* were a little nearer the reality of the years that followed than those who were talking themselves silly in the seclusion of Oxford. No doubt 'opposing bourgeois society, attacking religion, patriotism and the idea of the family', had its own measure of unreality, but it provided an intellectual starting point detached enough to be useful to a boy from the Salisbury Choir School. Indeed, one has to go back to the most inventive literary period of the century, the years preceding the First World War, to find anything like the incisiveness and the degree of disjunction from his immediate English predecessors which Gascoyne showed.

In these early years Gascoyne contributed many translations of Aragon, Eluard and others to the magazines that would accept them, and his own work was as surrealist as the English language allowed. That English could not accept the sort of small tornado represented by surrealism in France was partly due to the fact that our literature had long embodied an irrational element, even in Shakespeare himself, in a manner so little concealed that this particular revolution no longer seemed particularly exciting. The real object of Gascoyne's chase was not, however, the particular contemporary movement but the general 'phenomenon of a sudden upsurge of lyricism and of man's unconscious thought (which are individible)'. It was this which carried him to the German writers of the early nineteenth century of whom 'the Lakeland school of poets and their successors' were, he said, 'a lesser reflection'. It is not difficult to see why the work of Hölderlin should have a particular attraction for Gascoyne. In the introduction to *Hölderlin's Madness* he classifies Hölderlin with Rimbaud as belonging to 'the tradition of the *seer*. That is to say,' he explains, 'that their *ars poetica* was an offspring of the Platonic doctrine of inspiration. They believed the poet to be capable of penetrating to a secret world and of receiving the dictation of a transcendental inner voice. "Der Dichter ein Seher": "Je dis qu'il faut être *voyant*, se faire *voyant*."' This secret world is, in fact, Paradise, 'if by Paradise we mean a state of autonomous existence unsubjected to necessity, a state of perfect freedom, without time or age, and if the non-rational imagination of the poet is distinguished precisely by its ignorance of Necessity's irrevocable laws and its defiance of the aristotelian *ananke*'.

In the 1937–42 volume the poems of those years are re-arranged under five headings, and they had before that been conceived as groups rather than as entirely separate poems. The poet who has something profound and difficult to convey is bound to regard his work, more or less explicitly, in this way. In Gascoyne's work the unity is emphasized by a recurrent, one might say permanent, Christian reference, very different in kind from what is found in the later Eliot. There is no 'constructing something, on which to rejoice', but a continual tentativeness, as of a man testing his perception of the truth, so that it is present in the poems labelled 'metaphysical (or "metapsychological")' and 'personal' as well as in those explicitly classified as 'religious'. In an article recently published in *Two Rivers* (Winter 1969) Gascoyne says:

All my really intelligent friends, of whom there have fortunately for my own intelligence been a good many throughout my life, have suffered, and sometimes quite painfully, from much the same sort of strange and really ridiculous religious difficulties; and these were difficulties which in the final analysis may be said all to boil down to the same fundamental problem, which was indeed until quite recently a previously well-nigh insoluble one. The problem is as follows: How to *believe* such an obviously true and yet almost as obviously falsified tale (—dogma, or rigmarole, it simply depends on your habitual vocabulary)? And the answer is this: *It just wasn't rationally possible.*

He goes on to give the reasons why it wasn't possible, the first being that '*It was really true*, and we didn't recognize the fact'— a version of the *credo quia impossibile* of Tertullian. It cannot be said that Gascoyne's most successful poems are those in which he faces this problem most directly, though we get in *Tenebrae*

Thus may it be: and worse.
And may we know Thy perfect darkness.

And in *Kyrie*

Grant us extraordinary grace,
O spirit hidden in the dark in us and deep,
And bring to light the dream out of our sleep

—lines which indicate the sequence of thought from surrealist   257 beginnings. Gascoyne's searching of his own and others' wounds is very different from the rather cocky, so-called 'clinical', approach of Auden. Gascoyne values psychology as a possible route to the truth not as a technique which enables you to put somebody right.

> And when you pinned upon your mouth that smile
> Of purest malice by which you betrayed
> Your total lack of trust, how all too well
> I recognized its likeness to my own twitch of disgust.[1]

He writes of a friend who committed suicide:

> Yet even in your obscure death I see
> The secret candour of that lonely child
> Who, lost in the storm-shaken castle-park,
> Astride his crippled mastiff's back was borne
> Slowly away into the utmost dark.[2]

'Thought has a subtle odour,' Gascoyne says in *Odeur de Pensée*,

> Thought's odour is so pale that in the air
> Nostrils inhale, it disappears like fire
> Put out by water

and it is this subtlety which is somehow caught and which we perceive in his verse.

In the poems in *A Vagrant*, which are relatively few in number, this delicate, sure touch is felt more consistently. In the title poem Gascoyne describes his own role with a complete lack of pretension — a test few poets will pass:

> Awkward enough, awake, yet although anxious still just sane,
> I stand still in my quasi-dereliction, or but stray
> Slowly along the quais towards the ends of afternoons
> That lead to evenings empty of engagements, or at night
> Lying resigned in cosy-corner crows-nest, listen long
> To sounds of the surrounding city desultorily
> Seeking in loud distraction some relief from what its nerves
> Are gnawed by: I mean knowledge of its lack of *raison d'être*.
> The city's lack and mine are much the same.

[1] *To A Contemporary.*

258 [2] *An Elegy.*

The music of such verse is quiet but, to anyone with an ear for speech, unmistakable. It is one with the impression one has of the complete authenticity of this voice which is heard only when it succeeds in rendering the mind.

> When I am able to resist
> For once the constant pressure of the failure to exist,
> Let me remember
> That truly to be man is to be man aware of Thee
> And unafraid to be. So help me God.[1]

It is as far from the coated religiosity of the nineties as from the affectation of their speech. David Gascoyne is far from Lionel Johnson, but he is close to Thomas Traherne and to Henry Vaughan the Silurist.

[1] *Fragments Towards a Religio Poetae.*

Chapter Thirteen

Conclusion

History does not end; at least it has not done so yet. What the gap between 1950 and ourselves is filled with it is, mercifully, not for this book to say. MacDiarmid, Barker, Auden and Kavanagh extend themselves into this period. If Auden's later work lacks interest, Kavanagh wrote some of his best poems towards the end of his life, and Barker continues to be worth reading, whether asking whether he can

> ever truly comprehend the essential cynicism
> Of a society invented by beach boys and supported by girls
> without girdles[1]

or occasionally in the moods when romanticism does not lie:

> I hear the old bone in me cry
> and the dying spirit call:
> I have forfeited all
> and once and for all must die
> and this is all that I know.[2]

A man does not judge his juniors as well as he judges his seniors and his contemporaries, and anyone who wants to know how far aberration in this kind can go should look into the *Oxford Book of Modern Verse* edited by W. B. Yeats. It is hard to believe that Yeats did not know better, but probably he did not. In youth we learn most vividly from our immediate predecessors, and they hand us over to the dead, and it is of the long dead that literature is overwhelmingly made up. A versifier who knows only or mainly

[1] *Nine Beatitudes to Denver.*
260 [2] *At Thurgarton Church.*

the works of his contemporaries is likely to be a very frivolous man; there are some so frivolous as to admire no verse but their own. Contemporary literature can be read with understanding only by people with at least a hankering to know what has gone on at other times. Wyndham Lewis's verse is invigorating but it is not as good as Cleveland's. There are few names which do not erase themselves when set against appropriate touchstones. It was a merit in Pound and in Eliot that they continually put one in mind of such matters — rather explicitly, for they were Americans. Since then, the politics of the thirties, and the general apocalyptic miasma of the forties — not to speak of the evils of public patronage, and of the poetry and university trades after that — have obscured the fact that, so far as literature is concerned, the future is more likely to be found in the past than in the present. If Dante and Catullus, Horace or Raleigh, or some equivalent figures, are not of actual importance to you, in terms of pleasure and enlightenment to be got from their works here and now, then literature — the designation of the permanent elements in man — is not what you are interested in as you turn to the weeklies and the Sunday supplements. There is always the great, excitable flow of politics and fashion, but the point of literature is something different. It is the natural thing, not an affectation, for a poet like John Heath-Stubbs to echo or translate bits of the Latins, French or Provençal in the course of his work, as well as utter such underivative conversation as

Mr Heath-Stubbs as you must understand
Came of a gentleman's family out of Staffordshire
Of as good blood as any in England
But he was wall-eyed and his legs too spare.[1]

There is no incompatibility between learning and the poetry which is, so to speak, direct chat. On the contrary, a durable chat has to be made of something stronger than merely contemporary materials. The validity of poets who may seem to write more or less directly from experience — Brian Higgins or Cliff Ashby — depends not on their immediate experience but on the degree in which what they report is true of other people in other places and times. Of course the time and place of writing, the physiology

[1] *Epitaph.*

and the biography of the individual poet, all help to determine the shape of the little incision he makes into reality. Poetry is at once old and new — the one only if it is the other.

What did the poetry of the first half of this century amount to? In a sense, no more than the works of the individual poets amount to. Indeed, Dryden and Pope are more than the stamp they gave to the eighteenth century. In the same way, the idiosyncratic minds of lesser people — Edward Thomas or Isaac Rosenberg — are more than any general development of which they are a part. But the direction of a general development is of some importance. We all participate in the language and a new mind, however inventive, can only start from where the language is. Shakespeare can only be born in Elizabethan England and Dante only in mediaeval Italy. Any authentic piece of writing helps the communal task of keeping the language clean; every piece of rubbish — in verse, in journalism, in scholarship, advertising, in official reports or other fiction — adds to the muck-heap. The poets of the half-century, so far as they are genuine, have contributed to bringing the wayward big mouth of the public back to an exact speech which manages to correspond to the real movements of the mind and to reflect reality. Reality is more elusive than the more strident merchants of so-called fact would have us believe.

An age of sturdy, and to some extent clumsy, common speech, like that of the early sixteenth century, has a long period of refinement before it. The more accurate and agile handling of metric and stanza-forms has a place here, just as the polishing of heroic couplets has point until Pope has produced a surface which, in its kind, cannot be improved upon. The iambic pentameter — the standard English 'blank verse' — practically exhausted itself in the rapid evolution from Surrey (1517–47) to the Jacobeans. Shakespeare's own development of it, from *Love's Labour's Lost* to *Lear* and *Anthony and Cleopatra*, is a history in itself. The form is perfected and broken again, but the new breaking, in *Lear*, is a perfect form in itself — an irregular one, but with an irregularity which could be achieved only when all the tricks of mechanical perfection had been mastered. The twentieth century started from elaborate stanza-forms, in Swinburne, and Tennysonian blank verse. The facility of both was too great for further use to be made of them without modification, for part of the business of tapping the springs of poetry is in breaking through the surface facilities. But anything can become a surface facility, and much of the 'free verse' of the twentieth century has been just lines cut up in varying lengths, with no rhythmic hold—not in fact verse at all. The literature of metrical analysis can contribute little to the identification of these failures. The test is what can be held in the mind, as a rhythm, and that is why disputation on this subject will never cease. But if valid new work is not for everyone to detect, most people of any literary training can see in retrospect what has happened. The irruption of new, conversational tones in the nineties, in Kipling, and above all in Hardy, is not now difficult to perceive. One can see which of, and when, the imagists managed to give shape to what seemed to many of their contemporaries merely a broken phrase. No one now argues about Pound's or Eliot's main achievements in this field; indeed the disposition is rather to swallow the verse with the name of the master. After these great technical performances, succeeding poets had a new capital to live on. The poets of the thirties and forties are unthinkable without these recently-acquired riches. For a poet such as John Heath-Stubbs, who began in the forties but whose work lies in the main after our period, Eliot and Pound have receded to a place in the general succession. He does not show their influence particularly because he has digested much more, including them. The same may be said of David Wright, a less conscious manipulator of the new technical spoils, in whom, at his best, the unmistakable conversational tone of the century is in the service of a possessed imagination. There is a subdued tradition, and a subdued novelty, about *Kleomedes* (in the volume *Adam at Evening*, 1965)

> Both Plutarch and Pausanias tell a story
> That is a worry to imagination.
> It's of the athlete Kleomedes, a moody
> Instrument for a theophanic anger
> And for an outrageous justice not our own.

In Martin Seymour-Smith, who is ten years younger, the nerves are more exposed, and an extremely subtle intelligence combs among them. His poetry is the common speech of a highly sophisticated mind.

Looking back over the half-century, as well as one can at this distance, one sees that the real inventiveness was mainly before 1925. In this period poetry was corrected and improved by the canons of prose. By the thirties an ideological overlay has spoiled the outline. By the forties, a twentieth-century version of Lord Chesterfield's lesson in poetics is creeping back: 'Prose, as you know, is the language of common conversation; it is what you, and everybody speaks and writes… But poetry is a more noble and sublime way of expressing one's thoughts.' The dog returns to his vomit.

Postscript

Looking back on this history of fifty years, more than thirty years after the end of the period and more than ten years after the book was written, it seems to me that the outline drawn in it remains firm enough. I put the matter in this personal and slightly tentative way because, whatever the pretensions of historians, no history is ever clearer than that. I am far from admitting an absolute subjectivism to literary history or to any other, but all history is written from a certain perspective—the author's—whatever airs he may give himself of being the embodiment of scientific method.

The modest objective of this book, as set out ten years ago in the 'Introductory Note', was 'to show where the best English verse of the first half of the century' was to be found, what its qualities were and what sort of men wrote it. A reason for re-printing it would be that the verse indicated has been found in fact to be readable, or more than readable, to contain more of the life of the period than was always readily admitted at the time, and to point in a direction which interests us now. These conditions the book does, I think, satisfy. It may be said to have crawled under certain pretensions, always a good thing to do, and to have ignored reputations to favour instead the quality of work done. This method of proceeding was not without producing some unfavourable reactions, as in the indignant reviewer who thought it outrageous to mention a man known as an anthologist and editor, but hardly at all as a poet—A. H. Bullen—but look at pages 14-16 and at Bullen's few small, solid poems. Or why, somebody said, bother about Clere Parsons? Turn to pages 216-218 and see why. There was no pretence that either Bullen or Parsons were major figures, even of the limited dimensions required to deserve that description in a history of fifty years, which is not very long, as literature goes. But the ability to detect genuine performances, where only a name of no importance, or none at all, is attached to them, is the first prerequisite of critical writing, without which all else is vain, and there is in this book a minimum of critical super-structure—a form of construction certainly overdone in our time.

It can be claimed, I think, that the identifications and discriminations made in this volume will find rather more ready assent now than when the book was first published. Edward Thomas (pages 71-79) has now become the centre of marked academic attentions which merely confirm the more scattered enthusiasms of earlier readers. Some once rather inflated reputations, such as that of Auden (pages 202-212) will be found here in something which would now be generally admitted to be nearer their true size, because the life of the language and not the afflatus of the reputation was what interested the historian. The marked preference for the early work of T. S. Eliot (pages 125-154) will still be thought by some to be too marked, but there is no mistaking the drift of assessment in the direction here indicated. Eliot is treated as one of the three major figures of the period, but no service would have been done to the living literature of our own time, or indeed to the continuing reputation of Eliot himself, by putting the lucubrations of his later years on an equality with the inventions of *The Waste Land* and *Sweeney Agonistes*. And the over-sized magician, W. B. Yeats, was desperately in need of, and here got, a more sceptical and ironical treatment than was, until the very recent past, usually accorded to his flamboyant figure. It is in deflated form, with the wind of cult and fashion taken out of them, that even the greatest figures have to settle into history, and thirty years after the close of the period it is now high time to see its most splendid names as they look against the history of centuries rather than of decades. The importance of the period, 1900-1950, is that it is near enough to us still to have a considerable actuality, and far enough away to be seen as part of the corpus of English literature rather than as part of the goings-on of our own time. As such, its history can be a profitable warning, showing the need for scepticism about the contemporary literary scene.

To point the warning further, it might have been desirable to have said more about some of the work which dazzled the author for a youthful year or two, and then vanished to a point. At the age of fifteen there were Rupert Brooke and James Elroy Flecker. The timing is important. It was 1929, only ten years after the Treaty of Versailles which formally concluded the First War, or the Great War as it was then called and still deserves to be. In accordance with the ordinary school syllabuses of the day, the first and second generation of Romantics, which prominently included Keats and Shelley, were exercising their charms on my adolescence.

It was an easy transition to take on Flecker, whose work was derived from this tradition, the more since its over-ripe romanticism——'Waving cypress, waving cypress, shall we go to Saadabad?'—was lightened by a Georgian expansiveness about the countryside and by what must have appeared to my innocence as a certain sophistication. There were the seductions of:

> When shall I ever be at home again?
> Meadows of England, shining in the rain,
> Spread wide your daisied lawns

and

> Have I not sat on Painswick Hill
>   With a nymph upon my knees,
> And she as rosy as the dawn,
>   As naked as the breeze?

The fact that I knew Painswick, but without the nymph, helped, no doubt. Rupert Brooke was a more powerful sorcerer. There were some of the same elements of seduction, as in

> Thank God, that's done! and I'll take the road
>   Quit of my youth and you,
> The Roman road to Wendover
>   By Tring and Lilley Hoo,
>   As a free man may do

—no less remote from my own world. And the ordinary schoolboy of 1929 was far from being free of the mythology of the Great War; the growing up of anyone born in 1914 was indeed inevitably marked by it, in one way or another. Hardly wonderful that one should have been open to something like the original romantic force of:

> If I should die, think only this of me:
> That there's some corner of a foreign field
> That is for ever England. There shall be
> In that rich earth a richer dust concealed;
> A dust whom England bore, shaped, made aware

. . . and because it swept over me then I shall know the poem to the day of my death and never be quite free of it.

Such enthusiasms, seen in retrospect to be so much the accidents of time and fashion, are a natural and proper part of the development of any passion for poetry. Before anyone born in 1964 laughs too derisively he should reflect on the possible evanescence of some of his own youthful enthusiasms, however much they may have been supported by reputation and by the wisdom of schools and anthologies—advantages which Rupert Brooke and James Elroy Flecker did not lack in their time. A date of birth in 1964 would put a reader in the same position, in relation to the poetry of the second half of the century, as I was in relation to the poetry of the first half. At the age of seventeen I encountered the work of Eliot, then not academically much recommended, and certainly not at all in my circles. It was from that point that my more enduring orientation in the world of poetry began, and this book represents a considered view of the period twenty years after the end of it, that is to say when I had long absorbed what I was to absorb of the work of the generations immediately before mine and indeed of my own generation. It is perhaps as good a point of view as another from which to write a history of this kind. Others of course can make a different assessment, if they will, of some of the poets I have written about. I would only claim that, as a starting-point for new explorations, this book has at least the advantage of presenting an assessment based on the reading of someone with an involuntary desire to find what interested him and to discard the rest.

For anyone who writes or who is going to write poems himself, this process is closely linked with the evolution of his own work. An absolute ruthlessness in taking what seems good and rejecting what seems bad is required in writing as in reading, even though one knows that such discriminations are fallible, like any human activity whatsoever. In the case of either the reader or the writer of poetry, a direct relationship with the work is a *sine qua non*, and the prestiges of fashion, reputation, prizes, publications, anthologisings, and public praisings and blamings are all irrelevant. The discipline is a very hard one, so that anyone who thinks literature is an easy option does not know what he is talking about and is certainly not talking about literature. On the other hand, it is also a release, for no pressure of examinations or of a desire to say what is acceptable to the people around one can alter the fact that the reader and the writer have to find their own ways and that the satisfactions of literature, which are as real as anything in this world, in the end come only to those who do so.

268   The thread I found in the poetry of 1900-1950—that of the best

expression of the 'general, completely inartificial conversation among contemporaries' (page 14) was the same with what I was looking for—with what success or unsuccess time will determine—in my own verse. This does not mean that, in writing verse, I have set myself any such general objective, or any general objective. That is not what the process of writing is like. Whatever critical notions one may have, when it comes to writing a poem it is rather that something begins to be said, words in specific rhythms begin to present themselves, go on and stop, and the whole tact of writing is to recognise what belongs to the poem and what does not. It may be that when one looks at the draft one finds that one went on writing after the poem had stopped, or began fumblingly before it really began; there may be intrusions which do not belong, words or lines which spoil the outline of the rhythm and the sense. The human mind being infinitely devious, one learns to write things which deceive oneself and may for a time deceive others. Almost certainly the young poet will begin to write with things which are nothing more, or little more, than imitations of other things not his own, and not a direct saying, and most of what passes for poetry, in any age, is merely a more or less plausible exercise in this kind, or a factitious invention which does not correspond to a direct apprehension. The plausibility and the factitiousness may be very accomplished, and resounding public reputations can be built on this sort of thing. All mere fashions are built on it, however excellent and original their beginnings, and many a good poet has disgraced himself by ignominiously imitating himself.

Sooner or later the sleight-of-hand shows up in the dowdiness of the language. In the end it is the language and not the poet that matters, the common means of communication which joins us with our contemporaries and which does what can be done to join the people of different centuries, so that the past is not entirely thrown away and even our little present is not entirely thrown away in the future. But again, there is no room for grandiose plans in the making of literature, nor of poetry in particular, which deals only in the specific. No one is likely to be more aware than the poet how little can be communicated, and how rare real achievements of this kind are. One thing is certain, that in a world given over as never before to the loud and tarty, a world in which thousands and thousands of people talk or sing for money, the voice which is speaking because it has something to say will not be among the loudest. It might almost be said that, in the second half of the twentieth century, unobtrusiveness of language is a mark that something is being said which should be attended to. This history ends at the mid-point of the century and it is for someone else to write the history of the second half—and preferably, perhaps, someone who has grown up in it. Of the poets mentioned in the concluding section of this book, Brian Higgins died in 1965, leaving three slim volumes, *The Only Need* (1961), *Notes while Travelling* (1964) and *The Northern Fiddler* (1965), which are worth picking up if you can find them. Cliff Ashby, dating his work from a council estate in West Yorkshire, has produced in *In the Vulgar Tongue* (1968), *The Dogs of Dewsbury* (1976) and *Lies and Dreams* (1980) verse which, if at times diffuse and straggling, has the rhythm and the unpretentious language of a living speech—work against which the validity of much clever as well as not-so-clever discourse in contemporary verse can be tested. A third poet mentioned in the 'Conclusion', David Wright, with a heavier and more complicated load to disburden himself of, has done so in a language as unassuming as either's.

A correspondent out of the blue wrote to me that Wright wrote what might well be 'the language of the future', a claim which, familiar as I am with Wright's work, struck me at first as astonishing but which, on reflection, I think may be true. Wright started in the miasmic forties, and there is a rare volume of *Poems* (1947), the inspection of which he does not overmuch encourage, though it already contains more than a glimpse, here and there, of the 'ancestral imagination' of which I spoke in the 'Conclusion'. But Wright's development has been, distinctly, away from the miasma, towards a clarity and *non-peculiarity* which is what I imagine my correspondent had in mind in his prophetic comment. Wright's work can most conveniently be approached in *To the Gods the Shades: new and selected poems* (1976)—from which matter from the 1947 volume was excluded—and *Metrical Observations* (1980). I have written at some length about Wright's work in *PN Review* 14, which contains a symposium, on the occasion of his sixtieth birthday to which a number of poets, including Geoffrey Hill, David Gascoyne, W. S. Graham, Michael Hamburger, Cliff Ashby, Martin Seymour-Smith and Anthony Cronin also contributed. My own close association with Wright, which is acknowledged in that symposium and elsewhere, including my translation of Dante's *Divine Comedy* (1980, 1981), does not deter me from recommending his work. We were both too well on our respective ways when I first encountered him, during the brief and brilliant life of *X* magazine, which he edited with Patrick Swift more than twenty-five years ago, for either's work to be influenced by the other's. On the other hand, whatever merits this history of 1900-1950 has it has

270

because it represents the findings of a man groping to write poetry himself, so it would be odd if I did not value the work of a man whose practical comments on the trade have been so useful to me.

Finally, in an edition of this book which it is hoped will reach some beginners in the art of poetry, it might be permissible to say that, because it is an art, the work of our fore-runners is important, whether in the end we like it or not. The world is full of people who want us to read or listen to their own verses but who have hardly felt moved to enquire what better poets have done; the only comfort is that things seem not to have been so different in Horace's day, though then the numbers were probably smaller. But the real incipient poet is more likely to be found in the person absorbed in a volume of someone else's poems, than among those who fill sheets of paper but do not willingly open a book. For it is by reading poetry that you find out what it is and whether you are one of those for whom it is necessary. This book is the record of such a search, and it will serve its purpose if it sets others off on a similar hunt.

May, 1981

Index

Aiken, Conrad, 129

Aldington, Richard, 54, 55, 56, 60–64, 65, 88, 106, 128, 182

Ashby, Cliff, 261

Auden, W. H., 40, 139, 202–212, 226, 251, 260

Barker, George, 242–249, 254, 260

Belloc, Hilaire, 65

Bennett, Arnold, 65, 199

Blunden, Edmund, 81, 82

Bold, Alan, 227

Bridges, Robert, 13, 239

Brooke, Rupert, 89

Bullen, A. H., 14–16

Campbell, Roy, 226, 231–234

Connolly, Cyril, 214

Conrad, Joseph, 47, 138

Curtius, E. R., 180, 134

Davidson, John, 13, 17, 22–24, 39, 129

De La Mare, Walter, 47, 48, 49, 79

Doolittle, Hilda *see* H. D.

Dowson, Ernest, 17, 20–21, 22, 39, 120

Dreiser, Theodore, 128

Drinkwater, John, 130

Eliot, Charlotte, 125, 126, 145

Eliot, T. S., 11, 21, 35, 60, 64, 94, 96, 111, 117, 119, 125–154, 162, 182, 189, 196, 198, 202, 204, 214, 215, 217, 222, 226, 229, 233, 237, 242, 243, 249, 257, 261, 263

Empson, William, 218–221

Faber, Geoffrey, 128

Fenellosa, Ernest, 106, 117

Fletcher, John Gould, 56

Flint, F. S., 56, 57–60, 71, 87, 88, 94, 96, 111, 112, 113, 182, 225

Ford, Ford Madox, 44–53, 54, 56, 57, 60, 79, 96, 101, 109, 120, 121, 182, 197, 198, 223, 224

Forster, E. M., 193, 194

Gallup, Donald, 133

Galsworthy, John, 189

Gascoyne, David, 254–259

Goldring, Douglas, 224

Gorman, Herbert, 197

Gosse, Sir Edmund, 128

Graves, Robert, 187–193

Greene, Graham, 202

Grieve, C. M. *see* MacDiarmid

Grigson, Geoffrey, 209, 249

Hardy, Thomas, 25–32, 38, 44, 47, 64, 87, 106, 111, 139, 168, 189, 197, 225, 234, 263

H.D., 54, 56, 97

Heath-Stubbs, John, 261, 263

Higgins, Brian, 261

Higgins, F. R., 165

Housman, A. E., 38–43, 239

Hueffer, Ford Madox see Ford

Hulme, T. E., 56, 64–68, 94, 96, 101, 120, 140, 223

Hughes, Glenn, 56, 57, 58, 59

Huxley, Aldous, 193

Isherwood, Christopher, 202, 206, 208

James, Henry, 120

Johnson, Lionel, 17, 18–20, 21, 22, 25, 27, 39, 120, 174, 259

Johnson, Pamela Hansford, 250

Jones, Alun R., 67

Joyce, James, 56, 68–70, 111, 197–199, 201, 240, 242, 245

Kavanagh, Patrick, 251–254

Kipling, Rudyard, 27, 32–38, 48, 64, 111, 114, 160, 207, 210, 238, 263

Lane, John, 27

Lawrence, D. H., 47, 56, 132, 193, 199–201, 215

Leavis, F. R., 120, 194

Lewis, C. Day, 85, 202, 208

Lewis, Wyndham, 47, 64, 65, 66, 84, 111, 146, 168, 182, 193, 194, 202, 212, 222–231, 232, 233, 241, 261

Lowell, Amy, 56

MacDiarmid, Hugh, 24, 234–241, 260

Machen, Arthur, 47, 71, 111

MacNeice, Louis, 156

Mansfield, Katherine, 65

Marsh, Edward, 87, 91, 92, 200

Monro, Harold, 56, 94–95

Moore, George, 47

Muir, Edwin, 193

Murry, J. Middleton, 65

Nevinson, H. W., 72

O'Flaherty, Liam, 193

Orage, A. R., 65, 182

Owen, Harold, 81

Owen, Wilfred, 63, 80–86, 190, 215

Parsons, Clere, 216–218

Pound, Ezra, 11, 16, 20, 41, 47, 50, 54, 55, 56, 60, 64, 65, 66, 67, 71, 79, 88, 94, 96–124, 128, 132, 133, 134, 136, 146, 165, 166, 168, 182, 198, 202, 215, 217, 222, 223, 226, 237, 238, 239, 242, 261, 263

Read, Herbert, 65, 180–187, 193

Rees, Goronwy, 214

Rhys, Ernest, 104

Reid, Forrest, 49, 61

Richards, I. A., 140

Rickword, Edgell, 193–197, 207, 209

Riding, Laura, 188, 192

Roberts, Ellis, 232

Rosenberg, Isaac, 86–94, 96, 190, 203, 262

Sassoon, Siegfried, 82

Seymour-Smith, Martin, 263

Sharrock, Robert, 229
Shaw, G. B., 22, 64, 65
Sitwell, Edith, 141, 249
Sitwells, 128, 233
Spender, Stephen, 128, 202, 206,
    208, 212–216, 226, 249, 251
Symons, Arthur, 20, 22

Tate, Allen, 214, 215
Thomas, Dylan, 249–251, 254
Thomas, Edward, 71–79, 80, 85,
    94, 118, 262
Thompson, Francis, 18

Tolkien, J. R. R., 203

Welland, D. S. R., 85
Wells, H. G., 189, 199
Wilde, Oscar, 17, 22, 46
Williams, William Carlos, 56, 97
Wolfe, Humbert, 233
Wright, David, 232, 263

Yeats, W. B., 16, 17, 18, 22, 47,
    48, 95, 96, 104, 106, 110, 123,
    139, 155–179, 190, 202, 215,
    222, 251, 254, 260